MW00789182

EMILY GLASCOCK RAMEY

The Years of Anguish

Fauquier County, Virginia

1861-1865

Collected and Compiled
For The Fauquier County Civil War
Centennial Committee

By Emily G. Ramey, Marshall
John K. Gott, Marshall
Co-chairmen

FAUQUIER HERITAGE SOCIETY EDITION

With the editorial assistance of
Gertrude Trumbo and John Eisenhard
of The Fauquier Democrat

A HERITAGE CLASSIC

Published 1998 by

HERITAGE BOOKS, INC.
1540E Pointer Ridge Place
Bowie, Maryland 20716
1-800-398-7709
www.heritagebooks.com

ISBN 0-7884-0963-8

CONTENTS

Dedication

In Honor of The Men of Fauquier
Who Served The Confederacy
1861-1865

The Fauquier County Civil War Centennial Committee was appointed by the Board of Supervisors for the purpose of making a memorial observance of the hundred years since the close of The War Between The States.

Mrs. Emily G. Ramey, Marshall, Co-Chairman
Mr. John K. Gott, Falls Church, Co-Chairman

Mr. W. Hunter deButts, Upperville
Mr. Wallace Phillips, Middleburg
Mrs. J. B. McCarty, Delaplane
Mrs. Katherine Slater, Upperville
Mr. Thomas E. Frank, Warrenton
Mr. Charles G. Stone, Warrenton
Mr. Harry M. Pearson, Remington
Mr. Kenneth Eskridge, Catlett

For The U. D. C.

Mrs. J. E. Norman, Warrenton
Miss Emily Fletcher, Warrenton
Mrs. T. Elmer Woolf, Marshall
Mrs. J. G. Gibson, Upperville

With sadness, the Committee records the loss of three members who from their rich store could have added much of vivid interest and information to these pages —

Dr. William N. Hodgkin
Mr. Charles E. Jeffries
Mr. John W. Stone

The Board of Supervisors of Fauquier County

Mr. John D. McCarty, Chairman

Mr. W. Hunter deButts
Mr. James F. Austin
Mr. James S. Gulick
Dr. Evan H. Ashby Jr.

Foreword

This recall and record of fact and story is submitted to hold alive the part played by the people of Fauquier at the front and in the home during four dark years in history, 1861-1865.

Laying aside the style and objectivity of the historian, this commemorative tribute has sought to bring to the printed page the presence and living breath of those who lived day by day with the experiences of privation and sorrow. They should be privileged to tell their own story, in their own way, and in their own setting.

Much effort has been made through research and public appeal for a full response in the gathering of this personal record, and an effort has been made to use all such collected material. This does not mean, however, that the whole story has been told, in finality.

Let this publication be regarded as a part of a progressive project, for surely there are letters, notes and diaries yet not offered which could in our own time by others continue The Story of Fauquier.

In war there is no victory. The suffering and the bloodshed in the great conflict, now one hundred years gone, offer little substance for celebration.

This little volume is presented in a different spirit—as a commemoration of the valor and sacrifices of those troublous years. It is an effort to recall the names of those, many of whom lie in unmarked graves, lost in oblivion, who went forth from Fauquier County to fight for "Constitutional Liberty and the Sovereignty of the States."

—Clara S. McCarty

No Escape for Old John Brown

From the recollections, written in 1895, of Fielding Lewis Marshall, of Ivanhoe, opposite Oak Hill, near Delaplane. Mr. Marshall was the son of Thomas Marshall of Oak Hill and the grandson of Chief Justice John Marshall.

One Sunday, at Emmanuel Church, we heard the shriek of the engine on our railroad, an unusual sound as all Sunday travelling was forbidden under Uncle Edward's regime as President of the road. Soon a horseman dashed up to the astonished crowd and announced that Governor Wise had sent up Captain Turner Ashby to give the alarm that the Yankee Abolitionists had collected a large force of armed men to rescue Old John Brown, the fanatic, from the jail in Charles Town, Jefferson County; that the Black Horse Cavalry was on the march from Warrenton, and that the Ashby Mountain Rangers were also coming; and that we were to assemble with as many of my company, the "Wise Dragoons," (of which John A. Adams was Captain and I was orderly sergeant) as could be collected.

Brother Tom was our Lay-Reader on that day. Being the oldest in the congregation, I was the first to speak and say what it was our duty to do. Without a moment's hesitation I said I was going; Tom and James Jones said the same. Rebecca was not at church on that day; and the sad expression of her face, when I informed her of my determination to go, I shall never forget. She was delicate, and deficient in physical courage. But when I told her I was a member of a Volunteer Company, and that if I hesitated I should forfeit all claim to the blood of those who were ever foremost in defending their country, from the first French and Indian Wars through the Revolution, and to the War of 1812, against all assaults upon our liberties, she gave a reluctant though firm, consent, and packed my saddle-bags with a few articles of clothing.

At Piedmont Station I found Ashby had left a supply of sabres for us who were not provided with them. I never shall forget how awkwardly I buckled the long thing around my waist, and how near it came to getting between my legs when I essayed to walk. As I was in this act, a neighbor of mine—my junior by some ten years or more—said to me, "Mr. Marshall, are you going?" I said, "Yes, Joe; ain't you going too?" He said No, his wife would not let him. I suppose he saw something in my face, for he added, "A bullet that would miss you would hit me." I turned from him in disgust, only thinking that a ball that would kill me would lose all force before it got through the flesh his carcass was encased with. He weighed over two hundred pounds, and was fat accordingly. Finding that my captain was so far off as not to be able to collect his company, I volunteered, as Tom did also, as a private in Ashby's company. In the meantime the Black Horse Company came up, and their captain, out-ranking Ashby by date of commission, took the lead or head of the column. At sunset, we left Piedmont for Paris, a village at Ashby's Gap. There we halted to take some refreshment, and then took up our line of march over Ashby's Gap in the Blue Ridge Mountains. It was dark then, and as the rumor was that the fanatics were swarming in the mountains on each side of us we maintained close order, and not much more noise was to be heard than the tramp of our horses, and the clanking of our unmanageable sabres against their flanks. We passed through the dark valley of this Gap, forests on each side of us, with no enemy to be seen or heard; and arrived without an adventure at Berry's Ford on the Shenandoah River. Captain Scott, being in advance, moved on to take the ferry boat first to convey his troop across. Whilst he was thus engaged, our captain (Ashby) impatient at the delay, dashed into the river a short distance below an unused ferry and forded the river alone; and then, returning, ordered his company to follow him, which we did with alacrity. It was the roughest and deepest ford I ever crossed, our horses having to clamber over the huge boulders in our track. With saddles wet half way up our saddleskirts, we reached the opposite bank in safety, and awaited the arrival of the Black Horse under Captain Scott. Upon his arrival, it was announced that, as our captain had crossed before he did, Captain Scott had assigned our company to the front, the post of honor and of danger, heretofore held by himself. Our company was drawn out by 2's, as a recent flood had washed out about half the road, making a passage too narrow for us to march in 4's, as we had been doing up to this time. In giving the order to march, Ashby dashed up right opposite to where I was, and I saw his horse's hindfeet give way, and himself and horse slip several feet below us, in the gully washed out of the road. He was on his

Hathaway horse, and as he reined him up the horse reared to a perpendicular. In a moment Ashby slipped off him from behind, relieving him of his weight. His charger instantly regained his footing on all four legs, and in a second Ashby leaped into the saddle, and the horse and rider bounded out of the gully to the firm road. The whole thing happened in a moment, and Ashby continued his order without the least interruption. 'Twas the most superb act of horsemanship I ever saw.

Marching through Millwood a little before day, we arrived at Berryville, or Battle Town, as formerly called. As we stopped there a short time, some man aroused from sleep threw up his window and asked what all this meant. A wag of a soldier bawled out, "'Tis Yankee soldiers come to set John Brown free!" The poor terrified fellow pulled down the window and disappeared. At sunrise, we bivouacked in sight of Charles Town—where John Brown was safe in jail—not having lost a man or horse in our midnight and perilous march. We had a Governor more excitable than Wise; and we soon found there was no occasion for us to be there, who had no company of our own present; there being more than men enough to see that Old John Brown would surely be hanged. After resting ourselves and horses, we turned our faces home, to assure the anxious ones there they need feel no fears for us.

Thus began and ended my short but sharp campaign in the John Brown War, just a year or two before the bloody war of four long years of death and desolation to many of us who were on that march, so deeply engraved on my memory.

Ordinance of Secession

A rare, printed copy of the Ordinance was found recently among the papers of a Fauquier resident in Paris, Virginia.

BY THE GOVERNOR OF VIRGINIA

A Proclamation

The convention of the commonwealth of Virginia having adopted, on the 17th day of April 1861, an ordinance "to repeal the ratification of the constitution of the United States of America, by the state of Virginia, and to resume all the rights and powers granted under said constitution," and by the schedule thereto annexed, required polls to be opened for the ratification or rejection of the same by the people of this state, on the fourth Thursday in May next:

Now, therefore, I, John Letcher, governor of the commonwealth of Virginia, do hereby proclaim, that the annexed is an authentic copy of the said ordinance and schedule, and that all officers designated therein are required to conform to its provisions in every respect.

(L. S.) Given under my hand as governor, and under the seal of the commonwealth at Richmond this 24th day of April 1861, and in the 85th year of the commonwealth.

JOHN LETCHER.

By the governor:

George W. Munford,
Sec'y of the Commonwealth.

AN ORDINANCE

To Repeal the Ratification of the Constitution of the United States of America, by the State of Virginia and to Resume all the Rights and Powers granted under said Constitution.

The people of Virginia, in their ratification of the constitution of the United States of America, adopted by them in convention, on the twenty-fifth day of June, in the year of our Lord one thousand seven hundred and eighty-eight, having declared that the powers granted under the said constitution, were derived from the people of the United States, and might be resumed whensoever the same should be perverted to their injury and oppression; and the federal government having perverted said powers not only to the injury of the people of Virginia, but to the oppression of the southern slaveholding states:

Now, therefore, we, the people of Virginia, do declare and ordain that the ordinance adopted by the people of this state in convention, on the twenty-fifth day of June, in the year of our Lord one thousand seven hundred and eighty-eight, whereby the constitution of the United States of America was ratified; and all acts of the general assembly of this state ratifying or adopting amendments to said constitution, are hereby repealed and abrogated; that the union between the state of Virginia and the other states under the constitution aforesaid, is hereby dissolved, and that the state of Virginia is in the full possession and exercise of all the rights of sovereignty which belong and appertain to a free and independent state. And they do further declare that said constitution of the United States of America is no longer binding on any of the citizens of this state.

This ordinance shall take effect and be an act of this day, when ratified by a majority of the votes of the people of this state, cast at a poll to be taken thereon, on the fourth Thursday in May next, in pursuance of a schedule hereafter to be enacted

Done in convention in the city of Richmond, on the seventeenth day of April in the year of our Lord one thousand eight hundred and sixty-one, and in the eighty-fifth year of the commonwealth of Virginia.

A true copy.

JNO. L. EUBANK,
Secretary of Con'n.

Although I May Be Killed . . .

Letter addressed to Mrs. Rebecca Marshall, of Markham, Fauquier County, Care of Major Ambler. It is among papers in the possession of Mrs. J. M. Marshall of Priestly Farm, Marshall, Virginia.

Middleburg
July 22nd, 1861

Dear Mother,

Our regiment is now on the way to join Beauregard at Manassas J. I understand they are now having a desperate fight there and I write you a few lines to tell you not to believe any reports you may hear about Archie or myself being killed until it is fully confirmed. There are so many such reports. The people seem to be in the greatest state of excitement and report our loss has been very heavy. I may be killed in this battle but I hope to bear myself like a man. After it is over I shall try to return home.

Give my love to all the children and believe me to be

Your affectionate son,
Jas. Marshall

We are in a great hurry and I cannot write more. Am behind the company but I want to thank you for having stood in the place of a real mother to me. So much so that I have never felt the loss of my own and assure you of my love.

J. M. M.

No Time Off for Christmas

Excerpts from a letter of T. H. Foster to his mother, Mrs. James W. Foster, January 2, 1862.

Camp Smith
Jany. 2nd 1862

Dear Ma:

I find much difference so far as privileges are concerned between being in a regiment and acting only under a General. In the latter case you are governed alone by your Captain from whom you may obtain many favors if you have his ear, while in the former your Colonel grants and refuses requests and that company whose Captain stands high with him is the most fortunate.

Unfortunately for us the system and discipline of a regiment enforced as it is here has not given our Colonel a favorable impression of our officer who is now at home sick. There is nothing like having a good friend at Court, when one wants favors.

None of us could get off to take a Xmas dinner at home or spend a night. I saw none of the usual evidence that the old year was going out down here until the last day of the holidays when I beheld at Manassas some half dozen darkies clad in brand new linsey wending their way to a neighboring farmhouse. The moving of the regiment and the preparation afterwards for winter quarters during Xmas caused me to forget that another year had passed away and that the time for the celebration of the birth of Christ (always so improperly celebrated) was at hand. Nothing could be heard here but the call of the sentinel for the sergeant of the guard and the axe which is being used by the soldiers with a hearty good will to prevent the chilling blasts of winter from freezing them out. No joyous bursts of laughter or sweet sound of music went up from out these pines which completely hide us from observation. The same routine and discipline and daily duty was here. And yet withal no one complained or expected anything else. We enlisted not to spend pleasant times or go home when we wanted, but to endure the hardships of a soldier's life and shed our blood if necessary, in defense of our country's rights.

This regiment is encamped about one mile due east of the stone bridge over Bull Run and pickets at the same place that it did when two miles below Centreville. A Company goes every fourteen days and remains two nights and three days. (It is a wonder that more accidents do not occur in our army than do, for just as I finished the above sentence a ball popped through the tent where I am writing about one foot above my head, nearly striking Mr. Russell who is out now fussing considerably about it. Suppose it was accidental and as it struck nobody give myself no concern about it.)

Our Company goes on picket tomorrow, and when we return I am coming home to spend one night. Tell Cousin Medora not to go home until I come up which will be, I hope, on Tuesday or Wednesday. The Post Office of the regiment is Manassas. Letters should be directed in care of Capt. Adams *6th* Virginia *Cavalry* regiment.

The size of Mr. Kearn's head is the same as mine (7 1-8). He is much in want of his cap. I shall be very glad indeed to receive a box of edibles, and hope some opportunity will soon present itself for its transportation down. I am getting exceedingly tired of beef and bread. My Jacket fits well and will be enough for the winter. Give my love to all and accept for yourself the warmest affections of your

Son.

P.S. Excuse the abrupt termination of this letter. That accidental shot has created such a stir around me that I cannot write more.

The Border Between

EDWARD CARTER TURNER

Edward Carter Turner, of Kinloch, near The Plains, was a man of ability, affairs and influence. He was born August 6, 1816, and died March 3, 1891. A part of the diary kept by him during a portion of the Civil War, gives a graphic picture of how Virginia as a border State, and his section of it, suffered through being repeatedly raided and fought over by both forces. It also reveals that Mr. Turner used all his influence against the action of the Charleston Convention and favored an honorable settlement between the North and South, though opposed to any disgrace to his State. He had friends and relatives on both sides, and a brother, Thomas Turner, who became a rear-admiral in the Federal Navy.

It is not generally known that the Mt. Vernon silver and plate, which Col. John A. Washington (early on the staff of General Lee) was heir to, was taken away from the home he established after leaving Mt. Vernon, known as Waveland, near Salem, now Marshall, Fauquier County, at night, in an ox cart, and carried to Kinloch, where it was securely hidden in a pigeon loft in its old-fashioned garden. It remained there in safety during the four years of the Civil War, although Kinloch was repeatedly occupied by Northern and Southern soldiers, and often searched by the Federals. When it was removed after the war the sacks were so rotted that they fell to pieces, but the silver was intact. No one had apparently thought of climbing up to and looking among those innocent birds that had thus become its unconscious but effective guardians.

Mr. Turner kept farm diaries throughout his life. That only this war-time diary, from August 17 to December 31, 1862, inclusive should have been discovered among his effects, is supposed to be due to the others having been appropriated in the raids and searches that were made during the war. Some may have been lost or destroyed afterwards.

Monday, AUGUST 18, 1862

Beautiful morning. After breakfast I take the carriage and start to Oakley to bring my Mother to this place; my daughter Janie accompanied me. We go by way of Middleburg and arrive at Oakley to dinner. I spent the night at Oakley.

After breakfast we started for Kinloch, came by the way of Middleburg. My friends tell me that it is currently reported that I am going to take the oath of allegiance to the U. S. Government. The report it seems was circulated by Robt. Beverley. Dr. Cochran was kind enough to contradict it before the publication of the oath, as it is to be presented to the people under the 11th order of Gen. Pope. I always said when spoken to on the subject that there were some circumstances under which I would take the oath of allegiance, I would swear to support the Constitution of the U. S. rather than lose my life or be exiled from my family and home. But since the publication of the oath by which a man swears to support the Government of the U. S., whatever that Government may be, no man has ever heard me say that I would take it. Indeed there are but two persons on earth whom I ever told what I intended to do and in reply to the many who have asked me the question, I have said I could not exactly say what I would do but when the alternative was presented, would act in accordance with the dictates of conscience. I have been called on by a great many for my views and my advice. My views I have carefully withheld as I did not wish to be quoted in regard to the matter, and my advice I have never given because I did not wish to shape the course of others in so important and responsible an affair. We reached home in safety, but my Mother is much fatigued by the trip. Weather delightful.

Wednesday, AUGUST 20.

Bright morning. Weather for some days past has been too cool for corn. I have the wheat of last year's crop taken from the garners and spread on the barn floor to give it air, it is inclined to heat. Janie and I ride down to see the Skinkers. Mr. Skinker has been arrested and taken to Washington. We are at a loss to know what are the charges against the most amiable and excellent gentleman. We find his family more cheerful than might have been expected, conscious of their father's innocence and trusting in a just and merciful God, they seem not afraid of what men can do unto him, may God have mercy on him and them. (Weather growing warmer. Negroes continue to abscond. If it becomes probable that the Southern Army will return to this country, there will be few negroes left to receive them.)

Thursday, AUGUST 21.

I ride with Janie to Falkland to visit Mrs. Jno. H. Carter. We find them well. After a most delightful visit, we return to Kinloch. Hear distant sound of cannon, rumors of the falling back and retreat of the Feds. Fight said to have been going on for several days. May God have mercy upon us and deliver us from our enemies. Very light showers during the day.

Friday, AUGUST 22.

Cloudy morning. While I write at 6 1-2 o'clock A. M. the firing of cannon is distinctly heard. The heart sickens at the sound of this terrible conflict between men who in fact are brothers but who in feeling have become the most bitter enemies. The sound of cannon increases. The fire is incessant and seems to be getting nearer. The fight can not be further off than the banks of the Rappahannock. O! the precious blood that is at this moment flowing, the bravest, the best of our people are bleeding, while the most worthless are remaining ingloriously at home. The firing is continuous to noon when it seems to stop. We shall hear in a day or two the results. Report reaches us this evening that Gen. Jackson's army is in Warrenton. This is doubtful.

Saturday, AUGUST 23.

The corn has done well thus far but will begin soon to suffer unless we get rain. The fight is renewed this morning. Heavy and rapid firing to the south of us; sound of cannon distinctly heard in the direction of Warrenton Junction. I ride with Janie over to Gordonsdale, the sick there are said to be better. See two Confederate soldiers. They tell of a dash made by General J. E. B. Stuart last night on Catlett Station. Two hundred Federal prisoners, a large number of horses, trains of cars and fifty wagons were taken, the railroad bridge burned and the track torn up. General Longstreet and Jackson on this side of the Rappahannoch. Federal army said to be retreating towards Manassas. McClellan and Burnside reported to be with Pope. Gen. Lee said to be in command of the southern Army on the Rappahannoch. My hogs are dying rapidly, find three of the largest dead; others seem sick, can not account for the disease. Sheep look badly. They are, no doubt, suffering for salt, which is too scarce to be given to them as often is necessary. Heavy clouds hanging, but no rain here.

Sunday, AUGUST 24.

No sound of cannon this morning. It continued to a late hour last night. The war of cannon begins again but not so early as on yesterday. At midday it is terrible, said not to be a general fight but firing on the fords to prevent the Confederates from crossing the Rappahannoch. Mr. Adams and I go on a visit to Mrs. Jones and I. E. Smith. We dine with the latter. N. Loughborough is with us. County wild with excitement on account of the battle. Return to Kinloch at night. Jno. Chapman and W. Stuart spend night here.

Monday, AUGUST 25.

No sound of cannon this morning. After dinner I start for Washington City to dispose of the draft on New York for $2,470.00 sent in July from St. Louis. I think it important in view of the troubles to do something with it. Shall be governed by the advice of friends in the city. I also wish to get the money for wool which I sent to Balto. and which I learn has been sold. I go as far as Ariss Buckners.

Tuesday, AUGUST 26.

I am waked up at 2 o'clock in the morning by Mr. Adams who comes from home to apprize me of the arrival of Jackson's army in our neighborhood. This wonderful man is rapidly advancing toward Manassas to place himself in the rear of the Federals now on the Rappahannoch river to destroy the railroad and cut off their communication with Washington. This secret and unexpected movement it is supposed will prevent the falling back on the junction of the army and ensure their capture when vigorously attacked in front. Their retreat towards Fredericksburg is said also to be intercepted. They will be compelled, as the knowing ones say, either to cut their way through or surrender the whole army. Nous Verrons. I arrived at home shortly after sunrise Find my nephew Tom of St. Louis and Capt. Johnson of Baltimore here. At an early hour the head of the column comes in view advancing rapidly from toward Salem. All day long our house and yard are filled with soldiers hungry, thirsty, barefooted and some of them almost naked, but bright and buoyant asking only a mouthful to eat and to be lead against the enemy. The people everywhere relieve them to the utmost of their ability but having been severely plundered by the Feds., little and in many instances nothing is left to feast them on, they take gratefully however, whatever is given and go on rejoicing in the prospect of speedily driving the enemy from their soil and the return of sweet peace. Among those who arrive for a scanty meal are our two sons Tom and Beverley, our nephew Wilson and several of our Randolph cousins. We thank God from the bottom of our hearts for the return of our dear boys and for His kind protection of them during their absence. They remain but a few moments and move on. In a day or two they are to meet the enemy in deadly conflict. How many now passing with light and careless hearts will 'ere another week be citizens of the unknown world? May God have mercy upon their noble souls. Our own dear boys may never return to their once peaceful and happy home. With fervent prayer we commend them to God who alone has power to protect and save them. How marked is the difference between the Federal and Confederate soldiers. The latter bland and courteous, asking in the most respectful manner for the gratification of his simple wants and returning heart felt thanks for the trifle he receives. The former rough and rude, frequently domineering and insulting, demanding instead of asking to be fed and insolent and huffish after he is filled. The difference is easily explained. The Confederate in nine instances out of ten is the very cream and flower of our population. He is well-bred and cultivated. The Federal, if not a low foreigner is from the meaner class of the Yankee nation, than whom the world contains no people more selfish, unprincipled and degraded. The one is brave and patriotic; the other is cowardly and mercenary, the one is fighting for a principle dearer than life itself; the other for the miserable stipend allowed for his services. 'Tis not remarkable under these circumstances that victory in so large a majority of engagements perched upon the Confederate banner, even when the disparity of forces is equal to two or three and sometimes five or ten to one.

Wednesday, AUGUST 27.

Pleasant morning. Stragglers continue to call in for something to eat. The last of Jackson's division pass this morning. All light-hearted and hopeful. Yankee cavalry appear in force at The Plains. They pick up many stragglers. Reported that Jackson has taken Manassas with many prisoners, negroes and military stores, country in great commotion, people nearly wild with excitement. Longstreet's army arrives at The Plains. Gen. Lee accompanies it, the neighborhood is swarming with soldiers and the scanty stock of provisions on hand barely enough for the people is being rapidly devoured. The soldiers are as considerate as under the circumstances could be expected, but they are starving and will be fed as long as there is anything left for them to eat. Oh! what a gloomy picture does the future present. The heart sickens and hope departs to contemplate it. It is most confidently expected by the officers that the Federal army will be destroyed. They are said to be outnumbered and surrounded. God alone can see what is in the black future.

Thursday, AUGUST 28.

Morning somewhat cloudy. Crowds of men and horses are pouring into our gate by sunrise to be fed. The prospect of having our humbled stock of provisions devoured alarms us. They continue to come all day and the stream increases as night approaches. I visit Gen. Lee's camp this morning, find him looking very well. He is cool and they say confident. While in the General's tent a citizen arrived with information that the Federals are advancing from the direction of Warrenton. They are doubtless making for Thoroughfare Gap, which if they reach and possess themselves of, will give them great advantage. I communicated my news to the General. At noon we understand that the Feds have taken possession of the Gap. The Confederate forces did not arrive in time to prevent it. It seems that they were purposely delayed. To give up the Gap may be a part of a strategic plan of great ability, but to me it looks unfortunate. Skirmishing occurs at the Gap. Information reaches us of an engagement of Gen. Ewell's division at Bristoe Station. Gen. Ewell was compelled to retreat. This is said to have been expected and intended. The Federal Army has left the neighborhood of Warrenton and gone to Manassas. They are doubtless alarmed for the safety of Washington. General J. E. B. Stewart with this whole division of cavalry is said to be at Fairfax C. H. within sixteen miles of Washington. The Confederates have abandoned Manassas and it is again in the possession of the Feds.

Friday, AUGUST 29.

Bright pleasant morning. The army is still passing and crowds of soldiers are still arriving at this house, they seem weary and hungry and painful, as it is many of them are obliged to keep on without being fed. The country is covered with able-bodied men who purposely straggle in the rear to avoid battle. It seems bad management on the part of our officers to allow these unprincipled fellows thus to escape their duty. The Federal Officers are particular and keep cavalry behind their brigades to force stragglers up. I ride to the battle ground of Thoroughfare Gap. The dead are still unburied. From twenty to thirty Feds fell and were left. Others may have been killed and were taken off. Our wounded are at Stovers Mill, six have died during the day; others not expected to live through the night. The fight has been going on in the neighborhood of Centerville all day, but no tidings have reached us. At night our son Beverley is brought home wounded in the left shoulder by a pistol shot and on the head a saber cut. The ball has not been extracted, his wounds are said not to be dangerous for which we sincerely thank God. He was wounded in a charge of his company at Centerville.

Saturday, AUGUST 30.

Cloudy morning. Beverley is quite comfortable this morning. Rested well during the night. Dr. Cochran arrived this morning. I suppose to see Beverley. He was not sent for. Hear that General Ewell has lost his leg. Report confirmed by arrivals from the scene of conflict, three other Generals are said to have been wounded. The fight is going on in the neighborhood of Centerville. Cannon distinctly heard. No reliable information of how it is going. Pope reported to have got between the Confederates and Washington, will probably not be surrounded as was confidently expected.The fighting portion of the army has passed, but the whole country is swarming with stragglers or deserters who are making themselves extremely troublesome to the people. Our yards are crowded with them all day and the barn and stable lofts at night. They are begging food of people who have none to give and are insolent and revengeful when disappointed. From what I see in this neighborhood and learn from others there must be at least twenty thousand men who are skulking from their duty. Very few Virginia troops are among the stragglers. They are nearly all from the South, mostly from South Carolina and Georgia. Our poor Virginians are in the front of battle striving to deliver their homes from the ruin for which they are indebted to S. Carolina, the land of stragglers. Poor victimized Virginia! overflowing with patriotism and chivalry but ruinously blind to her interest. Whose fault is it that the army instead of being on the field of battle is greatly to the detriment of the adjacent country lounging in the fence corners and are within hearing of the war and musketry? It shakes our confidence in the Generals that such abuses should be allowed. What is an army without discipline? A law-less mob and such is literally the case with the thousands of vagabonds that are dragging after the rear of the present army of the Confederate States. When the Federal armies were passing, there was no stragglers, the men were compelled to keep their places and the people off the road saw nothing of the soldiers and were not annoyed by them. Their discipline is far better than ours and better discipline must eventually bring better success unless they are the worst cowards on earth.

Sunday, AUGUST 31.

Raining this morning. No rain after breakfast. Nathan Loughborough arrives. Between two hundred and three hundred Federal prisoners pass up for H. Ferry. They have been paroled. Reports reach us of fearful fighting. Our troups are said to be driving the Feds back. We hear today that Wilson Turner is wounded. It is also reported that Dr. I. F. Fauntleroy is dead. Hope neither account is true. Dark and cloudy at night.

Monday, SEPTEMBER 1, 1862.

Dark morning. I learn this morning that my nephew Wilson was killed on Friday and buried on the field of battle. This information gives us all the deepest pain. We are comforted however with the knowledge that he was a youth of the greatest purity of character and as gallant and true a soldier as ever drew a sword. I understand that he was buried by his comrades to whom he had by his manly virtues endeared himself. They gave him all that under the circumstances they were capable of giving, a decent burial in a soldiers grave. I go to the battle field in quest of his grave, search all day but do not find it, witness many evidence of the awful battle of Friday and Saturday. Ground literally covered in many places with dead men and horses. Do not succeed in finding the grave. Night approaches and am obliged to relinquish the search. Returned to Kinloch at night. A hard rain overtakes me and I am drenched to the skin. Find my house filled with stragglers and others.

Tuesday, SEPTEMBER 2.

Bright morning, wind fresh from N.W. quite cool. After breakfast I return in company with William Turner of Baltimore to the battle field to renew my search for poor Wilson's grave. We find it on the farm of Mr. Thos. Leachman who kindly undertakes to protect it until the body can be removed. No reliable information can be obtained of the situation of either army. They are moving towards the Potomac, it is thought, the Feds trying to escape and the Confederates maneuvering to circumvent them. A heavy column under command of General Ripley passes on, the air is filled with rumors. I return to Kinloch at night. Bev. Mason who was here to-day informed me of the death of his brother Randolph. He died of disease.

Wednesday, SEPTEMBER 3.

Bright, cool morning. The sick men who fell in here from the army seem to be doing badly. They are evidently growing worse. Two will probably die. Our army matters in some respects are managed badly. Able bodied men are allowed by thousands to straggle from the ranks and no account is taken of sick and disabled men who fall by the way. St. Louis Tom arrives at night. Rev. Mr. Duncan also arrives. Rev. Mr. Norton has been here sick for a week. He has typhoid fever. There are four or five cases of it among people who have fallen in here after the army. It will be a miracle if it is not communicated to the members of my own family. May God in his mercy protect us. Every breath we breathe is big with terror in some shape or other. Time was when we were well off and happy. Would to God our people had been aware of it. Those who survive these troubles will know how to appreciate God's blessings and how to thank Him for them in the future.

Thursday, SEPTEMBER 4.

Bright, delightful morning. No news of importance. We hope the sick soldiers are better. Bev's wound is getting on well. I separated the lambs from the ewes, have 230 ewe and wether lambs and 19 bucks. Some of the lambs are not good. The old sheep seem to be deteriorating, probably from want of salt. Washington Stuart dines here. G. W. Ball, Landon Mason and a young Mr. 'Hennon arrives here at night. House and stable always overflowing.

Saturday, SEPTEMBER 6.

Another beautiful morning. After dinner Landon Mason and I ride to Falkland to see Steney Mason who is there wounded. Almost every house in the country has one or more wounded soldiers to take care of. We find Steney doing well. Return to Kinloch at night.

Sunday, SEPTEMBER 7.

Another bright morning. Baltimore and St. Louis Tom Turners arrive here to dinner. Sick soldiers are improving. Positively asserted that the Confederate army is passing over the river into Maryland. What will be the effect of this important step? Will it be to exasperate the Northern people and make them more determined to prosecute the war and to this end supply men and money with vastly increased spirit, or will the approach of a formidable army burning for revenge for many injuries received alarm them for the safety of their own border and cause them to sue for peace? 'Tis generally believed that the latter will be the consequence, but I confess I fear the former. Compared to ourselves, the Northern people have not felt the cruel consequences of this war. They are still rich and powerful and if their heart is in it, as appearances indicate, they may carry it on for years to come. Why should they, any more than ourselves tamely submit to invasion. Unless I am greatly mistaken as soon as it is seen that our Generals have designs upon their soil, an army superior to anything they have yet raised will be instantly equipped to drive back the invader and if encouraged by the success which their advantages may give them, will be easily persuaded to follow the retreating army and try their luck once more on the soil of Virginia. This is a most interesting era in the history of the war. We may be approaching an Elysium of Peace or we may be plunging deeper and deeper into this most savage and bloody contest. I confess I fear the latter.

Monday, SEPTEMBER 8.

Weather still most delightful. Hear today of the death of my old friend Dr. A. Chapman. As the air is filled with false reports of every sort and kind, we are encouraged to hope that this account may also be untrue, but at a time like the present there is nothing to live for and no one ought to lament the death of good men. Dr. Chapman was a man of the purest character and if dead is far better off than those who survive him here. We hear today that the Confederate Army reached Frederick City, Md., and that large numbers of the Marylanders are flocking to join it. We learn also that deserters are numerous from the Federal Army. Wm. and Alfred Randolph arrive at night. The two Tom Turners took their departure this evening.

Wednesday, SEPTEMBER 10.

Dark morning, I ride with Alfred Randolph to Dr. Ewell's to visit Gen- E. S. Ewell who was severely wounded in one of the late battles and whose leg has been amputated. The General seems quite feeble but does not complain of pain. He thinks himself better. God grant that this truly good man may recover. Alfred remains in his brother William's camp and I return to Kinloch. My two hands continue to haul wood preparatory to winter. Landon Mason and Wm. Kennon are here.

Sunday, SEPTEMBER 14.

Bright morning. Rev. Dr. Packard preaches at this house today to a small congregation of our neighbors. I am still very unwell with inflammation of the intestines. Hear today that the N.Y. Tribune and other Northern papers have come out for peace. It is thought that General Wood will be surrounded at Harpers Ferry. He has been called on to surrender but declined. So says rumor.

Monday, SEPTEMBER 15.

Foggy morning. The sick men who for the last three weeks have been here are better, and go off this morning on a railroad car loaded with muskets, drawn by oxen and mules to the hospital at Salem. News today that Jackson has whipped Wood from Martinsburg and is besieging him in Harpers Ferry. My hogs are nearly all dead and are still dying. I shall probably not save one of them. Out of fifty fine hogs for the pen this fall I have lost about thirty and of eighty promising shoats, I have only fifteen left. This is bad luck with a vengeance. My sheep are evidently declining cause I suppose the want of salt. This farm has left the buzzards well fed this summer. I have lost more cattle than usual. I dare say the buzzards had as well have them, for had they lived, 'tis questionable if they would have done me any good. These are sorrowful times!

Tuesday, SEPTEMBER 16.

Bright morning. Rumors today of the capture of Gen. Wood and 8,000 men at Harpers Ferry. Of the suppression of the N.Y. Herald and that Lincoln has called for a million of men, we are in the midst of mighty events. While they are transpiring, black news is setting upon the whole country! A blight is upon everything! No single interest is flourishing! Country still swarming with idle men who with their horses are fast consuming the small quantity of corn on hand. 'Tis painful to think about the approaching winter and the suffering that must ensue. Should it be severe and long may God have mercy on us! I am still very unwell and Bev. is suffering considerably from his wound.

Wednesday, SEPTEMBER 17.

Dark morning. House and stable constantly full of men and horses ostensibly belonging to the army but who appear to be very little with it. My hands, a man and a boy all that I have left, continue to haul wood, laying it in against winter. Reported today that eleven thousand prisoners and two thousand negroes were captured at Harpers Ferry. Can not learn exactly what is going on in Maryland or in Washington. Can not hear whether the Md. people are flocking to the Southern Standard or not. I am still far from well. Wm. Randolph and L. Mason arrived here last night.

Thursday, SEPTEMBER 18.

Another gloomy morning. No rain as yet but very threatening. (Ther. 68 degrees.) Gen Ewell arrives here to dinner on a litter. They are conveying him to the interior for safety. Report reaches us at night the Feds have arrived in the neighborhood a mile or two below Waterfall. It is supposed they are in search of the Gen. as he came this morning from the same neighborhood from Dumblane the residence of Dr. Ewell. The General was doing well until the arrival of this messenger at about 10 p.m., after which he sleeps but little, and spends a restless night. House, yard, stables full of men and horses.

Friday, SEPTEMBER 19.

Bright morning. By light the Gen. is placed on his litter and conveyed away in the direction of Culpeper C. H. They go by the way of Salem. Account of last night concerning the Yankees confirmed this morning. They are said to have gone toward Aldie. Report today that Burnside has been whipped and his army captured. Thirty thousand prisoners said to be taken. (Weather warm.)

Saturday, SEPTEMBER 20.

Dark morning. Servant arrives from Dr. Ewells with a letter stating that the night after Gen. Ewell left Dumblane the house was surrounded and searched by Federal cavalry for the General. Had he remained there one day longer he would have been captured and hurried off to Washington where in all probability he would soon have died of his wound. His escape seems Providential. Wm. Randolph arrives at night. Weather has been dark all day with occasional light showers. The City of Cincinnati has not been taken as was reported. There is much alarm for its safety.

Monday, SEPTEMBER 22.

Bright pleasant morning. Hear today that the Feds have passed up the Little River Turnpike in force. Skirmishing occurred to Upperville in which they were twice driven back. Some think their object is to get possession of about three thousand army cattle grazing in that neighborhood; others think that it is a movement towards Winchester to get in the rear of Lee's army. I sell the remnant of my cattle to Anderson Smith. I get $5 for eleven at Rockley and $32 for eight at this place. My two hands continue to get wood. Weather very pleasant.

Tuesday, SEPTEMBER 23.

Dark morning. Mr. Braxton Selden arrives here on his way home. He was captured in Maryland and paroled. Various rumors good and bad and indifferent reach us. We know not which to believe. Army said to have left Md. and returned to Va. Maryland people said by some to have been friendly; by others to have been unfriendly. In some of the villages Southern troops said to have been fired on from the windows by women(?). I sell my dun mare "Fanny" to Cassius Dulany for $450.00. This is nominally a great price, but paid in money that may prove worthless. I would willingly give it all for one half that sum in gold. The country is literally flooded with new Confederate notes. Everybody's pockets are stuffed with it and all being jealous of it, are anxious to dispose of it and offer fabulous prices for every species of property. Horses for example are bringing in this money fully three times as much as they were worth before the war and the same is the case with almost every other description of property.

Wednesday, SEPTEMBER 24.

Bright morning. I got a letter from Wood and Brown, the men who got my wool for which they promised to pay in cloth, stating that they cannot comply with their contract and proposing to settle with me in money at $1.25 per pound for the wool. This disappointment subjects me to great trouble for unless they let me have the cloth and c. which my family require for clothing, we shall be in much distress, as it will be impossible to obtain it elsewhere. If I get clothing for my family I shall not object to letting them have the rest of my wool on the terms proposed. Wm. Randolph left here this morning.

Thursday, SEPTEMBER 25.

Another bright morning but much cooler. I start this evening for Wood and Brown's factory in Fredrick County. I go as far as Rokeby, on the way find the family at Rokeby sick with Diphtheria. No very severe cases. Went this morning to Middleburg and got off B. P. Noland a check on the treasurer at Richmond for $816.00 amount due for cattle sold Anderson Smith, $65.00 of the amt. goes to Mr. Adams for a cow of his.

Friday, SEPTEMBER 26.

After breakfast I leave Rokeby and proceed on my way to the factory. Hear on the road from St. Louis Tom whom I meet near Millwood. My son Tom was captured by the Feds in Maryland and paroled. Tom informs me that he is in Winchester. I reach the factory at two o'clock and after securing cloth and c. for the use of my family sell the residue of my wool for $1.30 per pound and am paid cash in Confederate money $1,975.35. I spent the night at Mr. Wood's where I am made very comfortable and treated with much kindness. Frost this morning for the first time this Fall, and weather, though delightful, is quite cool at night.

Saturday, SEPTEMBER 27.

Delightful morning—Another frost. After breakfast I leave the Factory for home. I come by the way of Snickersville and Middleburg. Dined with Dr. Cochran and reached home at dusk. Find my son Tom here. He gives an account of his capture by the Feds. In his endeavor to escape, they shot his horse and his own deliverance from death was miraculous. God was not forgetful of the prayers regularly offered for his preservation and protected him. Oh! that my wicked and ungrateful heart could feel sufficiently thankful to God for this remarkable instance of his mercy to me. On reaching home I find my family well and happy. A queer fellow who calls himself a spy for Gen. Lee spends the night here. He probably is crazy.

Wednesday, OCTOBER 1, 1862

Dark foggy morning. I understand that Lincoln has declared his intention to liberate all slaves in the South as far as his lines extend and confiscate all rebel property and the work is to begin the first of January, 1863. Our hope is that a just God will thwart his design, at least as far as the innocent are concerned.

Friday, OCTOBER 3.

Bright morning. Hear that Longstreet's division is below Aldie. This if true is a sudden move. (Continue to cut corn.) Force small, work goes on slowly. Rev. Mr. Baker gives up the parish and comes to take leave of us. We are now without a pastor, even nominally and the churches are fast going to ruin. One of the bitter consequences is the total neglect of the education of the rising generation. No schools, public or private, in the country and the neglect of educational advantages to children formerly considered so lamentable is now scarcely thought of. We hear that our cousin, Mittie Randolph wishes a situation as governess and we are endeavoring to engage her. The prospect of falling again within Federal lines may deter her or anyone else from coming to this country. The present prospect of affairs is gloomy and depressing. We can only pray that God will not utterly forsake those who try to put their trust in Him.

Friday, OCTOBER 10.

Another fine morning. Remains cloudy all day with occasional light showers. I go today to estimate the damage done Dr. Chapman's property by the Confederate Army as it passed his place in August. Damages all told are valued at $1,069.23. Federal soldiers (Cavalry) appear in the neighborhood. Skirmishes yesterday and today at Aldie. Mrs. Ida Dulany is visiting here. Mr. Atlas still holds on. He is crazy and a most disagreeable guest. Heavy clouds at night. St. Louis Tom is here. Our house is ever full to overflowing.

Tuesday. OCTOBER 14.

Another dark morning. After breakfast I start with my son Tom for the Shenandoah Valley. He to see about his exchange and I to look after my cloth promised and paid for at Woods & Browns Factory. We go with the carriage and on reaching Snickersville are stopped by the Confederate pickets who say they have orders to let no one pass. We stop for the night with Mr. Osburn where we are kindly received and made comfortable.

Wednesday, OCTOBER 15.

Clear and pleasant morning. The pickets agree to pass my son in consequence of his business being of a military character, but refuse to pass me. Tom takes the carriage and goes on to attend to his business and mine. He takes about thirty pounds of wool to dispose of at the factory which he loses on the road and thus sinks for me about $45.00. I go to Mr. Jno. L. Powells where I expect to remain until Tom returns unless he stays too long for my patience. I pay the moderate bill of $200.00 (Confederate) to Mr. Osburn for our entertainment and walk to Mr. Powells distant four miles where I am most kindly received.

Friday, OCTOBER 17.

Bright morning after the rain of last night. I leave a message for my son to come on and after breakfast and a most delightful visit I take leave of my kind friends and start on foot for home. I walk as far as the Pot House where I am overtaken by Tom with the carriage but no cloth. Wood has twice deceived me and given me much trouble besides great disappointment, as I know not how to clothe my family for the ensuing winter. He protests however that it is no fault of his and blames the military authorities whom he says have taken possession of his factory. He had ample time to comply with his contract before the troops came, but the prospect of their coming and a high price for his cloth I believe made him withhold it from me. We reached home in the afternoon. Feds arrive at The Plains at night.

Saturday, OCTOBER 18.

Bright morning. Fed soldiers over here early this morning for corn. They take a small quantity for which they pay nothing. They are polite. Two soldiers visited Avenel to get corn and finding a horse in the stable branded U.S. proceeded to halter and lead him off. This horse was captured from the Feds at Harpers Ferry and by some means became the property of my nephew St. Louis Tom who was visiting at Avenel and being informed that the soldiers were taking his horse ran down to the stable and fired on them with his pistol and put them to flight saving his horse and the Yankee halter. Tom made his escape. In a short time three Yanks returned and supposing that it was the owner of the property who had fired on them rode their horses into the house and otherwise insulted the family. They also searched the house to find the offender but finding no one and being assured by the servants that Mr. Beverley had been absent from home for several days and that it was a Confederate soldier who had fired on them, they departed, taking with them a good mare, the property of Mr. Beverley. It is supposed they are gone towards Centerville. We are gathering apples. A light crop.

Thursday, OCTOBER 30.

Another bright morning. A Company of Feds come along this morning and take me from my own farm. They keep me about an hour and release me near Rock Hill. I can not account for their conduct. They were civil, but not communicative. They took two other citizens whom they released with me. Our position at this time is of all others the most unenviable. We occupy the skirmishing ground and are liable to daily visitations from scouting parties of both armies. Our situation is truly distressing. God grant that the day which shall break our bitter cup is not far away.

Friday, OCTOBER 31.

Another sweet morning. I go to Pr. W. in search of a cow driven off by an Irishman who found her in the commons near The Plains. I find her with the son of the Irishman who makes no objection to my claim. Rumors today of the falling back of the Confederate Army and the advance of the Feds. They are said to be crossing at Point of Rocks and elsewhere on the Potomac and advancing in large numbers up the Little River Turnpike. God forbid that any of them should pass through this neighborhood. They are said to be sweeping the country of stock particularly horses as they go.

Saturday, NOVEMBER 1.

Another most delightful morning. Finish gathering potatoes. Crop small but quality fine. It seems not to be doubted that the Confederate Army is falling back, and this country will probably soon be taken quick possession of by the Feds. The act of conscription has taken out of the country all men under the age of 35 years . . .

Monday, NOVEMBER 3.

Wind clouds this morning. A great fight has been going about Upperville today. Hear nothing from it. Immense clouds of smoke seen. Constant firing heard.

Tuesday, NOVEMBER 4.

Bright morning. Some Fed. soldiers appeared here last night on horseback. I find this morning that my stable was broken into and my horse Waggon and my saddle were stolen. I go after breakfast to the

Federal Camp near Thoroughfare for the purpose of recovering my property. I am detained in the camp all day.

In the afternoon I see my horse in the Federal cavalry. I show him to Capt. Hasting of the 74 P. N who undertakes to speak for his release. The horse is returned to me but the saddle I do not recover. This division of the Army seems almost entirely composed of Germans and is commanded by Gen. Shurtz. Some of them are gentlemanly and reasonable; others rough and brutal. Capt. Hasting is particularly courteous and is unquestionably a kind hearted good man. He treated me with the utmost politeness. I reach home with my horse late at night. Find that all has been quiet here today, for which I thank God.

Thursday, NOVEMBER 6.

Many wind clouds. Federal Army arrives in large force and encamp in Mr. Beverley's woods near Mr. Welch's. The soldiers spread all over the country and commit all manners of depredations. They begin on me by taking two of my most valuable horses; the horse that Gen. Shurtz returned to me on Tuesday being one of them. I go to headquarters at Mr. Welch's and ask Gen Newton for a guard which he readily orders to be furnished. I go to Salem to beg of Gen. Stoneman by whose men my horses were taken to have them returned. On my arrival there I find that Gen. Shurtz had moved off in the direction of Orleans. Being very uneasy for the safety of my family I am afraid to follow him and return to Kinloch. On reaching home I find hundreds of men on the place killing my stock. The guard was protecting my interest about the house but was not strong enough to prevent the destruction of my cattle in the fields. Night sets in with a multitude of thieves all over my farm, around my barn, in my garden and in every out house not immediately under the eye of the guard. A most black and miserable day is followed by a restless night. All night long the work of destruction goes on.

Friday, NOVEMBER 7.

Dark, cloudy morning. Begins to snow early in the day. This morning the work of destruction is renewed with increased spirit. Several officers among whom is a Capt. Scott of N.Y. came to the house and seeing our situation are kind enough to exert themselves in our behalf. The guard is increased and a Provost Marshal, a Mr. High is exceedingly active with his guard to give us protection. We gather the sheep, cattle, horses, and colts in the yard and succeed better in guarding them than on yesterday. Still they are occasionally stolen and killed before our eyes; so great is the multitude of thieves that beset us. Snows on all day. At night the ground is white.

Saturday, NOVEMBER 8.

Looks like clearing up. Find this morning that two more of my horses have been stolen, my Cobham Stallion and a valuable young mare. All day long the soldiers continue to destroy property not strictly guarded. Many hundred of sheep, cattle and hogs and every description of poultry are destroyed. People generally are entirely stripped of their subsistence. God only knows what is to become of them! The Provost Marshal Mr. High is kind and attentive. He does all in his power to save our property and but for his activity nothing would be left us. I shall never cease to thank him. At night the thieves venture into the yard to steal my calves and one of them is shot by the guard, severely wounded in the arm. A surgeon comes and his wound is dressed.

Sunday, NOVEMBER 9.

Dark morning. High wind. This morning at an early hour the army begins to march and by the middle of the day have all disappeared. The wounded man and a nurse is left here for us to provide for out of the scanty remnant of food left in our possession. 'Tis hard to estimate my losses. As well as I can judge, I have lost 100 sheep, 34 hogs, 5 yearlings, 4 very fine horses and a large quantity of poultry.

Tuesday, NOVEMBER 11.

Fine, pleasant morning. I start early to Warrenton to see if I can recover my horses. I find I can do nothing and return to Kinloch. No molestation of my family in my absence for which I thank God.

Friday, NOVEMBER 14.

Bright morning. Great white frost. Charlie goes to Warrenton today and brings a report that my name has been mentioned in a letter published in N. Y. Herald and written from The Plains as a thorough going Union man, the author of this letter whom he may be had no authority from me to publish any such thing. If he supposed that I am a Union man in the Northern sense of the word, or if he thinks I would wish the Union restored with infraction of the Constitution or disgrace to the South, he is egregiously mistaken. I was a Union man for several reasons. In the first place I had no confidence in the party that advocated secession. I saw as its leaders men whom I had always considered erratic, unprincipled and dangerous, men who were the authors of all political heresies that for several years past have been disturbing the peace and endangering the safety of our country and I did not choose to act with them, or to be found in their company. The Charleston convention was composed of such men. The edict of secession was the work of its hand. I had no confidence in its virtue, wisdom or patriotism and did not choose to be governed by its action. In the second place my border locality would ever deter me from being a secessionist, because I know that ruin to myself, my friends, and my state must be the inevitable consequence of a dissolution of the Union. In the third place I had many friends and among them two brothers, one of them an officer in the Federal Navy on the Northern side' and I did not desire a state of things that would separate and make us enemies. Fourthly I had a holy horror of seeing the Government which our fathers established and cemented with their blood and as the richest of all legacies bequeathed to us disrupted and destroyed by a party destitute entirely of virtue, principle or patriotism. These were the principal reasons operating to prevent my being a secessionist and to bind me to the Union as our fathers made it. I opposed the ordinance of secession with all my influence and do not regret having done so. Indeed in view of the ruin that surrounds me, the fruit of the measure, I am proud that I did oppose it, and am comforted to think that I am not responsible for one particle of the trouble that our unhappy people, myself among the rest are at this moment suffering. In conclusion I own that while I would rather see the last man of my section stretched in death than see the Union restored with disgrace to my State, it is the wish nearest my heart that an honorable settlement may at length be effected and the States one and all North and South cluster again around a common government and resume their march upon the road to prosperity and power.

Saturday, NOVEMBER 15.

Bright morning, (Ther. 40 degrees.) Dreadful state of things today. 33 M. P. arrive in the neighborhood. My house is twice searched in the same hour by different parties of the same Regiment. Col. Maggie a bull headed Italian. Myself and son Thomas are arrested without charge and taken to the Thoroughfare and released at 8 P.M. without a question being asked us to return through the dark (my son on foot) home. Other most worthy and excellent citizens are likewise arrested and treated in the same way. The troops here today committed no robbery or outrage other than searching the house. May God grant us patience to bear as good Christians the chains that we have forged for ourselves and not murmur against His Providence for trouble of our own making. I arrived home late at night and am happy o.ıce more in the midst of my family.

Tuesday, NOVEMBER 18.

Dark morning. Little rain. Count my sheep and from 800 have been reduced to 600. My losses by the Fed. Army during its three days visit in this neighborhood was three or four thousand dollars. Rains more or less all day. Our dear son Tom takes leave of us today to join the Southern Army. We give him up with sad hearts and with earnest prayers for his safety in soul and body, commend him to Almighty God! Nothing remains in this vicinity of the Northern Army but small parties of Cavalry acting as scouts. We rejoice at their departure and pray that they may never return. Mrs. R. E. Scott we learn is reduced so low that she has been obliged to ask for food at the hands of the Federal General in chief commanding at Warrenton. Application was made by the Hon. S. Chilton to Gen. Burnside to supply Mrs. Scott and her children, whom the Federal soldiers had robbed of every thing, with bread. Gen. Burnside replied to Mr. Chilton that starvation was one of the consequences of civil war, that the people had brought it on themselves and that he, Mr. Chilton, being a lawyer was too well informed to suppose that he, Gen. Burnside had any right to give Government provisions to starving rebels, or words to that effect. Mr. Chilton replied that he had not considered the application in a legal light but made it in the name of common humanity. When the Army departed the Gen. ordered some stores that could not be removed to be left for the benefit of Mrs. Scott. O! how humiliating is the fact not only to this proud family, but to the whole population of this county that the children of their great and their idolized Scott should be reduced to the necessity of asking bread of the murderers of their father, the enemies and destroyers of their country.

Friday, NOVEMBER 21.

Another dark morning Clears up in afternoon. Shuck corn, but for whose benefit God only knows.

Saturday, NOVEMBER 22.

Bright, pleasant morning. We kill a beef today weight 500 net. Hear every day of outrages perpetrated on our poor people by the Federal soldiers when in this vicinity. Houses robbed and burned, bread and meat taken to the last morsel. The last cent of money taken from the pockets of defenceless people. Our most amiable relative Cassius Dulany was robbed of $2500.00 in cash and suffered greatly in other respects

Thursday, NOVEMBER 27.

Bright, pleasant morning. I go this afternoon to attend the funeral of my old and very dear friend Dr. Alexander Chapman. The Doctor after a long and painful illness died at his sisters (Mrs. Blight) near Warrenton a few days ago. His disease originally was Typhoid Fever, but his lungs become involved and he may be said to have died of Consumption. Thus has passed to its rest as noble a spirit as ever animated a tabernacle of flesh. He was amiable, gentle, generous, brave, magnanimous. He was buried at the Thoroughfare in his families grave yard and in the midst of a Federal encampment recently abandoned, in the ground where the skirmish of the 28th of August took place and near the spot where many Federal soldiers lie, covered in their shroudless graves.

Friday, NOVEMBER 28

Bright morning. We learn today that Seward, Blair and Smith have resigned their places in Lincoln's cabinet. Do not believe the report.

Tuesday, DECEMBER 2.

Morning hazy. We pen corn today. Federal cavalry constantly appearing in the neighborhood. The heart sickens at the sight of them from fear of a repetition of their cruel atrocities. What manner of men can they be who call themselves soldiers and give the enemy a wide birth and exercise their valour in the persecution of old men without arms, and women and children. If their business is to suppress the rebellion, why don't they march like men against the rebels and disburse them? Do they expect to put down the rebellion by insulting females and killing pigs and poultry and stealing horses? Judging from present appearances their policy is not to fight, for not withstanding the immensity of their host they seem afraid to risk a battle with the rebels who are inviting them to the contest.

Wednesday, DECEMBER 3.

Reported today that the war in the North between the Democrats and Republicans has commenced. McClellan said to have been put in irons. Do not believe the report.

Thursday, DECEMBER 4.

Bright morning. Learn today that Lincoln in his message to Congress has revoked his proclamation granting after the first of Jan. 1863 liberty to all slaves within that portion of the Southern territory dominated over by the Federal Army. This report may not be true indeed most probably it is entirely without foundation in fact, but true or false it makes but little difference as the principle was in force long before the publication of the proclamation. From the day that the Northern Army first invaded Virginia to the present moment, it has been its habit to entice slaves to abscond and in some instances where they have been faithful to their lawful owners and refused to run, they have been forceably taken away. That this habit will continue in full force as long as the army occupies our soil, no one doubts. Of what interest then is it to us whether the proclamation be renounced or not?

Tuesday, DECEMBER 9.

Bright morning. We prepare to kill the remnant of hogs left us by the Yankees only 8 in number. My brother Henry arrives at night from Washington. Another one of those delightful visits he sometimes pays us. Illumining the dark horizon which surrounds us at times like this, such visits from valued friends are inexpressibly grateful. My brother has come on for the purpose of removing the remains of his son Wilson who fell at the battle of Bull Run on the 29th of August last.

Thursday, DECEMBER 11.

Another very fine morning. I start with my brother after an early breakfast for the neighborhood of Groveton where lies the body of his poor boy Wilson. We arrive at the grave on the farm of Mr. Thos Leachman at about 11 o'clock, assisted by several of the kind people of the vicinity, we without much trouble exhume the body from the shallow grave in which it was hastily placed without a shroud or coffin by his mournful comrades and put it in a box furnished by the undertaker for the purpose. My brother starts with it for Washington where it will be placed in a metallic coffin and sent to its last resting place in St. Louis, Mo. I return to Kinloch. We salt down our handful of pork and begin to get wood for Christmas.

Friday, DECEMBER 12

Bright morning. I omitted to state in the record of yesterday that I had sent by my brother Henry to St. Louis $3,000.00 for investment. This money is obtained in the way of interest on my funds already loaned in that city and which since the commencement of the war has been accumulating. A loan of $7,000.00 made to Mr Lucas of St. Louis five years ago fell due on the 25th ult., which my brother tells me Mr. Lucas will not consent to keep unless he can have it at 8 percent which he says is all that money is worth in his city. Governed by my brother's advice, I determine to let him keep it on his own terms as he considers it much safer than any other investment that I could make, and authorize him to renew the loan to Mr. Lucas for three years at 8 per cent. He will let Mr. Lucas have the above named $3,000 also at the same rate. I take my carriage to Falkland for Miss M. Loughborough who is going to Washington. She takes with her a memorandum of articles which she has kindly undertaken to get for us. Janie goes to Falkland on a visit. We hear today that the Federal Army has been severely whipped, more completely defeated than on any former occasion. This is probably true if an action has taken place, but situated as the armies have been with the Rappahannock River between them, the armies occupying the opposite banks, I doubt if a general engagement has taken place. The report also says that all Burnside's wagon train has been captured and that the remnant of his army is retreating to Washington and that Centerville and Chantilly have been evacuated and that the Feds have destroyed all their stores. Such results, though they may not put an immediate end to the war will no doubt so far cripple the army as to keep them at home for sometime to come, and our poor people for a season at least will be relieved from their insults and thefts. My sister, Mrs. Powell arrived tonight.

Thursday, DECEMBER 18.

Bright morning. Beverley goes to Woods Factory to make another effort to get our cloth. I have no hope that he will succeed, for I have many reasons to believe that I have unprincipled men to deal with who, having been paid for the cloth, will keep me out of it forever if they can. Cannons heard in the direction of Washington City. Report of Confederates victory at Fredericksburg confirmed. Feds reported to have lost eight to fifteen thousand men. (Weather very delightful.)

Saturday, DECEMBER 2.

Bright cold morning. Continue to haul wood, Beverley returns without having been to the factory. We hear however, that some of our cloth is at Dr. Cochran's in Middleburg. Northern newspapers acknowledge a great defeat at Fredericksburg.

Sunday, DECEMBER 21.

Bright beautiful morning but biting cold. I go to Middleburg and find at Dr. Cochran's a part of the goods which Wood and Brown undertook to furnish me for the clothing of my family. I get no letter from them explaining why the balance was not sent or when it will be forthcoming. They are most unsatisfactory men to do business with. If I am so fortunate as ever to get clear of them I shall endeavor to keep so. Beverley who has been to Falkland informs us that Miss M. Loughborough, who went to Washington in our carriage and who kindly undertook to bring us a small supply of necessary articles, has not returned. I heard also in Middleburg that many of the people of that neighborhood had gone to Washington but that no one had returned, and the impression is that they are detained.

Monday, DECEMBER 22.

Cloudy, damp morning and quite mild. I get a letter from Jno. D Rogers informing me that my Mother's boy Bob is with the army and in his possession and proposing to hire him for the next year. He offers me $15 per month for him. We finish getting wood for Xmas. Weather very warm today. Rogers mentioned in his letter that our son Thomas had been taken prisoner in the Fredericksburg engagement. He was left in the custody of a guard whom he killed, thus makhis escape. This is spoken of as a handsome achievement and so it may be, but to me it is aiarming to see how reckless our young men are becoming of human life. No more is thought of destroying a man's life and launching his immortal soul into eternity than of killing a dog. It is doubtless the right of a soldier to make his escape by killing his guard. No one can blame him for so doing, but will not such things result in petrifying the heart and freezing to death every feeling of humanity? How much to be lamented it is, that our young men should be exposed to such poisonous influences, undoing in the twinkling of an eye the pious work over which God-loving and God-fearing parents have labored for years. But such is war. May God have mercy on us!

Thursday, DECEMBER 25.

A beautiful Christmas morning. A most quiet Xmas. No merry making as of yore (Stagnation even among the negroes. Too few are left to get up a frolic and their thoughts are probably occupied with matters more serious. The day has almost arrived when president Lincoln says they are to be free. The first day of January, the great hiring day, when all the negroes of the country and the white people too used to assemble at Warrenton to settle accounts of the past year and make arrangements for the new, is the day in which Mr. Lincoln has proclaimed all the negroes shall be free. That a large proportion of the few who remain are looking forward to that day with hope that this promise will be realized and that as free men they will remain here and do for themselves, I do not doubt, others and in my opinion much the smaller number have no desire to change their condition and will probably go on as usual with contentment to themselves and satisfaction to their owners. What will be the state of things with the expectants after that day is an interesting question. *Nous Verrons.)* Rumors afloat today that the Yankees have returned to Warrenton, Winchester, etc. Firing of cannons heard toward the South. "Farewell to the sweet sunshine." Christmas Day closes in a cloudless night. The clouds are upon the hearts of the people.

Friday, DECEMBER 26.

Another sweet morning. We learn today that Miss M. Loughborough has returned. She had much difficulty in getting out of Washington, so much, that she says, she will not try it again. She succeeded in bring-out the articles she kindly undertook to get for us. The Federal authorities are always much more strict and exacting after a defeat. The border people are made to feel their rod with ten fold severity whenever they are whipped by the Confederate soldiers. It seems to them some comfort to turn their arms against women and children. O Valiant Nation!

Saturday, DECEMBER 27.

Cloudy morning but very mild. I am riding all day and scarcely meet a single individual on the road. The country is almost deserted. In former and happier times Christmas week was a time of general hilarity. Merry making was going on under every roof in the neighborhood. The air was filled with joyous sounds. At every public place the people, white and black, were assembled and with laughing, singing and dancing beguiled the time. At present, there is scarcely to be seen a sign of human life, much less of human enjoyment. At the cross roads and public stands you look in vain for the usual throng; you listen in vain for the sounds of mirth. A solemn silence reigns on all the surrounding ruin.

Sunday, DECEMBER 28.

The clouds of last evening have disappeared and we have a bright, beautiful morning. Our poor wounded boy Beverley leaves us this morning to resume the arduous and dangerous duties of a soldier. His wound is far from well. He can make no use of his left arm. He expects a place on Gen. W. F Lee's staff. It has been promised him. I ride as far as Huntly with him on his way. The army is near Fredericksburg, and he expects to find Gen. Lee somewhere in that neighborhood. Weather delightful all day.

Monday, DECEMBER 29.

It is reported that I have been to Washington and received payment for the damage done me by the Federal Army while in this neighborhood in November. The old report that I had taken the oath of allegiance to the Lincoln Government is no doubt revived. These reports are circulated by enemies, men whom I have never injured in thought, word or deed, but on the other hand, have at various times been of essential service to. If it does them any good or affords them any pleasure thus to slander an innocent neighbor, let them indulge their ill will. I hope I shall not suffer seriously from their calumny but by pursuing as I have always endeavored a just and honorable course, outlive the prejudice it may engender.

Tuesday, DECEMBER 30.

Somewhat cloudy this morning. Gen. Stewart's command arrives in this neighborhood from another raid upon the Yankees. He attacked them at Occoquan, captured a large quantity of their property, took many prisoners and is now returning with his booty. Several of the officers among them Gen. Rooney Lee, his brother Robert and Hill Carter, Jr. of Shirley come here to spend the night. The army seems to be in finer health and spirit than it has ever been. We hear of no sickness of consequence and the robust and ruddy appearance of the men and officers present a pleasing and striking contrast to the attenuated forms and cadaverous complexions so commonly seen in the army a year ago.

The soldiers so far as I have seen are well clothed and well shod. Wonderfully well provided for in these respects considering the great difficulty with which such things are obtained. They get corn and hay of me for which they pay in cash a high price $7.50 per bbl. for corn, $150 per hundred for hay.

Saturday, APRIL 4, 1863—

Hear that the Yankees have advanced in considerable force up the Little River Turnpike to Aldie and Middleburg. They have been greatly annoyed by Mosby's and Farrow's raids and will probably keep in this and Loudoun Counties force sufficient to protect the Army in Fairfax from further annoyance. This being the case, the people of this country will doubtless suffer much. Buckner remains with us today. I make preparation for leaving home tomorrow and shall certainly go unless the weather is too stormy to admit of my starting.

Sunday, APRIL 5.

This is Easter Sunday and as usual a violent storm is prevailing. Snow about six inches deep and still falling. This is by far the worst storm of the winter. Ther. 31 degree. By comparison with the records of other Springs, this is by far the most inclement and backward that I have ever known. Scarcely a furrow has been run for corn and not a seed of any sort put in the ground. No appearance of verdure on the sods and no sign of buds on the earliest trees. Snows furiously all the forenoon. Stops about midday. Nine or ten inches of snow on the ground. Partially clear in the afternoon. Snow melts. Hear that the Yankees arrested on yesterday all the white men they could find in Middleburg and took all the horses. Things are looking darker and darker for our unhappy and unprotected people. The Yankees are said to have returned to Aldie. Night sets in pleasantly with much snow still upon the ground.

Monday, APRIL 6

Pleasant morning over head. I leave home this morning for my long talked of visit to the South. My object in going is to find a place of safety for my stock and family, should the conduct of the Federal Troops which seems to be growing more and more cruel and insupportable render it necessary for me to fly. I take with me my Mother's servant, Joshua and my stallion Agrippa.

Friday, MAY 1, 1863.

Having returned from my visit to the South, I resume my journal. With a heart bowed down with grief I record the events of the last twenty-four days. On the 28th day of March my son Tom arrived here with letters from Gen Stuart to Captain Mosby. He informed me that he was no longer of Stuart's staff but had been sent by him to join Capt. Mosby in his guerilla warfare upon the Federal forces protecting Washington and stationed in the county of Fairfax. (This announcement was anything but agreeable to me. In the first place I did not respect the service in which Mosby was engaged. Its object was mercenary rather than patriotic. A number of adventurous men, and I feared men of desperate or doubtful characters, had united under Mosby for the purpose of making raids upon the enemy. In order to encourage them and to make them active, vigilant and dangerous, the Government allowed them the privilege, the extraordinary privilege, of retaining and converting to their own use all property they captured from the enemy. In the capture of horses, arms, etc. their profits were great and excited the cupidity of many with whom a love of country and genuine patriotism are secondary consideration. That my son should be associated with such men for such purposes I say was not agreeable to me. I disapproved also of the change on account of the great danger to which he would be exposed of losing his life in this irregular and desultory species of warfare. I cared nothing about the glory others seemed to see in reckless feats and hair breadth escapes. I only wished my son to do his duty as a christian soldier as long as the war lasted, and earnestly prayed that at its close he might be returned to me as I had given him up, safe and sound in body and soul. In this prayer I have been disappointed, sadly, bitterly disappointed.)

On Saturday, the 25th of April my dear son and four others of Mosby's men were sent from the neighborhood of Upperville to the vicinity of Warrenton on a scout. At eight o'clock P.M. they arrived at the house of Mr. Chas. H. Utterback, three miles from Warrenton. A party of from twenty to thirty Yankees, concealed in a body of pines saw them approach and when engaged in conversation with Mr. Utterback and suspecting no harm, the little party were stolen upon by the Yankees under cover of the night who approached within ten steps of them before they were discovered, and fired on them exclaiming simultaneously with the discharging of their pistols "Surrender you g-d scoundrels." My poor son was shot near the shoulder of the left side and the ball entered his lungs where it was supposed it lodged. His horse ran off and he fell from his back in about twenty steps from the spot where he was shot and about fifty from Mr. Utterback's door. The rest of the party except one made their escape. A young man named Frankland was captured and taken off a prisoner. His murderers approached my son lying on the ground in a state of insensibility and supposing he was dying took him into Mr. Utterback's house and left a note of which what follows is an exact copy:

"Private Thos. Turner, son of Edward Turner, shot by me. You are to take charge of his effects and hand them over to his father." Signed E. I. Farnsworth, Capt. 8th Ill. Cal. After taking him into the house, the Yankees left hastily, taking with them his pistol and saber. My son's horse ran off and was not captured and was brought to this place on Sunday. At half-past one A.M. on Sunday morning I was waked out of a sweet sleep by a loud rap at my door, and a note was handed me by a servant sent from Mr. Skinkers to inform me of the sad event. The note was short, merely stating that my son was mortally wounded. Never shall I forget the pain occasioned by this awful announcement. Inexpressibly bitter to myself and still more so to my poor wife. I dressed myself in all haste and started to find my dear boy hoping as I rode through the darkness and praying earnestly that it might not prove as bad as it had been represented. I reached my good friend's Mr. Skinker about daybreak, and he rode with me to the house of Mr. Utterback, where I arrived at sunrise. I found my son alive but suffering severely. His mind was perfect but his body below the wound was entirely paralyzed. He spoke cheerfully and affectionately and was delighted to see me. Dr. Moss who had been sent for came soon after my arrival. He examined and probed the wound, and that the examination might be made we were obliged to cut the clothes from his back. The doctor stated that the ball had entered his lung. My dear son then asked him to be frank with him, and if he thought the wound mortal to tell him so plainly. The doctor told him he thought it a very dangerous wound and Tom listened with composure to the announcement. The doctor subsequently told me that he thought then there was no hope for him. A litter was procured and at 3 o'clock P.M he was placed upon it and carried by the neighboring people (who most kindly turned out for the purpose) to Mr. Skinkers on the way to his own loved home. He had borne well his removal and was to all appearance better. Indeed he was suffering but little when taken from the litter and placed on a bed in Mr. Skinker's parlor. He rested tolerably during the night, taking forty drops of laudanum every six hrs. In the morning he was free from pain and his throat which had been obstructed, sometimes painfully obstructed by coagulated blood and matter from the lungs, so as to render respiration difficult, was comparatively clear. Indeed he seemed better and but for the paralysis in which there was no apparent change, we had every reason to be hopeful of his recovery. The doctor thought him well enough to continue his journey homeward, and after breakfast his friends and neighbors gathered in to bear him forward, on his litter. The morning was warm, but the force was good, for Tom was a great favorite and many friends came to assist him, and the litter moved steadily on, the men spelling each other at intervals and stopping occasionally to bathe his face and hands and otherwise to refresh him. The laudanum administered to him on starting kept him quiet and free from pain and he slept sweetly most of the time. We reached Kinloch at about one o'clock P.M. He seemed little exhausted when transferred from the litter to the bed from which, poor fellow, he never rose again. Tuesday morning he spoke cheerfully and said he was quite well. He sometimes fancied that sensation was returning to the parts paralyzed, said he thought he could move his legs and complained of their feeling cold. He also thought he could feel when they were touched. This was imaginary, for in order to test their sensibility I pinched his legs without causing him to complain of pain. Late in the afternoon the Federal cavalry appeared in force on the hills around "The Plains". About the same time Mosby's Company of 120 men advancing on the road from Hopewell to "The Plains" halted in sight of the Yankees about opposite to our ice pond. Here they stood for some time eyeing their enemies who at the same time kept an eye on them. They were little over half a mile apart and their . . . approached to within a few hundred yards of each other. The number of Federals greatly exceeded Mosby's number. The odds were too great to risk a battle and Mosby retreated rapidly toward Mt. Garrison where he got into the mountains. He was not pursued. After Mosby had gone out of sight, the Yankees began to dash about the neighborhood visiting the different houses and plundering the people of such articles as they valued, meat, horses, corn, poultry, etc. A party dashed up to this house about six o'clock and asked if soldiers were not in the house. They were told that no soldiers were here but one who was badly wounded. For the first time in my life I kept myself out of their sight, fearing that they would arrest and take me away from the bed-side of my dying son. On hearing that there was a wounded soldier in the house, they rushed in and demanded to be shown to his room. My wife entreated them most earnestly not to disturb her dying son. Assured them that his wound was considered mortal and a visit from them would probably lead to the worst results. Nothing that she could say, though she said and did everything short of falling on her knees before them, moved them and they rushed madly into the room with cocked pistols in their hands. The Capt. of the party, a rough and unfeeling man, suspected my son and family of duplicity. He said my son was a healthy looking man and would not believe that he was wounded unless he could see the wound himself. My wife assured him as did my daughter and our cousin Miss M. Randolph that he was desperately wounded and all entreated him with tears in their eyes not to disturb him with an examination of the wound which could not be done without causing much pain. Their entreaties and tears were of no avail and though they showed him blood on his shirt he would not be satisfied until he had rolled him over in bed and looked at the wound with his own eyes. After asking him many questions and addressing to him many unfeeling and insulting remarks, he left the room and with his company rode away. In a short time they were seen returning to the house at full speed Again they dismounted and rudely entered my son's chamber, the same rough Capt. leading the way. This time they were attended by a surgeon who said he had been sent by the General to make examination of the wound with a view of his removal if practicable. My poor wife and daughter again besought them not to arouse and excite my son, reminded them that he had been examined and begged that no further investigation should be made. To their entreaties the surgeon replied that he had no discretion, his orders were peremptory and must be obeyed. 'Tis just to the surgeon to say that he did his duty with humanity, handling him gently and giving no unnecessary pain. He apologized for what he did and repeated that the general's order had imposed the unpleasant duty. He pronounced him too ill to be removed, advised my wife to keep him as quiet as possible, and the party mounted their horses and rode away. When I returned to the house from my place of concealment I found my son calm but visibly weaker. Night came on and the Dr. (Cochran) did not return. He had fallen in with Mosby who informed him that the Yankees were in this neighborhood, and he was afraid to venture forward. I must not omit to relate that while the officers of the party were in my house engaged in the examination of my son, the privates were prying into every hole and corner on the premises seeking what they might steal. They with false keys tried the meat house door. Demanded of the servants the whereabouts of my son's horse; broke into one barn by splitting to pieces the door; into another by forcing out a glass window. Fortunately for us their keys did not fit the meat house lock and nothing of value had been left in the barns that was portable to men on horseback. So they got nothing and had to content themselves with wantonly tearing the canvas curtains from the top of a new wagon they found in one of the barns. I take great pleasure in recording the fidelity of my servants on this occasion. The boys ran with the horses to the woods. The young women and girls were vigilant to protect such small articles of value about the house as might be packeted. The old servants replied gruffly and unsatisfactorily to their impudent questions. And Wilhelmina, the best and most faithful of servants, the kindest and most affectionate of friends, with characteristic solicitude was everywhere that her presence was required. She boldly confronted them to keep them out of the house She presented herself to them alongside of her mistress to prevent their entering the chamber of our wounded son, and as she could find opportunity she visited my retreat to keep me posted on their presence and their proceedings, and when they had finally gone 'twas she who came and apprized me of the fact. Indeed, to her alone it was known where I had hid myself for she suggested the place of concealment.

My son's saddle and bridle were hid and Dr. Cochran, whose last horse had been taken a short time before, was riding his horse and thus they were foiled in what they greatly desired, getting the wounded soldiers horse and accoutrements. As the night advanced, our poor son became more restless; so distressing to us and so painful to him was this disquietude that in the absence of the physician I ventured to administer an additional dose of laudanum. The opiate caused him to doze, but there was no rest or comfort in his sleep. He was frequently disturbed by unpleasant dreams, would start from his slumbers ask for some water and fall to sleep again. Thus he continued until near day, when he awoke and asked excitedly where he was. I replied "You are at Kinloch," and asked him if he did not know that he was at Kinloch. His memory seemed to revive and he answered: "*Yes, this is Kinloch.*" Suspecting that his mind was failing, I asked him if he knew me. He answered "Yes, you are Henry Dulany." His mother at that moment approached his bedside and I asked him if he knew who she was. He replied "Aunt Maryetta." His mother then said "Tom don't you know me?" He replied "Oh yes, mamma that is you." His breathing had become very difficult, but it had been more or less so all the while from the accumulation of matter in his throat which from time to time he expectorated and though he was gasping for breath we hoped that he would presently clear his throat as he had constantly done before and were not particularly alarmed at this symptom. After daylight I left him with his Mother and went to my office to dress myself. While thus engaged, a servant came with a message from my wife to come immediately to Tom. On reaching his bedside I was struck with the change in his condition. He was gasping most painfully and throwing his hands wildly about. He attempted to speak but could not articulate. He was dying, and surrounded by his weeping friends, his spirit in a few moments took its flight. His death occurred at a quarter past six o'clock on the morning of the 29th day of April. He lacked only nine days of being twenty years of age. He was born on the eighth day of May, 1843. Thus had fallen another victim to this most unholy, unnecessary war; a young man of the purest character and the finest promise. Oh! unhappy, victimized, ruined Virginia, how hast thou suffered in the loss of the flower of thy youth, in the destruction of the cream and essence of thy population.

Led blindly into a war from which under the most favorable circumstances thou hadst nothing to expect but ruin, thy people butchered, thy property squandered, thy territory wasted, thy altars profaned, history must necessarily record the folly, and thy children yet unborn read the humiliating fact that thou allowed thyself to be made a cats paw of by others who to save themselves, plotted and accomplished thy ruin . . .

Diary of A Confederate Soldier

HENRY BENNETT

Research by M. D. Gore, Sumerduck, Virginia, November 18, 1937.

JANUARY 22nd, 1863—It is still raining. We received orders last night to hold ourselves in readiness to march in a moment's notice as the enemy made strong demonstrations near Fredericksburg, but as yet nothing has taken place. All quiet on our lines here.

27th—Pickett's division moved today and camped northwest of Fredericksburg. It has rained all day.

28th—It has snowed very fast all day. Detail from our Regiment made to work in the trenches. It is night and the hum of the camp has ceased and no sound breaks the stillness but the wintry blast that sweeps by rocking the sturdy oaks and the patter of snow flakes on our blankets which we have spread over poles for shelter.

29th—Clear and mild. The snow is ten inches deep. I am of the opinion that all active operations have ended along our lines for the present. The roads are now in horrible condition and it is almost impossible to get out. We returned to camp today and we were happy to see our comfortable huts again. We felt it was getting home again. I was very tired as I had marched all the way, ten miles with a heavy load, without resting. I hope after a night's sleep to feel all right again.

FEBRUARY 8th—Continued to rain until 12 o'clock, cleared up warm. Snow has all melted. We were relieved today and returned to camp. We had a miserable march, the roads are in horrible condition. I got to the 11th Va. about 6 o'clock and stayed there all night with my brother Oscar.

14th—Clear and cool. Wind east. It has the appearance of rain today. We had no drill today. Got a load of wood and chopped it up. I am quite comfortable in my new domicile which consists of a tent stretched over an excavation of earth with a fireplace and chimney with a barrel on top to prevent smoking. We have no news from Hooker, and whether he intends to force a passage of the Rappahannock in his insane attempt "on to Richmond" or change his base by turning at the mouth of the river and come by way of Suffolk, remains to be seen.

15th—We broke camp this morning and commenced our march towards Richmond. It commenced to rain about day light and rained hard for several hours. We marched thirteen miles. The roads are in awful condition. Capt. Kirby and myself stopped the night at Mrs. Marshall's, we were very tired but after a hearty supper of good fried ham and cornbread, and a good night's sleep we were much refreshed, and set out early in the morning to rejoin our company.

19th—Still cloudy and misting. We marched three miles below Winchester on the Petersburg Pike and camped. The ground is low and very wet. Where we are bound for I am not able to say.

1st. of March—Rain this morning but cleared at noon. We marched from Chester three miles below Petersburg. Many pretty ladies waved to us as we passed through the city, and cheered us on our toilsome way.

2nd—A lovely day. The sun shines bright and warm, and the song of a bird reminds me that spring has again returned. I do not like the face of the country as it is flat and marshy, but occasionally presents a fine appearance and seems to be well cultivated. There are many fine residences which betoken wealth.

3rd to 10th—We are still in camp near Petersburg. Gen. Jenkins' Brigade left for Blackwaters this morning, the 9th inst.

18th—Cloudy and rain about noon. We had brigade review, and inspection today. We have heard of a cavalry fight at Culpeper. Fitz Lee's Brigade was engaged and drove the enemy to the north bank with much loss. Our loss is also heavy. I suppose that Clay was in the engagement.

23rd—Very cloudy and disagreeable. Jim Fisher and Dick Payne left on a furlough this morning. We left camp at noon and marched nine miles. The roads are in horrible condition. The face of the country is anything but inviting, flat and swampy and covered with water. The plantations seem to be in a backward state. The tenements are old and dilapidated. To judge from Prince George Court House there is not much enterprise in the country here and very little use for lawyers. I saw but two houses beside the Court House, jail and Clerk's Office.

24th—We marched fifteen miles over the most desolate and forlorn country. The land is only fit for frogs and snakes The few farms on the road are very small and badly managed, which bespeaks but little improvement either in civilization or enterprise. We waded through water up to our knees for miles. I had no conception of such a vast waste land so little adapted to cultivation and improvements.

25th—We marched 20 miles today through Sussex and a corner of Surry and Southampton. The face of the country is much improved here, and I saw a good many fine farms, well tilled. I saw many fine peach and apple orchards which is a good sign of thrift and enterprise. We camped at Ivor Station on the Petersburg and Norfolk Railroad. I was very tired and jaded.

26th—We did not move today as we are near our post where we will picket. I am much improved and am now ready to resume marching or any duties that may devolve upon me. The Yankee pickets are at Black Water River about four miles below. I am not advised as to the force we have here, but presume it is ample to keep in check any advance movement of the enemy. The sun rose clear and bright this morning and continued so all day, the first clear day in ten days.

8th April—Cloudy and cool. Regiment inspection this morning. Our company got praise for having cleanest guns. Reported attack on Charleston. Kemper's Brigade is now at Franklin. I hope we will get close together before long. Reynolds left on his discharge this morning. I sent a letter by him to Orange Court House. Company drill this evening. I bought a pound of dried apples and stewed them, which ate most excellent indeed. We live very badly, getting very little to eat. My legs pain me very much with rheumatism. I hope they will get well when the weather gets settled. The spring is very backward for this state.

10th—We camped near Franklin, a small village on the Seaboard and Roanoke R. R. I had the great pleasure of seeing my brother Oscar here. His brigade came here on Monday. It must be some move is on hand as our troops are concentrating at this point. The weather is getting warm. We have come through one of the most disagreeable, wet winters it has been my lot to see.

11th—We took up the line of march before light this morning and crossed the Black Water River at South Quay. Nothing of importance transpired on this march. The country is much improved on this side of the river. We camped seven miles from Suffolk. Our advanced troops captured the outposts of the enemy.

12th—We bivouacked early this morning near Providence Church. Captured at this post five pickets. It was quite warm.

13th—Heavy skirmishing all day. Our regiment, the 17th, went on picket duty tonight. Very cold and disagreeable. Am very tired.

15th—We were surprised this morning before light. The enemy is in strong force, cavalry, infantry and artillery. We had a sharp fight and were compelled to fall back. Tom Saunders and Dr. Huffman of Company, were wounded. Rained hard all day. We were reinforced and occupied our position about noon.

16th, 17th, 18th, 19th—Threw up breastworks. The 11th is now with us on our left.

20th 21st, 22nd—Still hard at work. The Yankees burned a house right in front of our lines.

23rd—Another house was burned today. Our company on picket duty had quite a sharp skirmish this evening. Rained hard all day.

24th—The enemy appeared in heavy force. Our pickets were driven back with some loss. Several were wounded on both sides.

25th, 26th, 27th—Clear and cool with high winds. All very quiet on our lines.

28th—Rained today. All quiet on our lines. Nothing of moment. Our scouts captured three Federals this evening.

29th—Cleared up about 10 o'clock. Quite warm, prospects of a thunderstorm. All quiet up to six o'clock this evening. Whether we shall have a fight or not remains to be seen. The enemy seems satisfied that we are not attacking them, and I think they have no disposition to attack us. If they should they will pay for it as we are well entrenched and still strengthening our works

3rd—Clear and warm. All quiet on our lines. We fell back tonight and crossed Black Water River about 10 o'clock. The enemy did not follow us, only their cavalry picked up some stragglers.

9th—Clear and warm. We marched from Petersburg today and camped near the R. R. seven miles below Richmond We will remain here only a short time. All quiet on the Rappahannock. I am very tired and hope to have a few days rest to recruit my exhausted strength.

10th—Clear and warm. Gen. Jackson died today at 2 P. M. This sad intelligence filled us with great sorrow. The great Capt. sleeps his last sleep. No sound can wake him to glory again. The spirit that led his invincible legions to victory will not die. His men will still fight to avenge the death of their Chieftain.

11th, 12th—Clear and warm. We are still camped in the woods.

15th—We got marching orders this morning, and all appeared pleased at the idea of getting on the north side of the James River. We left camp at 2 P. M and marched near Richmond.

16th—We resumed our march before 6 A. M. and passed through Richmond in good order. The sidewalks were crowded with ladies who waved to us. We camped twelve miles above Richmond on the old telegraph road. Our destination is Hanover Junction, but we do not know how long we will remain there. There is a rumor that Hooker has crossed again and is at the Hamilton Crossing. I am very tired but hope with a good night's rest to have strength to march again tomorrow.

12th June—I have permission to go home. -Left the Regiment at Waller's Tavern. I met several old friends on the road. I got home at night, very tired, as I walked thirty-five miles. It is warm and dry.

13th—I am at home, am too tired today to meet my Regiment. The Division is in camp near Culpeper Court House. I was too tired to accompany them on a walk.

14th—Went to Raccoon Ford today to join my company, but to my luck the Brigade had been ordered back to guard the railroad at the Junction, so I went back home. Father preached at Craig's Church today.

17th—I left early this morning and traveled quite fast. I got back to camp after dark, having marched 27 miles. I was extremely tired.

18th—I went on guard this morning. It has rained all day.

23rd—The first of the Yankee prisoners passed by this morning. 1000 captured by Gen. Ewell at Winchester. We had news today of another victory at Vicksburg.

24th—Cloudy this morning, slight sprinkle of rain. More prisoners went by today.

25th—We left the bridge this morning. Ordered to Gordonsville. We took the train eight miles above the Junction. Rained hard all day. The cars were all wet and muddy inside and very disagreeable as we had no room to sleep. We got to Gordonsville at day light this morning and camped in the woods one half mile from there.

28th—Cloudy. Orders tonight to pack up. We took the cars at dark and got to Richmond at daylight.

1st July—We got to Gordonsville this morning and camped in a beautiful grove on the Orange Road one mile from the village. Rained hard all day. We get very wet as we did not have time to put up our tents. No news of interest.

9th—Commenced our march again at 8 A. M. We had to wade many streams as the bridges had all been swept away. The roads are rocky and full of water. We camped in the mountains. We had marched 18 miles today.

10th—Crossed the mountains today and came to the Luray Valley, which is a splendid country. The crops are abundant and everything is in a flourishing state. War is not known in this section. We marched 20 miles and camped near Luray.

11th—We commenced our march again early this morning. The day was extremely warm. I was overcome by the heat, and had to fall out of the ranks and rest. We marched 18 miles today and camped eight miles from Front Royal.

12th—Crossed the river at McCay's Ford. Water waist deep. Crossed the north fork four miles below Strasburg. We camped here this evening. Marched 12 miles. Nothing of interest.

13th—Rained very hard, and we got soaking wet. We passed

through Middletown and Newtown on the Valley Pike. We camped near Winchester. Marched 10 miles today.

14th to 19th—Still in camp near Winchester. News that Gen Lee has recrossed the Potomac. Troops camped at Bunker Hill.

20th—Today we marched to Cedarville near Front Royal and camped there. Very warm. Gen. Pickett is on the march

21st—We left camp at four o'clock this morning and crossed the river which was quite rapid and came near washing us down. Corse with the 30th, 29th & 15th, took possession of Chester Gap losing two men and one wounded. The 17th took the road to Manassas Gap. Our pickets were all captured. The enemy made a dash at the reserves but were handsomely repulsed. Three were killed and one wounded and one a prisoner. They kept a brisk fire on us until late in the evening. Having been reinforced by Garnette's Brigade, we advanced 2 miles, when our pickets discovered the Fourth Regulars advancing. Our Regiment filled in the bushes and formed, and advanced in line of battle as soon as we got sight of the foe. We charged them down and drove them from the field with three killed, one wounded and several prisoners. Our loss only three wounded.

22nd—Reed's Division relieved us this morning. We rejoined our Division at Chester Gap. Woodford's Brigade, Molaw's Division drove the enemy out this evening.

5th August—Marched today. Camped on Mountain Run. I went home and found all well. Father had gone to preach at a funeral.

6th—Returned to camp today.

21st—National fast and prayer day which is being generally observed in the army. Meetings are held in all the Regiments. Much seriousness and solemnity seem to pervade the entire army.

9th September—We got marching orders yesterday evening after a month's rest We left camp this morning at an early hour in the direction of Orange Court House, passed that point on towards Gordonsville, camping five miles from the latter place. We marched 15 miles hot and dusty. Many rumors are abroad as to where we shall go but no one seems to know.

13th—We marched through Richmond by company. Halted an hour. Took the train and arrived in Petersburg at 5 P. M. and camped near the city. Armistead's Brigade is here. Kemper and Hunt are below Richmond.

15th—We got to Lynchburg at noon, and after getting out rations we took the train for southwest Va. The country is all hills and vales shady groves and fine farms with luxuriant crops The Blue Ridge Mountains are in the distance.

16th—We got to Camp Zollicoffer tonight. The country is fine. The people flocked to the road to see us pass and to cheer us.

19th—Still cool. In line of battle all day. The enemy went to Bristol and destroyed all the commissary stores, and burned a bridge and returned here.

20th—They made an attempt to get to our place but met with a vigorous resistance and retired. Our loss, two killed and four wounded. The Cavalry had several wounded. The loss of the enemy is not known, several died at Blountville and several were left on the road wounded.

1st November—Lt. Slaughter, Embrey, Cologne, Winter, Pemberton, and myself cut poles and logs for timber to make boards for our house. Am very tired.

2nd, 3rd, 4th, 5th—Clear and warm. Have finished our house and now have very comfortable quarters.

12th to 20th—Still here in camp. Nothing to relieve the monotony of camp life We have battalion drills in the morning and company drills in the evening. No news of Lee's or Bragg's armies. Embrey and myself changed our quarters to a tent as it was so crowded. Weather clear and warm.

20th—Embrey went to Richmond. I received letters from home. I went on guard this evening.

21st, 22nd—Rained all night. No news.

2nd December—The Yankees landed at Smithfield last night. Our regiment under arms We marched 2 miles on Broad Water road to the ferry late this evening. Not more than sixty Yankees landed. Col. Herbert's horse fell with him today and hurt him badly

3rd—Resumed our drills. Report that Longstreet captured Burnside's army at Knoxville. Grant has fallen back at Chickamauga. Gen Bragg has been relieved of his command of the army. Hardie is now in command. Gen. Morgan made his escape into Canada with six other officers. Meade has retreated across the Rapidan, Lee is in pursuit.

17th to 26th—Clear and cold. Stanfield went to Richmond on conscript duty. Embrey detailed as scout. Spent Christmas in camp, nothing of special interest occurring to break the monotony of camp life. My sincere prayer is that this may be the last of Christmas our army may have to spend in camp.

30th—Dress parade this morning. Court martial cases heard, of which there are quite a number, many of them very severe. Some of the sentences: shaving half the head, wearing a twelve pound ball and chain for a year, to be kept in close confinement when not at work. One poor fellow from Company C. has to forfeit his life for desertion, will be executed before the regiment on January 8th. The officers of the 17th with others from other commands gave a ball after a tournament which was quite interesting. Capt. Barnes of Co. D was the successful competitor having taken the ring every ride. If I am to judge by the great noise of the late hour, Capt. Barleycorn was acting a conspicuous part among many.

1st January 1864 to January 24th—We have remained in camp drilling when the weather would permit. Nothing of special interest has taken place.

23rd—With many regrets we had to leave quarters today. We went aboard the train at 3 P. M and arrived at Petersburg at night. We remained in camp until Thursday, then took the cars for North

Carolina arriving at Weldon late in the evening. We then went aboard the train and reached Kinston late at night. We marched two miles and bivouacked. Kemper's and Barton's brigade have gone to the front today in the direction of New Bern.

30th—Our regiment with the 15th are detailed for special duty. We left Kingston at 3 P.M. and marched till midnight. We marched 25 miles, and our feet are blistered.

1st February—We were aroused at 2 o'clock and resumed marching. Our duty was to storm a fort, but after reconnaissance it was found to be too strong for us.

2nd—Lt. Wood with his marines boarded a gunboat and captured it and burned it. The troops on our right captured five hundred prisoners.

3rd—We commenced retreating today and reached Goldsboro on the 7th, where we are now encamped. The weather is mild and pleasant.

7th to 18th—We are still here in camp. We are now drilling. A young man in Co. B was killed instantly by one of his own company. They were snapping guns at each other, which they thought had no charge in them, when one went off and killed the poor fellow outright.

24th—Co. drilling this morning. Cleaned our Co. ground. Dress parade this evening. We received orders at sundown to move. We left camp after dark and took the train for Lexington, in Davidson County, North Carolina. Had a nice time on the trip as we were in passenger cars. We passed through several towns and reached Lexington about noon and went into camp.

26th—We marched through the town and had a dress parade and were then dismissed for an hour to look around the town. Then we marched back to camp

27th—We left camp before light and went aboard the train, and got back to our old camp at daylight the next morning. Nothing unusual occurred on the trip.

1st, 2nd March—Co. and Battalion drill. News of a Yankee raid by Kilpatrick around Richmond. They were repulsed with some loss. We have orders tonight to be ready to move at a moment's notice.

3rd—We commenced our march towards Kinston this morning and marched twelve miles when had orders to return. We got back to Goldsboro about night . The 29th Regiment started for Richmond about dark. While waiting for the train the orders were countermanded. We came to our old camp on the morning of the fourth where we are at present. Kemper's Brigade came up from Kinston last night and camped on its old ground. They expect to go to Richmond.

5th—The Brigade has gone to Wilmington, North Carolina. The boys did not want to go much. I went to Goldsboro and bought a gallon of peas and paid four dollars for them

6th—Cold and cloudy. Received orders this morning to remain in camp. Our tents were struck this evening and carried to Goldsboro. We expect to march, and I hope we will return to Virginia.

7th—We left camp this morning and marched to Goldsboro and took the train for Kinston. We arrived at 11 A M. and camped just south of the town. Had to clean up our camp.

15th—I left camp at 4 o'clock this morning on a furlough. Took the train at Kinston at 6 o'clock and reached Goldsboro at 8 A. M. Changed cars there which gave me a seat to Petersburg, and which city I reached at 3 P. M. Left Petersburg at 4 P. M. and reached Richmond at dark. We now had an exciting race for the transportation office where we had to wait for two hours for transportation clerks to give us proper traveling credentials. We now went to get lodgings for the night. We were conducted by a negro boy to the Monticello House where we got supper and bed for ten dollars. I left my couch at an early hour and went to the Fredericksburg Depot and after waiting a great while, the cars at last commenced moving and soon we were on our way and without any detention we reached Guyeys Depot at 10 A. M when I took it on foot and after many hours got home, the heaven of my present anxieties. I was very glad to see my brother Clay as I had not seen him for 13 months. The weather has been very bad since I came home. A great snow storm set in about 2 P. M. and snowed all night. It fell some 15 inches deep.

The Home Front

By JOHN A. C. KEITH

In every conflict since the beginning of history women and children and old people have endured suffering and hardships beyond number at the hands of invading enemies. In our own Civil War these innocent noncombatants were subjected to all the horrors of occupation in various parts of the South, but those in Northern Virginia had four long years of them with only brief intermissions.

Prince William, Loudoun, Fairfax and Fauquier Counties all shared hardships and devastation.

Fauquier, however, deserves particular attention in its sufferings because it was the largest of the four counties composing the territory which has been called the "Debatable Land" and "Mosby's Confederacy". Stretching more than 50 miles from the crest of the Blue Ridge nearly to tidewater it lay within a few miles of many major battles and suffered from their impact.

Wounded from the fields of Manassas, Ball's Bluff, Fredericksburg and Chancellorsville flooded churches, court houses and private homes, to be cared for by Fauquier women. Marching Confederate armies had to be fed with local farm produce, while the invaders merely took what they wanted. In addition to being separated from their menfolk serving in Lee's army and caring for wounded and burying dead these people had to provide for their families and what servants remained, to try to hide their livestock from the invaders when they came, to carry on what farming they could and to try somehow to live normal lives, and just survive. It took courage, determination and ingenuity. Doctors were scarce and medicine all but unobtainable. Old people and children became ill often from malnutrition. Food was always a problem and an old letter says, "We'll have a cake at Christmas if we can get some molasses." If they had hogs to slaughter the problem was where to find salt which was as rare as gold. Any type of clothing was either not available or too costly for people who needed their few dollars for food. Finally, they often received almost brutal treatment from the invaders. Women were insulted, houses and barns destroyed. No place, however fine, was safe from all manner of enemy depredations.

In attempting to give some account of the Fauquier home front from 1861 to 1865 I have had to draw largely on family stories and family letters, but since my kinfolk were spread out from Upperville to Gold Vein I believe their experiences were similar to those of most others in the county. As a child I saw Colonel Mosby and such gallant ladies as Mrs Norman V. Randolph who when a young girl had taunted the Yankees occupying Warrenton. I knew my uncle, Captain Edward Carter, who was lame all his life from a wound received in Pickett's Charge at Gettysburg, and another uncle, Judge James Keith, a man of huge girth whom I could not envision as a trooper of the gallant Black Horse Cavalry. Old Man Furr came to our house when in need of financial help because he had been in my grandfather's company. In my bedroom stood a monstrous wardrobe on top of which a Confederate soldier had hid when the Yankees raided Glen Welby searching for Mosby. The old people never tired of telling war stories and I listened, and I shall quote from my grandparents' letters and those of other relations

On a humid afternoon in July 1861 young Jack Payne of "The Pines" and a friend lay in the grass on Warrenton's Academy Hill and listened to a rumbling off to the northeast. It could have been thunder but it was the guns of First Manassas, that battle which presaged a great change in the lives of Fauquier people. That lovely land of rolling meadows and fertile farmland was about to be laid waste and become a veritable desert

For four years armies marched and remarched across it. Fences went down, crops were destroyed, livestock butchered, buildings destroyed until in 1865 all that was left were "our bare acres" as Mrs. Isham Keith of Woodbourne wrote to a Kentucky cousin. Almost immediately after Manassas, Warrenton was deluged with wounded. The school house, churches and private houses were full and every woman became a nurse. Many of the brave boys from South Carolina and Georgia died and were buried in the town cemetery, each with a neat wooden cross bearing his name to mark the grave.

In the winter of 1863 the Yankees occupied Warrenton and used the crosses for firewood, leaving our heroes nameless. Immediately after the War these unknown dead were placed in a common grave under a fine marble shaft dedicated to "Virginia's Defenders" and proclaiming, "Here they sleep as sleeps a hero on his unsurrendered shield."

In any of its manifestations war is frightful but it is much much worse when a population is occupied by a hostile army and separated from its own fighting men. The Confederates retreated from their positions at Centreville in the early spring of 1862 and the Union forces moved into Fauquier where they remained until their defeat at Second Manassas in late August of that year They came back again that winter and withdrew after our victory at Chancellorsville in May only to return after Gettysburg to stay until after Appomattox.

Confederate soldiers could visit their families only by stealth, and communicating by letter was difficult to say the least as the Confederate postal service could not operate in occupied areas and most letters were carried by hand. No one got newspapers. News of the battle of Gettysburg reached Fauquier a week after the event and then only by rumor. People were frantic to know if their loved ones were dead, wounded or captured.

All normal life was disrupted as even religious services were irregular in the rural areas. When the Rev. Mr. Granberry, a Methodist divine, arrived at a country house it was an event and as many neighbors as could gathered to hear him preach. Food and livestock were carried off not to be replaced while a dearth of farm help prevented the raising of crops. In 1865 Mrs. Ambler of Markham felt it sufficiently important to note in her diary that she had had a chicken for dinner.

A further complication of civilian life was the presence of unionists. As in many border areas a great part of the population had been staunchly opposed to secession. After Virginia had joined the Confederacy, however, the great majority went with their state wholeheartedly. There were nevertheless a few recalcitrants who remained loyal to the union and were suspect by their former friends. Some of them were secret union sympathizers who gave information to the enemy. Old, cantankerous Henry Dixon, the only man in Fauquier who voted for Mr. Lincoln, was also an informer and was the cause of at least one man being arrested as a spy. This was an unfortunate German who gave music lessons in the Salem neighborhood and was probably completely innocent. Dixon charged him with giving information to Mosby and the poor man spent the rest of his days in the Old Capitol Prison.

Much has been written about the daring exploits of Col. John S. Mosby and his dashing partisans. Many of their most gallant deeds were done in Fauquier where they had numerous friends and hiding places, a number of the troop being natives of the county. There is no doubt that the rangers inflicted an enormous amount of damage on the Union forces and supply lines and that they rendered valuable assistance to the beleaguered Lee. At the same time, it must be admitted that many local people suffered from helping him or from being suspected of doing so.

The occupying forces were beside themselves with fury at the way in which this will-o'the-wisp could strike them and then be off before they knew what had hit them. In their fury they wreaked their vengeance on any local citizens they felt to be in league with him. This revenge was the cause of burning Joseph Blackwell's house at Piedmont Station, of punitive raids on Mr. Ludwell Lake's at Rectortown, Mr. Hathaway's near the Plains, and on Major R. H. Carter's at Glen Welby. Mosby hid in the Glen Welby woods from which he staged a successful raid on a Union baggage train. Col. Gallop. in a frenzy, rushed to Glen Welby and gave its inmates two minutes to get out before he fired the house. The gallant conduct of the Carter women saved the old home but the barns were destroyed and remaining livestock carried off.

This always present danger did not deter the people of Fauquier from helping Mosby when they could. An instance of this is Bert Pollock's ride. Roberta Pollock, an intrepid horsewoman, was a first cousin of General Lee and lived at Leeton Forest just outside Warrenton. One winter's evening she was in the village and by chance overheard a Negro giving the Union soldiers information as to when they could surprise Mosby at a hideaway near Salem. Without waiting a second she mounted her horse and dashed off into the snowy dusk to warn the partisan. Accompanied only by a faithful servant she made her way across View Tree and over a spur of Wildcat Mountain sometimes getting lost and finally almost being shot by one of Mosby's pickets. But she gave him warning only a few minutes before the Yankees arrived.

Warrenton being centrally located and the county seat was generally occupied by a sizeable Union force, but even so it was subject to Mosby's raids. Mrs. Norman V. Randolph (Janet Weaver) who as a little girl lived in the house now known as Carter Hall said that often she and her sister would lie awake tensely at night listening to horsemen riding up the lane under their window. If they heard the clank of sabres and other accoutrements they would know they were Yankees. But if they heard only the foot falls of carefully guided horses they knew that they were their men and tingled with pleasurable excitement. The Federals were perfectly aware that the townspeople aided the Confederates whenever possible and were on the alert to arrest anyone suspected of helping them. On one occasion they rounded up a group of local suspects and brought them before the Provost Marshal. Nothing definite was charged against them and first of all they were asked to give their names. They did: Fox, Wolfe, Lyon, Frogg, Bear and Rabbit (all local names). The Provost was so confused and confounded that he let them off.

On many occasions Union officers and men were kind and considerate in their treatment of the civil population and there are many stories of friendliness on both sides. People in Northern Virginia had friends and relations in Baltimore and Philadelphia, some of whom appeared among them in Federal uniform and were well received. The North, however, recruited many new immigrants in its armies, rough uneducated people who had no feeling of pity for the unfortunates who were at their mercy. Plunder and destruction were their only aims.

In the summer of 1863 old Isham Keith lay dying at his home outside Warrenton. He had had a woolen mill at Waterloo which made cloth for the Confederate Army. The Yankees burned it, so he sold the land and went to Richmond, partly on foot, to put the proceeds in Confederate government bonds. Upon his return he became fatally ill, nursed by his wife and the young women of the household. His two sons were in the army. One afternoon as he approached his end word came that the Yankees were next door at Innes Hill where they fired the house and stole John M. Forbes' library. In a short time they were at Woodbourne but not before Mrs. Keith had locked the young women in the attic. They rifled the house, broke up furniture and finally ripped open feather beds and mixed the feathers with molasses on the parlor floor. In her dilemma Mrs. Keith looked out of a window and saw a group of officers on a hill at the edge of Forbes' woods. She waved a sheet out the window, an officer saw it and came spurring to the house. This man, Major Hitchcock, was shocked at the scene he beheld. He took the flat of his sword and beat the brutal Irish and Germans out of the house. Later he apologized to Mrs. Keith and took a United States flag which he placed in an angle between the house and a wing, assuring her that as long as it remained she would not be molested. Until 1930 the marks made by Yankee sabres were visible in the bars of the cellar windows at Woodbourne.

Stories of hardship and gallantry on the part of Fauquier women in these trying years can be repeated without number. Some of them, including Mrs. Ambler at Markham and Mrs. Henry Dulany at Oakley, kept diaries giving graphic accounts of these stirring times. Not only did they suffer from the depredations of regular troops but even worse they feared deserters and hangers-on.

Robert E. Scott, being too old for active duty, had helped to fit out a company of infantry of which his son, R. Taylor Scott was elected captain, and Edward Carter, a student at VMI, first lieutenant.

Fanny Scott Carter, daughter of Richard H. Carter of Glen Welby near Salem, was the wife of R. Taylor Scott, son of Robert Eden Scott. When both her husband and her father went into the army Mrs. Scott and her young children went back to Glen Welby to live with her mother and sisters. She wrote whenever possible to her husband and excerpts from her letters may be taken as typical of those written by Fauquier women to their men in the army.

"Glen Welby, March 11, 1862.

"Last night we had a stampede from here, every body but Henry Rich and Jim, both Johns, Charles, Sam, Bill, Henry Saunders, Wallace and probably Selden. (Family servants). I fear they have carried off Pa's horses, Sophie had an offer of $150 for her mare, it is missing. I am rather surprised at some of them, but now have my confidence shaken in all. Mr. Allison (overseer) went down to the Plains for Belle Carter and Mrs. Wilson and I hope they will come. We want a good many here with us. Mr. Robert Wright's house was searched in every part for him, all his poultry, meat etc. was taken."

"Glen Welby, April 3, 1862

"Saturday last our *neighbors* left Middleburg and came to the Plains, since then rumors are abundant of their doings and sayings. They have several times visited Salem in large and again in small parties. Col. Geary makes Mr. Tom Foster's his headquarters. They eat at the table with the family and I am told behave very badly. The Col. threatened to have Kate arrested, said it would not be long before the stars and stripes were waving over the whole South. She replied for a while perhaps over Virginia, but over the entire South never with some emphasis. He was quite enraged and very violent in his language. They have arrested Mr. Jacquelin Smith, upon what grounds I cannot hear, I am told the spectacle presented as they passed through Salem with their prisoner was quite ludicrous, his personal appearance particularly. I understand they had a little skirmish beyond Salem on Tuesday near Blake's Mill. Several Yankee prisoners were taken and one or two killed. Alick (J. Alexander Carter who lived at Meadow Grove, near Marshall) has seen the Yankees several times and had conversation with them. Sophie had a letter from Kate Powell (a sister of Mrs. Henry Dulany, of Oakley, later married George Carter of Oatlands, in Loudoun County) at Oakley. She says they have suffered a great deal since Upperville was occupied by the enemy. They took a great deal of corn, 17 head of cattle, a Waggon and four horses, all the fowls, and four women servants went off. The family were constantly intruded upon and when the windows and doors were bolted and locked to keep them out they were violent in their threats, shook the windows, struck the sashes with their bayonets and charged around generally, took possession of the kitchen and ordered dinners. Ida (Mrs. Henry Dulany of Oakley whose husband was a first cousin of Mrs. R. H. Carter of Glen Welby) positively refused to give them anything. They took what they could get and left for the time, though they returned and were at Oakley every day for two weeks. The Stephensons in Upperville were treated badly, Mrs. S. locked in her own dining room, her daughters shaken by the shoulders and threatened with arrest. We have been looking for them daily, so far none have arrived. The Salemites are much excited, none more than Mr. Hall."

"Sunday Glen Welby, April 6, 1862

"We went to Salem Church this evening, Sophie and I in the Rockaway, Alick (J. Alexander Carter of Meadow Grove, later served in the C. S. Navy), Edie and Mr. Williamson (a Methodist minister) on horseback. Had a sermon from the 103rd Psalm "Like as a father pittieth his children, so the Lord pittieth them that fear him." Mr. Williamson returned with us and will remain several days longer. I will write to Oakwood by him when he goes to Warrenton. The enemy, I believe, are not there yet. We remain undisturbed. The Yankees have left the Plains, gone back to Upperville scared off by the capture of eight of their men at Salem and the rumor that the Rebels were in the Free State. It was quite exciting to the Salem people, the race, capture, surrender etc. took place in the streets of the city. It was supposed a large number would quarter in Salem; they went to all the churches, examined them it was thought with intent to use them in quartering their men. Dr. Harry (Presley R. Harry, Dentist) is still with the Southern Army; they threaten to hang him as they think he was the cause of their capture. We have not been molested at all. I told you earlier that Bill Monroe had returned and is now here at the Glen. The rest of our servants I expect from his account have crossed the river. At any rate, none have returned to their allegiance."

"Glen Welby, April 7 1862

"I sent you two letters yesterday, my dearest Taylor, one to Culpeper C. H to be mailed and the other to a gentleman of this neighbourhood who said he would send it direct to the camp (at Orange), but I have just heard that Mr. Balthrope (Next door neighbor of Glen Welby) will leave this evening and as he kindly offers to take a letter I cannot allow so good an opportunity to escape. I judge you by myself, a letter is always acceptable. Henry Arthur Hall sent those directed to his care to me by Royston. . . . The enemy have been around us in every direction, behaving often very badly and with great insolence and profanity to ladies, much of this I have from the ladies themselves. At Oakley they sent word to Ida that if they did not find dinner prepared for them and whatever they ordered ready they would walk upstairs and know the reason why. They vow vengeance upon Salem and say they'll burn every house to the ground Of course, the inhabitants are much excited. I saw Judge Norris yesterday who gave me an account of the way they behaved. Numbers of servants are leaving the neighborhood. Night before last Dr. Withers lost every one, men, women and children. Mr. Allison (Overseer at Glen Welby, Texas and Major Carter's other farms) prophesies that Bill Monroe will not stay and that in a month from this time there will not be one on this place . . .As far as I am individually concerned I am reconciled to giving up my own servants. I think it a very great responsibility bringing them up and managing them properly. There is a large number of the enemy in Upperville. They behaved at some places outrageously. Col. Geary is a perfect liar, a ruffian and devoid of all decency. I hear horrible accounts of him everywhere and don't know how he could ever have been mistaken for a gentleman. . . Everything seems to be at a standstill, little or no farming going on, scarcely anyone ploughing, fences pulled down, fields many of them in commons, stores closed, no one traveling about, the public roads deserted; a few travelers on old, broken down steeds that no one would care to possess himself of, may occasionally be seen crossing fields. All looks sad and desolate. War is terrible and yet I fear the worst is to come."

"April 19, 1862

"While you were on your march to Richmond during all that bad weather we were flooded with Yankees, the most miserable set that ever I put my eyes upon, the scum of the earth, and from every Nation and every tongue in one regiment. They spoke 17 languages but most of them were Dutch and wild men. Your father tells me they eat fowls of every description raw, strip off the feathers and eat them down. Puppies were a great delicacy. They stole and ate every one they saw. The neighborhood was greatly annoyed by them. We as I told you in a former letter escaped miraculously and our loss was comparatively small. Gen. Geary is now about here and his headquarters at Luke Woodward's above Rectortown . . . We are completely cut off from our own army and can hear nothing relative to their movements. I have never seen a newspaper since you left. I am anxious to go to Oakwood (12 miles away) as soon as it is deemed safe to travel and pay my long talked of visit to Grandmamma and your father and mother. At present you can hardly move for Yankee picketts. In order to go in and out of Salem (two miles away) we must obtain a pass. Alick and DeButts (two young brothers) occasionally go out; we never do, as it is not safe. This morning Mary Bland (a house servant) is missing. Harriet came for her last night and they went off together, taking with them some of our best clothes, Ma's (Mary Welby DeButts, Mrs. R. H. Carter of Glen Welby) black silk cloak, etc., etc. a number of my things. Harriet came out from Salem a few days ago. I talked to her firmly but kindly and required her to go back, told her always to come to me when in trouble and I would do all in my power for her. She promised to behave and left me but I felt convinced she would go off and was careful of my clothes. But yesterday when your father (R. E. Scott) arrived, I ran down and left my keys. She stripped us."

"Glen Welby - Monday 6th July 1863

"Where are you, my dear husband (Major Scott was on Gen'l. Pickett's staff and had been at Gettysburg) what are you doing and what is going on. We live in utter ignorance of everything and everybody, outside our immediate neighborhood. We rarely see a Southern paper and never hear anything definite of our army. Yesterday, we heard there had been a fight in Pennsylvania and that we had whipped the enemy. Of course, we are all anxiety to hear more. I live daily and hourly in dread of a battle. 'Has Longstreet been engaged? Is Edward safe (her brother Captain Edward Carter, who was wounded and captured in Pickett's Charge.)"

"Glen Welby, Tuesday, July 28th 1863

"Our losses have been very heavy and I fear will be still heavier. The Army (Union) has passed for six days. We had them constantly in two incessant streams to and from the house. Oh! it was a dreadful time. Your "Chief of Staff" is safe but looks rather worsted. We are all well, but entirely without male protection. Even the boys are absent. I fear our sheep are all gone. Sophie's and Belle's colts were taken and old Bob; the others escaped. All our meal was taken from our mill, some of our hogs were killed, we know not yet how many, one colt (the best from Texas) (now Sudley) and perhaps some of the young cattle, we cannot ascertain positively. Some of our fowls also perished. These are our losses so far. We are thankful and consider ourselves fortunate and are thankful to have a house left and to have suffered no personal violence. Some have lost all, a few I've heard from had their houses burned and their all destroyed. At Meadow Grove they had a guard but lost their only horse."

After Gettysburg nothing was heard for weeks about the fate of Captain Edward Carter in Pickett's Division, who had not returned from the immortal charge. Also nothing was known of the fate of his cousin Thomas Gordon Pollock of Leeton Forest, a grandson of Attorney General Charles Lee. Finally, word came through that Captain Carter was desperately wounded in a hospital in Chester, Pa. His mother could not go to him, so his sister, Mrs. Scott did.

She finally secured passes through the lines to Washington and traveled thither on a flat car of the Manassas Gap Railroad. In Washington she had interviews with Secretary of War Stanton and President Lincoln who assured her of a safe conduct to Philadelphia.

Even with these safeguards Mrs. Scott was accused of being a rebel spy and would have suffered arrest but for the intercession of Mr. Maxwell Wyeth, a prominent Philadelphian who had married her cousin, Henrietta Horner of "Mountain View" near Salem. Mr. and Mrs. Wyeth befriended her during her sojourn in Pennsylvania and she was able to nurse her brother back to health before he was sent on to prison for the remainder of the war.

Mrs. Scott was able to return to Fauquier in late October 1863. She first got to Alexandria where she had to obtain a military pass to go to Warrenton and then went on "the cars" to Calverton Junction. There she was met by Mr. Bragg, a Warrenton livery stable operator who took her in a wagon to Oakwood, her husband's home. From there she went on horseback across Watery and Wildcat Mountains to Glen Welby, a distance of 12 miles and a journey which took all day. In her absence her sister Sophia DeButts Carter reported on conditions at home to the men folk in Lee's Army. Writing to her brother-in-law, Major Scott, she tells of the futile search for Tom Pollock's body.

(Sophie Carter to R. Taylor Scott)

"Glen Welby, September 24th 1863

"Nannie Pollock has gotten back from Pennsylvania she had no difficulty whatever. I was in Warrenton last week and spent the night at Leeton Forest and was there when she arrived They have given up all hope of Tom and believe him certainly dead. I felt the deepest sympathy for Cousin Elizabeth and the family for their grief is very great. Edith Carter is much distressed at Richard's death as she has no other family The object of my visit to Warrenton was to sell some flour, which is in great demand by the citizens, in order to get some Federal money for sister Fanny. I went down twice, Cousin Margaret Peyton (of Gordon's Dale) my companion both times I went first to obtain a protection from General Sedgwick for the ox team which he readily granted. A day or so after Alick and West went down with the flour, and I in the carriage with Cousin Margaret. We met with a ready sale for the flour and got $50 for the four barrels. Colonel McMahon who was so kind in obtaining sister a pass to go North asked for her direction and said he would obtain a pass for her return and send it, as he did for Nannie Pollock. When I went down the second time he had sent it the day before which was September 3rd."

In May 1863 Major Scott wrote from Richmond to his wife at Glen Welby: "I was sorry to hear of the arrest of so many of our friends in the County and the loss of so much property. Truly our enemy seem determined to wage a war of subjugation upon us. I have collected a few newspapers which I enclose with this letter . . . On Sunday night last I heard Mr. Doggett and Dr. Moore preach General Jackson's funeral sermon. Monumental Church was so crowded I did not trv to obtain a seat."

As the War dragged on to its tragic end the people of Fauquier seemed to become inured to hardship and danger. For the young people it was almost the way of life, as is pointed out by a letter written by Johnny Scott to his brother Major R. Taylor Scott. Johnny was a delicate boy of 15 living alone with his aunt Mrs. Robert Eden Lee at Oakwood, isolated and alone. He writes thus:

"Oakwood, 14 February 1864

"We have not been disturbed by the Yankees lately except they came about twelve o'clock Monday night and beat at the door. When I went down and opened the door about half a dozen caught hold of me and pointed their carbines at my heart. They then arrested our guard, whom General Gregg had given us and after beating open the back door about twenty came in and stole everything they could lay their hands on. Fortunately, we put on a very bold front and prevented them with the assistance of our guard from taking very much. I was never so flattered in my life. They took me for a Confed, and if I had obeyed my first impulse and kicked some of them off the front steps I should have been shot, for a more cowardly set I never saw . . . A Yankee lieutenant and four men captured one of our boys the other day and took away from him two pistols and a sabre. The lieutenant then cut him twice with his sabre, but while they were carrying him along he suddenly pulled a pistol out of his boot, shot the lieutenant who afterward died of his wound, and escaped on his horse. It must have been one of Mosby's men, for no others have so many pistols, and Jimmy Keith says that they shoot as much as a whole brigade when they go into action. The Yankees have not taken my colt yet but I am afraid they will for it is old enough to ride."

Hunger and harassment beset the people of Fauquier through the dreary months of 1864 and 1865. They fought against a sense of hopelessness to survive. The months dragged on. Everyone was hungry, everyone was cold, some were homeless.

Then in April 1865 hope died with the surrender at Appomattox. People felt that never again would the hills of Fauquier be as green or its fields as fertile. And yet life must go on and in the season of spring when the fruit trees blossom and things grow despite all discouragement it is impossible to be entirely without hope.

In mid-April 1865 young Mrs. Isham Keith was in the overgrown vegetable garden at Woodbourne scratching the hard ground with a derelict hoe prior to sowing a few precious seeds. But the warm sky was kindly and although hungry she had hope for the future. In a bit, she looked up and saw her strapping brother-in-law Jim Keith just back from Appomattox where he and the rest of Fauquier's gallant Black Horse troop had surrendered with Lee's army. He looked down at her seriously and said, "Sarah, Abraham has gone to Abraham's bosom." The shot at Ford's Theatre had ended what was begun at Fort Sumter four years before. Fauquier and the rest of the South could begin to build again.

When Hungry Soldiers Swarm

MRS. HENRY GRAFTON DULANY

Excerpts from the journal of "Aunt Ida"—Mrs. Henry Grafton Dulany — of Oakley, Upperville, 1862-63. Her notes were sketched in a ledger, an account book, whose long, thin pages are now speckled and brown.

Aug. 20 1862—This morning I got up very early, having had a headache all night and thinking a morning ride would do me good, started for Upperville to get some medicine from the Doctor for Margaret. I took Rozier behind me on Cricket. Finding the doctor still in bed I went to Dr. Williams to pay him for pulling Mary's tooth, and then back to Dr. Gunnel's to wait till he came downstairs. He had just come down when Mr. Carr put his head in the door and said in the most distracted way: "Mrs. Dulany, Mrs. Dulany, the Yankees are coming, coming fast—you had better—better—you had better—" "I had better secure my horse," I said, "and will thank you to lead her into the back yard, please Sir." This he kindly hastened to do but the doctor was before him and Cricket was hardly out of sight when the Yankees came racing and tearing through the village. They pulled up just in front of the doctor's, and soon every kitchen in town was full of them calling for breakfast, and the stables were broken into and provender taken to feed their horses.

I trembled for Oakley, knowing they would have seen the gate. On the whole they behaved tolerably decently for Yankees, taking only two horses and some goods from Gibson's store. They took Cricket, but the doctor recovered her and lost his own good horse. While I sat at the window in his office with the blinds closed, one soldier opened the blind and stared at me but when I turned my back walked off. They only stayed in town to get breakfast and then returned the road they came. They were some Maryland companies and were looking for some droves of cattle they heard were in the neighborhood. Stuart Bolling escorted me home.

Our having twenty-seven of his officers in close confinement has so cut General Pope's comb that he has published a proclamation so modifying his infamous order No. 9, that he might as well have cancelled it entirely. No soldier is now at liberty to enter a private house under severest penalties.

Aug. 24, Noon. I cannot doubt but that a great battle has commenced. Since ten o'clock there has been one incessant roar of artillery in the direction of the hostile armies. Each instant, as I write, a solemn boom of cannon falls on my ear and my heart sickens at the thought that for every such sound I hear it may be many of those fighting for our homes and liberties are stricken down.

Afternoon. The firing slackened after one o'clock and had ceased altogether by three, and now we shall have to wait for days to hear the issue and then it will come to us so misrepresented through the northern papers that it may be weeks before we hear the exact truth. The fighting cannot be more than twenty-five or thirty miles off. I think if I were a man, a whole community so deeply interested should not remain long in ignorance of what had occurred; but it would never enter the heads of any one of these stay-at-home gentlemen to get on his horse and ride in the direction of the firing.

Night. I was mistaken in thinking that the firing had ceased. A strong north wind prevented our hearing it. As soon as the wind lulled we heard it again constantly until the sun went down.

Aug. 26. A few moments after I got up this morning I heard Uncle Nathan Loughborough's voice calling me in the yard, saying he was in a great hurry. I threw a shawl around me and went to the window. He was so excited that his voice had an unnatural sound as he told me that Jackson with forty thousand men was at Salem, en route for Manassas it was supposed. Our own dear General, our own beloved army, within ten miles of us once more. I could well sympathize with his excitement and had any one been here to go with me I would have ridden all day to cheer my eyes with the blessed sight.

Uncle Nathan had heard that Jackson had sent word to the people around to send all the provisions they could as he was making a forced march and carried nothing with him; so I immediately sent word to Mr. Kidwell to get the spring wagon and my two old mares (all the Yankees have left me), and he was soon under way with corn, hams, tomatoes, a barrel of flour, and as much as the wagon could hold.

It seems that while Lee was amusing the Yankees with a feint of crossing the river in one place, Jackson and his army were actually crossing much higher up, and here they are in the enemy's rear, while they suppose him before them across the river, baffled and disappointed. Many conjectures are afloat as to the result of the move. Glorious old "Stone Wall"—I am now expecting Mr. Kidwell back from The Plains where we thought he would arrive just in time to meet the whole army.

Aug. 29. Mr. Kidwell, (our overseer), came back very late from The Plains. I did not see him till the next day, when he came in bringing me, to my no little mortification, *money* for the provisions I had sent to the army. He got to The Plains too late to see the main body of the army which by that time was far on the way to the Junction. Shortly after he left the house Mr. Bolling came with Cousin Addison Carter, Henry Harrison, Stuart and Anna. Mr. Bolling had been to The Plains, had seen all our boys, Tom, Willie, Bev, and all were well. Everyone is jubilant at the move, expecting great things.

A note from Cousin Mittie Herbert today tells that Gen. Ewell has been wounded, and one of our Turner cousins—she does not say which—and that *Clarence Whiting* is safe at Welbourne.

Yesterday we went to Middleburg and just before entering the town caught up with a long train of our army wagons going to Jackson. Our poor soldiers looked so dirty and tired. I longed for something to give them, and thought with regret of the milk, eggs, etc., at home that they would have enjoyed so much. They were received with the greatest enthusiasm by the ladies of the town, plates of provisions were handed from every house and every demonstration of welcome shown them.

At Cousin Catherine Cochran's we heard the sad news of Charlie Powell's and Cousin Randolph Mason's death. Charlie Powell I did not know, but can feel sincerely for his parents whose only son he was. Cousin Randy Mason was one of the best-loved friends of my girlhood and it is with keen regret that I think I shall never see him again.

This evening I heard the clank of a sword on the porch and knew instantly a soldier had come. It was Walker Armistead. Hal, he tells me, is in Halifax county on a visit to Dr. Carrington. I am very much afraid he will miss this chance of coming home.

Notwithstanding the buoyancy of our soldiers I cannot help feeling very anxious for our army.

Aug. 30. This morning after attending to my household duties and teaching the children I mounted Cricket and with Rozier behind went to Upperville to learn the news. There I heard that Gen. Ewell had lost a leg, for which all are sincerely sorry, he is a gallant officer. I feel particularly sorry for he was so kind a friend to "St. Louis Tom," that I shall feel greater uneasiness about him now than ever. Bev Turner has been severely wounded. Many wounded are being brought to Middleburg and it is said some may come to Upperville. Dr. Williams sent to me for aid in sending him a wagon load of provisions tomorrow. I only wish I lived near enough to the hospitals to assist in nursing.

Dear old fellow, Walker Armistead is with us, it looks like good old times to see him sitting in our circle once more.

Sept. 1. Yesterday having heard that a great battle was fought the evening before near Manassas, in spite of its being Sunday and raining a little I mounted Cricket and with uncle Joshua as an escort I started for Middleburg thinking I could gain a little information.

I also wanted to tell Kate, who is there, to look out for people going to the battlefield, as we might hear from our boys as soon as possible in case of their being wounded. I met a good many of our soldiers on the way and had one adventure in being thrown over Cricket's head in the dust. Fortunately I was not hurt. In Middleburg I saw Cousin Burr Noland and Willie Wilson who had come home the day before. Everybody looked so happy there I could hardly believe it was the same country it was two weeks ago.

Brother Richard and Mr. Weidemeyer were at Cousin Burr's. I rode back behind their carriage and found when I got home that Hal had come in my absence. So now my satisfaction is complete.

Sept. 3. Yesterday morning Uncle Nathan came over to tell us of dear Wilson Turner's death. He was killed in the battle Saturday. Mr. Bolling came over; Hal, my dear husband, was starting for the battlefield to see about Willie's body, but Mr. B. having just come from there told us the body had been buried and the place marked, and that Uncle Ned had gone down to remove him to Kinloch. Every such sacrifice only increases my detestation of the wicked government that has caused such needless suffering, and intensifies my love for the cause daily becoming more and more hallowed by the dearest and noblest blood of our land.

Sept. 11. Everything is a complete change—I can hardly believe myself in the same land. We see our own soldiers every day. Where the Yankee army is I do not know. . . . We have a hospital full of wounded soldiers for whom we are providing food and clothing and in Middleburg there are 1,500.

Sept. 28. I cannot write regularly now. The house is crowded from day to day with our soldiers, most of them, I am sorry to say, stragglers from the army who had better be at their posts. Some of them (and these I am delighted to see), weary marchers calling for a meal and night's lodging. Many of them prove nice gentlemen whose acquaintance it is a pleasure to have made. Our boys, the Turners, are here all the time. Last night even the floors were covered with mattresses.

The Yankees in quite large force made a raid through this neighborhood last week. They did no damage except paroling some of our wounded in Middleburg and killing one man and wounding four in an engagement with the Sixth Cavalry above Upperville. A good many gentlemen were staying here who might all have been captured very easily as the first intimation we had of their being within fifty miles of us was the reports of musketry from the skirmish.

Provisions are getting low with us. My sugar is all gone, there is no coffee, and the corn is alarmingly low in the granary. The churches all being used as hospitals, we have no services.

Nov. 2. Nearly two months have passed since I last wrote. Battles have been lost and won, friends have come and gone, our country has been occupied by our own troops generally but occasional raids by the Yankees have produced temporary excitements. On two occasions we have had the mortification of seeing our cavalry retreat before equal or inferior force of the enemy. In the last ten days there has been much excitement among us. First, Walker's Division of two Brigades, and then Hill's whole Division have been encamped around Upperville. Stuart's famous cavalry have been in the neighborhood. The day before yesterday they sent in sixty prisoners captured near Union. Yesterday Hal was present at an artillery skirmish near the same place. This morning we all went to church but were hardly seated when Hal came in to say that Gen. Hill recommended the removal of women and children from the village as the enemy was advancing. We came rapidly home, meeting the infantry pickets and wagon train. Since then we have been listening to the artillery. Just now it has ceased but Hill's whole Division is drawn up in line of battle on Vineyard Hill, and we expect a general engagement.

Not only have we had the horrors of war to contend with but disease has been carrying off numbers in our midst. For weeks I have been alternating with Ma helping to nurse Uncle Nathan's little children. Of his six daughters four are dead from diphtheria, and many other children are dying and dead in the neighborhood. (Aunt Ida had three young children of her own, but we see that it never occurred to her or her mother to fail to come to the rescue of their neighbors.)

Cecil Gray and Mr. Fletcher, our kind old friend, have died in the last week, and Lizzie Powell and Katie Taylor. As I sit at the window and write, the road is alive with stragglers and Hal just brought in a sick soldier and put him to bed in the little room. Four cavalrymen are at the front door.

Eleven o'clock: The house has been crowded with poor hungry sick soldiers since I stopped writing a few hours ago. Gen. Stuart's cavalry fell back slowly before the enemy, disputing every inch of the way, the enemy occupying the ground as he retreated. I sat on the balcony of my room and watched the battle which became very distinct from the flashes of the artillery as night came on. With the aid of a spy-glass we could see many movements of our men, the enemy being entirely concealed by the woods. It is strange for us in our sheltered, quiet country, to hear the roar and see the flash of artillery, to watch the movements of an army and feed at night dozens of soldiers wearied with a hard day's fight.

Nov. 4 Yesterday was a day of days. First as we sat down to breakfast a courier rode up to say that the Yankees were advancing. Soon after breakfast the soldiers in the house prepared to leave. With a sad heart we said good-bye to Brother Richard and "St. Louis Tom" and all the rest. Then they went off to enquire the news and soon Tom came riding back to say our army was falling back toward Piedmont and had no intention of giving battle to the enemy. We could tell from the sound of the batteries as they approached each change of position. First they were at Fletcher's, then in the woods below our house, and so on the Yankees regularly advancing and occupying the position our men had left. About eleven o'clock Hal rode up with Welby Carter and others. I hastily prepared lunch for them and we watched the skirmishing, our field being entirely covered with videttes and our pickets at "Number Six." Soon we saw the pickets move from Number Six, then the videttes going across the fields toward Upperville. The soldiers here and Hal with them rode at this time away—suddenly I saw them start their horses in a gallop and from the right I saw our videttes coming in more rapidly. Then looking to the hills beyond Number Six I saw them covered with Yankees, and soon the field in front of our house was filled with sharp-shooters. Soon we saw a battery on Cousin Robert Carter's hill just in front of Oakley, which began to play on our men and then there were no more southerners in sight. The house was surrounded by Yankees. For an hour I watched the battery pouring out shells against our battery which was planted in the Vineyard. The shells from both batteries burst in full sight of us, frightening the servants nearly to death. I was forcibly reminded of their startled exclamation in Baltimore on the 19th of April—"Fo' Gawd, dey gwine 'shoot.'"

After a while the Yankee battery followed by a large body of cavalry moved across the front field. In passing a soldier rode in and dismounting rang the bell. I went to the door and, receiving a polite bow, was asked whose house it was? On answering, I was asked if I had forgotten the soldier who returned me my filly last year? I then recognized Major Chapman who had been really very kind. But so sad did I feel at seeing our men go and the Yankees take possession that my reception was rather chilling. He seemed to feel it for he stayed only a few moments saying that he had always promised himself the pleasure of calling on me if it were ever in his power. I had some cause to regret not having taken advantage of the incident to obtain protection. Soon after he left I saw Hal coming to the house between two soldiers. He told me he attempted to come home the Piedmont way, but when by uncle Dan's cabin the Yankees began firing at him very rapidly. He waved his handkerchief for a white flag and rode up to them. He was carried to Major Chapman, who, finding out who he was, introduced himself, and told Hal he must consider himself under arrest. He gave his parole and was released. He was quite sick when he came home and lay down but had hardly fallen asleep before our troubles began.

I first saw the Yankees taking off the turkeys, then the bridles, then the chickens, and fearing everything would be taken I wakened Hal, who went after them and succeeded in getting back nine hens with their heads off. He contended with the marauders till eleven o'clock and then worn out went to bed. When we woke in the morning there was not a turkey on the place, only two ducks and about a dozen left out of two hundred chickens. The first thing I saw in the morning was the men in the yard chasing and shooing the chickens. I saw others with dogs chasing the sheep. I called to an officer who stopped it so our sheep were saved this time, though five were killed the night before and some hogs.

Yesterday Mrs. Loughborough came over to see what we were doing to protect ourselves. She was in the greatest distress, every sheep, every fowl of any kind, almost the last hog, and every horse and colt they had, gone. Uncle Nathan has gone in pursuit of his horses and colts. Here they have broken into the corn house and taken off as much corn as the horses can carry, and are as insolent and overbearing as they can be. We are told that the army has moved, but our fields are alive with soldiers, and Vineyard Hill white with their tents. The cavalrymen are going by my windows now with horses laden with our hay. The three last horses that are worth anything are locked up now in the meat house and Mr. Kidwell is watching the others in his yard. Hal is guarding the hog-pen while Katey and I take turns watching the sheep.

Nov. 9. Several days have passed since I wrote. Not one moment could be spared from contending with the plunderers who have surrounded us day and night reminding me more of ravening wolves than of anything human. One night at least one hundred were here, and by morning of our large flock of improved sheep only fifteen could be found, while from one end of the field to the other their white skins were dotted about on the grass. They killed the hogs and every shoat and took most of the cabbage out of the garden. We had to butcher four sheep left badly wounded.

One night Hal brought home the Chaplain of the Regiment nearest to us thinking his presence might be some little protection. He was a wordy old fellow who thought the loss of horses, chickens, hogs, sheep and everything we have, a small matter when considered in connection with the great question of the integrity of the Union. I could but observe the spirit with which he described the trouble *he* had had, and the indignation *he* had felt, when some undiscerning thief treated *his* old gray mare with as little respect as if he himself had been the most obstinate rebel of them all, leaving him in the same condition as most of our gentlemen, namely, a-foot.

I am struck with the difference in the conduct of the servants during this last invasion. Last spring they were more or less disposed to take advantage of the times, but now their indignation equals ours. It is true these last are no respecters of persons, but make way with *their* chickens and other goods as unscrupulously as if they had been the original secessionists, and when you interfere with a darkey's "things" you cut him to the quick.

Hal has just come in from Welbourne bringing the first intelligence from the family that we have had since this invasion. Both at Crednall and at Welbourne they have been stripped of everything.

We hear that the Confederacy has been recognized by England, France and Russia, but do not know whether or not to believe it.

I find it impossible to get clothes for my servants. As to myself I get on with little or nothing, but my great perplexity is how to keep Hal covered. The children had a supply laid up. Shoes are the great difficulty—my feet are literally on the ground and I have not the least hope of getting another pair.

Nov. 14. Having heard that the widow Fletcher had sent into Loudoun for some groceries I rode down to enquire what chance there was of my getting some, and so was off the farm for the first time since this invasion. The whole country is a vast common, not a rail fence to be seen for miles, and the stone fences pulled down to let the armies pass, until they do not serve at all as enclosures. When we got to Mrs. Fletcher's her wagon had not come and while we waited her son showed us the results of bombardment near her house. Shells had burst in the yard, the plaster and windows were broken. A shell entered the window of Mrs. Fletcher's chamber and tore the room to pieces. A general made her house his headquarters and had with him a Miss Chaste (?) who took off with her when she left, brushes and combs, bed linen and towels, Mrs. F.'s side-saddle, etc., etc. They killed sixty hogs and forty sheep and most of her poultry. Everyone tells the same story, and many poor men are left without a mouthful of meat for their families.

Yesterday evening Brother Richard sent his bugler to me to send him some cold meat and bread. His whole Regiment was in Upperville. Mrs. Loughborough was here and had me send to her house for a round of corned beef she had. I sent Robert with apples, walnuts, bread and meat and butter. Talcott Eliason was here today, wanting to purchase Hal's horses, especially his bay mare. I would greatly prefer Hal taking her to some safe place. She is too fine an animal to sacrifice.

Dec. 28. We are in the midst of all the disagreeables of Christmas week. The poor children have had a dry time of it, no toys, no bonbons, no parties. As to me I have had but one idea for weeks, to find homes for all these servants, so that none may be left here to sit in idleness at home for the coming year to consume the scanty supplies laid in for the family. All have found homes but Patsy who is as hard to get rid of as a counterfeit shilling, and in fact not much more useful.

Great events are taking place every day, our great victory at Fredericksburg, the backward move of the Yankees toward Washington, successes in North Carolina and Tennessee and the dissolution of the Lincoln Cabinet; Jefferson Davis' severe but admirable order retaliatory upon Butler combined with our relief from the presence of enemies, excite our hopes and cheer our spirits. My little Mary and Fanny are staying with Jenny. Jenny is looking prettier than I ever saw her, bidding fair to eclipse her elder sisters before very long.

We had a visit from Cousin Robert Beverley and Eliza a few days ago and it happened that Hal had been lucky enough to have shot a wild turkey and as it was the only turkey we were likely to have at Christmas time we asked Uncle Nathan and Mr. Bolling to come over and help us eat it. The country is full of game and Hal is a very good shot, so if we can only get ammunition I shall consider it a special provision of Providence equal to the supply of manna and quails given to the Israelites; by which reparation is made to us for the loss of all our domestic fowls.

Jenny returned from her visit on Friday. She was detained by a party of Yankees stopping her at the main road. Jenny's tears lie very shallow, so when she found that her assertion that she was only a little girl on the way home to see her mother had no effect, she began to cry. Lena Noland, who was with her, tried to move the soldiers by earnest entreaties, accompanied by vehement complaints of the cold, to let them pass, which finally they did, preceded by about eighty cavalrymen.

May 1, 1863. The winter has passed away, the dreariest, coldest, wettest, saddest winter followed by the latest spring within the memory of man. Not one tree in leaf, the garden not even cleaned. Everyone dressed in winter clothes—curtains up—carpets down. No corn in the ground and very little grass in the fields. The unusual lateness of the season and delay in farming operations causes serious uneasiness. President Davis has issued a beautiful proclamation urging upon the people of the whole South to turn all their energies to producing food and to think more of supplying the army and people generally with provisions than of their individual gain; to give up cotton and tobacco and cultivate corn and wheat, and raise livestock.

The two armies have been during the winter principally *in status quo* but we hear at last that Hooker has crossed the Rappahannock and a battle is anticipated almost immediately. In our own neighborhood we have no lack of excitement. General Fitz Lee has been not far off and Major Mosby with his one hundred and twenty-five Partisan Rangers occupies the country immediately around Upperville, the village itself being the rendezvous when a raid is contemplated. The men live upon the citizens and consequently there is not a house where they are not quartered, and as a change of residence takes place after every raid, we have strangers every few days, and the house always full to overflowing. The impression seems to be that we are protected by them from the Yankees, but I fear it is just the reverse for after every raid by Mosby's men there is retaliation by the enemy, in which the citizens suffer severely, as Mosby and his men must always get out of their way, seeing he is always out-numbered. The broken bridge on the turnpike has till this time been some protection to us, but the people of Middleburg and vicinity have suffered severely.

Mr. Barnes, a young Marylander, and many of the men, stay here. He always, the others coming and going. It is a comfort to have our own soldiers around us and a pleasure to administer to their wants, but the utter breaking up of all family privacy is much to be lamented. I fully realize the inconvenience of living in a roadside tavern.

I have been to Baltimore and succeeded in getting clothes for the family and the servants but could get no groceries. I sent a man to Harpers' Ferry and he got me some brown sugar, which we are using in tea, having no more coffee. The blockade is very strict, nothing can be gotten across the river and we feel seriously the pinch of the times. For months we have had nothing but salt pork on the table, potatoes and rice being equally unattainable, hominy therefore is our only vegetable, varied by fried mush and occasionally carrots. A dish of asparagus today was a real treat but the family is so enormous that it will be days before we collect enough for another dish.

The prices in Richmond are fabulous. $75.00 a cord for wood, $8.00 for a small turkey, $3.00 a yard for cotton and calico, $30 a pair of lady's shoes—

The horrors of the war are increasing every day. Only last week "Kinloch Tom" left us, bright with enthusiasm, glowing with health, to go on a scout for Mosby and was shot through the lungs by a party of Yankees in ambush. Fortunately he was near enough to Kinloch to be carried home on a litter. The wound was pronounced mortal but the end was hastened by the Yankees coming to the house and insisting on taking him off. He died a few moments after they left his room.

(There were so many of the Turner boys in the war that they are distinguished by the names of their homes. "St. Louis Tom" of General Ewell's Staff was the son of my Aunt Ida's Uncle Henry Turner, who lived in St. Louis, Mo. "Kinloch Tom" was Uncle Ned's son, who lived at the ancestral home near the Plains.)

Mosby left for another raid yesterday, his object being to burn some bridges; it is a hazardous business and I feel anxious for the result.

While I was in Baltimore Katey engaged herself to George Carter and will be married in October. But for this war her prospects for happiness would be very great, but these times of death and terror cast a gloom over all things.

May 8. A few days ago Major Mosby started on a raid towards Drainsville, the object being to surprise a Yankee camp. This he accomplished, capturing a whole regiment of cavalry. But just as the men were remounting, some bringing off prisoners and some collecting plunder an alarm was given and lo! a whole Brigade was upon them! The prisoners were of necessity released, most of the plunder relinquished, and the whole party had to scamper for their lives. The loss in killed, wounded and prisoners, estimated at between six and twenty.

Yesterday was appointed a rendezvous for the company in Upperville. Mr. Buchanan and Mr. Barnes left us in the morning expecting a possible raid. About one o'clock Mr. Barnes rode hastily up, saying the Yankees were on the Union Road and that one of the Turner boys had volunteered to go in pursuit of them. He armed himself and went off. At dinner Hal came in with Mr. Ellzey. Robert Gray had borrowed Mr. Ellzey's horse to join the scout. We had just done dinner when Mr. Barnes rode hurriedly up. "We ran right into the Yankees—Upperville is full of them—Buchanan is shot."

Everything was again in confusion, horses had to be hurried off, meat concealed, silver and jewelry secreted, etc., and every preparation made to escape the rapacity of the enemy. Yet all the time my mind's eye never for a moment lost sight of that poor fellow suffering and bleeding who had left my house so well but a few hours before. It rained such torrents we could not send for him that evening but Hal went over to see him and thence to Upperville to get a doctor. The town was full of "Blue Devils" and no doctor to be found. I had to be content with sending Robert to stay all night with him giving him most minute directions as to dressing the wounds. This evening Hal took six men, an ambulance and litter and brought him home. Mr. Barnes, Mr. Gray and Mr. Ellzey are still among the missing, but I expect they will all return here some time tonight.

May 10. After another week's spell of cold rain a beautiful bright spring day, bringing out rapidly the poor cramped weary vegetation, pale with its long confinement and longing to burst its prison bounds. And with the glorious beauty of the spring day comes the soul-gladdening tidings of a great victory (Chancellorsville) over Hooker on the Rappahannock—"a greater victory than we have ever had before," says General Lee's dispatch, for which our hearts ascend in thanksgiving to the Lord God of Hosts. The list of wounded is headed by the name of Stonewall Jackson. Could he know—perhaps he does know—how beloved he is by every Southern man, woman and child, he would feel richly repaid for all he may have to suffer.

Mr. Buchanan is doing very well, poor fellow. I hate to see him shut up in his little room while all the others are riding, walking, and enjoying in every way the loveliness of this sweet day. He is as bright and cheerful as possible and seems to be content.

Many rumors come from the Rappahannock, but it is useless to record them all. Long before anyone thinks it worth while to read my journal History will have placed it in the power of every half-grown boy and girl to contradict every word I say.

A report has come that the Yankees are advancing in large numbers from the direction of Snickersville, and I see people running in all directions taking their horses to places of safety in the woods and mountains, but I have determined not to stop the all-important work of cornplanting, so Hal rode out to reconnoitre. He was long in coming back, so I made myself easy.

Not the least evil of these troublous times is the agitation produced by reports of approaching Yankees. We have so little left us that we cannot risk it, so at every rumor we have all the meat taken from the meat house, the stock run off to safer places, silver, money, arms, etc., concealed, and generally it amounts to nothing. I have not seen a Yankee for months. With our reduced force this extra trouble is no trifle. Mr. Buchanan is not so well today. Dr. Gunnell expresses some uneasiness.

Helping Mosby's Men

MISS AMANDA VIRGINIA EDMONDS

These excerpts from a diary were contained in a talk given to the Piedmont Chapter of the United Daughters of the Confederacy by Mrs. B. C. Chappelear, and were first published in The Fauquier Democrat, Warrenton, in January 1951. Amanda Edmonds Chappelear of Belle Grove, between Delaplane and Paris, was the mother of Curtis Chappelear, local historian, whose notes were published posthumously in 1954. The Amanda Edmonds diary covered the months March 1864 to February 1865.

Saturday, March 26, 1864: Mr. Magner with us again, bringing some news. Although coming from our nearest neighbors we had not heard of it until his (Mr. Magner's) arrival from Mosby's headquarters and revealed it in his excitable, wild manner. Mosby making a raid across the Shenandoah with five men, captured four Yankees and made good his return, reaching Mr. Triplett's after night. Going into the house leaving the prisoners with one guard at the stile where they were dismounting and securing their horses. One of the Yanks pretending to be tying his horse at the same time was untying Mosby's horse which he mounted instantly, and with Mosby's arms buckled to his fine saddle rode off with great speed. One of the other Yankees who had not dismounted followed and both made their escape, after being pursued some distance. Mosby greatly laments the loss of his fine horse, and I should think it will be some time before he recovers from his shock and surprise. Truly that was a rich Yankee trick and played on the gallant Colonel too, makes it look almost incredulous. I enjoy a hearty laugh over it, not at his loss or because the prisoners made their escape, but from the scene pictured in my imagination—seeing the flight of the two and the rebels standing awe-struck and Mosby's utter surprise, with his blood fairly boiling. It is better it were his horse than that of one of his men, for he has others to fall back on and is well able to lose it.

The ranger who was left to guard the prisoners when Colonel Mosby's fine and favorite horse was ridden off by one of the prisoners was Sergeant James W. Wrenn, who made his headquarters at the Triplett home. This place was also the headquarters of his brother Lieutenant Albert Wrenn. The Wrenn brothers were natives and residents of Fairfax County. The night of February 17 and 18, 1864, a body of Federal cavalry left their camp at Warrenton about 11 o'clock for the purpose of surprising members of Mosby's command at their several homes or headquarters in the upper end of Fauquier County. They were led by a deserter from the command, who was well acquainted with the section of the county to be raided, and knew the places where members of the command would likely be found. It was an intensely cold night. A detachment of the raiding Federals arrived at the Triplett home just before daybreak, but before they could surround the house, the Wrenn brothers left it dressed only in their night clothes, and went barefoot over the frozen ground and a frozen creek to Mount Edie, a high hill located about a mile southwest of the Triplett house. Here they stayed in the bitter cold until the Federals disappeared from the scene. All the horses in the stables on the Triplett place were carried off by the raiding party.

(Miss Edmonds tells something of what took place at her home, Belle Grove, when the raiding party of Federals visited her home on that cold night in February, 1864.)

February 18, Thursday—the ever memorable Thursday. How! oh, how shall I begin to pen here all that has happened since the day dawned upon us this morning. Much to our surprise, mortification, and sorrow, the slumbers of the household broken by what has never marred our peace and rest before at such an hour: rattling of swords, and the clatter of horses' feet, which fortunately made known to our dear soldiers that something was wrong. Bud (Edward G. Edmonds) jumped from his bed and there to his utter surprise were Yankees dashing up. He with Mr. Alexander and George (Sam Alexander and George Triplett, both of Fairfax County, who made their headquarters at Belle Grove, and were members of Mosby's command), dashed downstairs where Ma and I met them, frightened nearly to death, but on they dashed to a secret hiding place, followed by their overcoats, pistols, and everything they had left behind in their hurry, which I could grab up, for time was short then, the Yankees were all around the house, and every moment I expected them to bolt in.

All was done in a moment, and now, when I look back, I shudder and tremble to think how narrow an escape they made. The next move Ma and I made was for our room and had just entered (still in our night robes) when six of the horrid wretches entered with a 'good morning'. I guess they received no response from me more than a rebellious stare. They opened the other door and there met Clem (Clement West Edmonds). They clamped him and Ches (Chester Edmonds) as though they had secured a prize in Rebel soldiers. The devil Captain ordered Clem under arrest and left one of the imps to guard him. I hurriedly dressed and followed the rest of them up stairs; at the same time I thought Ma would have gone frantic. All of us thought Mr. Triplett, Mr. Hunt, and Jack (John I. Edmonds) were in their hands, and certain that Syd (Sydnor Edmonds) was taken for he had not more than a few minutes before left the house, but rumors from the servants quieted our fears for a while, telling us that they were all safe. Syd was tending his horse and mounted the loft just as a Yankee opened the door. Oh heavens! what a satisfaction, what a relief, to know that they were all safe; but still we were completely surrounded and we could but tremble for their safety.

I joined the wretches as they were searching the boys' rooms. They had gathered an armful of clothes, with some of Mr. Alexander's and George's, which they unfortunately left in their hurried retreat. Ches then joined us, and we all had a guard over us. I flatter myself to think that my pleadings overcame his Yankee heart, and he yielded from his first determined resolve to carry Ches off. The release of Clem was still to be considered, and Ma was successful with words of entreaty. Still they pretended to believe him a soldier. (Clem Edmonds, a brother of Amanda Virginia Edmonds, was only 17 years of age at the time and Ches Edmonds, his brother, was still younger.) There in our presence we had to stand and look at the rogues search the pockets of the jackets they brought downstairs with them. Oh! how I longed to snatch them from their hands, for I felt as though they were contaminated, even after their eyes rested on them, much less when their hands had held them. I gratified them with a search in the cellar, appearing as indifferent as possible and pretended I was anxious they should gratify themselves. For my life, had a pistol been held to my head I could not have held my tongue. I knew it was wrong to sass and give vent to my indignant feelings but oh!, I could not help it to save my life. The wretches certainly were very lenient for Yankees. Ma, during the time, was in perfect agony and never left her room, having things there that demanded her presence to secure their safety.

Having satisfied themselves in searching the premises, I stood on the kitchen porch nearly frantic with joy to see them mount and about to be off, then I saw a stir among them and they rode around in the yard again. I imagined they were going to search again when lo, I heard one of them yell 'Bring him out——bring him out.' Great heavens, who have they found; and in a moment more I heard one of

Mr. Hunt's familiar laughs. Still confident that Mr. Triplett was safe, until a moment later both of the poor Rebels stepped from their dear old retreat, and bid a long, long adieu to all pleasure that their humble roof had ever afforded them. As soon as I saw they were about to leave without coming to bid goodbye, I went down to them.

Mr. Hunt bid me 'Good morning,' remarking that turn about is fair play, taking it all in his usual good nature, but my poor friend (Mr. Triplett) got permission to come to the house under guard. I relieved his mind in regard to the other Rebels, whom he anxiously inquired after. There was no smile about him. He deigned to lavish one upon the surrounding scene. I felt as if my heart was stone when he bid me goodbye so kindly. I was wrought up to such a pitch of excitement I could not have shed tears had my brothers shared the same fate. Not a bit of anguish then, all was excitement and anger with the black hateful looking wretches, who were carrying off two who had never known the utter loneliness of those far off prison walls. I watched them as far as I could discern two gray coats from the mass of blue. I turned and went to the forsaken retreat; there I found Jack. I threw him some clothing as he had left all behind him except his coat. Syd and the rest came from their covert, all eager to go in pursuit of the Yankees in hopes of capturing their lost property—six horses—leaving enough for the Rebels to pursue them, besides the work horses. We were sure at first every horse was gone, and we felt thankful to them for the horses they left behind.

The Gibson boys, who narrowly escaped capture (at their home Fleetwood, later the home of Channing Delaplane) came by and joined our boys and off they went. A little later we saw two hundred more Yankees march around from the byroad. (This detachment of the Federals, after a division of the raiding party below Piedmont, now Delaplane, went round by way of Markham and came over the road leading through what is now Apple Manor Orchard and rejoined the first detachment at Paris.) How I clapped my hands to see the Rebels charge them and give them a volley. Just then the Yankees turned into the gate and formed in a line. Here they had a warm contest with the Rebels, who had gathered in their rear as they came along the road, but no one, I think, was hurt on either side. What a little handful of Rebels to attack such a large number. Bravo! to the little band. We gladly saw them all pass without disturbing us and join the other party at Paris."

Friday, February 19: "Three days of the coldest weather I ever felt, but in view of that we have a house full of soldiers—some of them frolicking over the ice pond and, indeed, some disgracing themselves with King Alcohol. Joe, John and Douglas (Gibson) spent the evening and night with us."

Saturday, February 20: "Another day of excitement and anxiety. Rumor came early that Yankees were at Upperville. All the soldiers in the neighborhood set out in pursuit after meeting the gallant Lieutenant

Colonel Mosby, who arrived from Richmond yesterday with an additional star on his collar. The morning passed full of care and anxiety to all here. I wandered about the yard looking and listening but all was quiet."

(**Note:** — The Federals who came to Upperville on February 20 were a squadron commanded by Major Cole of the Second Battalion, Maryland Cavalry. His command of 200 men was followed and attacked by 50 of Mosby's Rangers at Blakeley's Grove School House and defeated, with the loss of seven killed and seven captured. Most of their wounded were carried off by the Federals.)

Passing Through The Lines

HENRIETTA BRAXTON HORNER

This recollection by Mrs. Maxwell Wyeth is datelined September 21, 1895, Mountain View, near Marshall.

In March 1861, I went to Philadelphia to have some small operation performed on my eyelid. My brother, Richard H. Horner, accompanied me to Washington where I was met by Mr. Frank H. Wyeth. How little I dreamed what was before us, and that my farewell to my brother and home would be for years.

The operation on my eye was successful, but while the healing effects were being carried on by my good physicians, Drs. Henry H. Smith and Hughes Agnew, terrible events were being enacted in the South. Fort Sumpter was fired upon, the bugle sound "to arms" was heard throughout the land; every city became a moving mass of troops, and the spirit againt *all persons* from the South who were in their midst was violent.

Philadelphia was in the hands of a raging mob for days, and those who were at all suspected of holding Southern sympathies were compelled to take the oath of allegiance to the U. S. Government.

Being a woman, I was exempt but my cousin, Mr. Alfred Horner, at whose house I was, was made to hang out a U. S. Flag and keep it out.

I immediately decided to return home, coming to Washington to the house of my cousin, Mr. George Whiting, expecting to go on next morning to Alexandria, and thence to my father's home when morning came.

Terrible was the scene in Washington; Ellsworth had been killed in Alexandria; the Long Bridge was taken possession of by troops. The cry and fear was that the Southern troops would take Washington. It was then I had my first sight of Abraham Lincoln, the dreaded enemy of every Southerner, dashing by our house in a carriage with Secretary Seward.

Finding I could not get home, Mr. Wyeth came for me, taking me back with a heavy heart, for home, parents, loved ones, all were behind me and in danger. Several dear homes of friends and relatives were opened to me; the one accepted for the summer, or until I could get home, was that of Mrs. William S. Horner, widow of my father's honored relative, Dr. William E. Horner.

No words can ever express the love and kindness, generous kindness I received at her dear hands. She knew I had no funds and was cut off from home and friends; she took me as her child, supplying a summer wardrobe and every needed comfort, then as the entry to Virginia and friends were still blocked, she invited me to go as her guest to Narragansett Pier, Rhode Island, which I did, remaining with her until August, 1861.

Hearing of an opportunity "Through the lines", I returned to Philadelphia with Mrs. Horner's kind brother, Mr. Samuel Welsh and his daughter, Fannie. The opportunity failed me, and I was homeless. Mrs. Dr. Henry Smith and Mr. Welsh invited me to be their guest, the latter as long as I needed a home.

The War was then raging. "Bull Run" or Manassas had become famous and dreadful, and I remember shortly after the battle of "Bull Run", Mr. Welsh, or "Uncle Sam" as I had learned to lovingly call him, were dining with others at Dr. Smith's when to rouse up the little Virginia rebel, the Doctor asked if I were not a F.F.V.

I replied, "You ought to know, Doctor; you married one of my family." He said, "I only wanted to tell you that the appellation of 'First Families of Virginia' had been changed to 'Fleet Footed Virginians'."

"Indeed," I said, "Well, fleet footed as they are, they could not keep up with your troops when they left Bull Run lately for Washington." The gentlemen applauded, and the Doctor was advised to let the little rebel alone.

In November and December, I made several attempts to obtain a pass through the lines but failed. My dear good friend Mrs. Horner gave me a home all the time. My last attempt was the most interesting of all, though I must not forget one other made to General Banks' headquarters, accompanied by Judge Casey, the friend of Mr. Wyeth's father, Mr. Francis Wyeth of Harrisburg.

The Judge introduced me, "Miss Horner of Virginia". General Banks very courteously listened to my story but said, "I can't give you a pass, much as I would like to oblige you". Then I said, "General, could I not be passed off as a Yankee?"

"Never, Miss Horner, with your Southern voice and pronounced Southern accent."

Then all laughed at me good-naturedly. At this moment, General Carl Schulz was announced and was introduced to me. Why should they give me a pass, when General Schulz was the bearer of the fact that the day before Miss Buckner from my own neighborhood had been captured, and her petticoat found to be thickly quilted with quinine for Southern use?

Heartsick and homesick, I returned to Philadelphia. All this time my intended husband was tender, loving and devoted to me in my loneliness.

In January 1862, I again went to Washington, determined to make one more attempt to go home before yielding to Mr. Wyeth's urgent entreaties to end our long engagement and be married. He accompanied me this time, and finding that Secretary Seward was the one to apply to for a pass, we went to his office, were first taken into his son, Fred Seward's presence.

I was my own spokesman. Mr. Wyeth's firm being the employees of the Government in supplying medicines for the Army, I did not wish in any way to compromise them, and in those dreadful times one had to be so particular, yet I could not help being saucy when I got a chance.

On hearing what my business was, Young Seward said, "Well, there's no use in your troubling the Secretary. He'll not give you a pass."

"All right," I said. "I'll see him all the same and if refused, will get it from headquarters and not from one of his employes," ignoring the fact that he was the son, and I did see the Secretary, too. After listening to my petition, briefly made, to be allowed to go into Virginia, he said, "I am very sorry, Miss 'Horner, but your family living in and around Warrenton, are a large influential family, and every male member in the Confederate Army". (One brother Dr. Frederick Horner, was in the U. S. Navy)

"Yes," I said, "that is so, and if there were one who was not, that one I would disown," but before this, he had told me he was not issuing any passes through the lines and I believe for this reason, they were about to remove their noble McClellan from the command of the Army of the Potomac, and in a few days he was relieved at Salem, Fauquier Cty.

Then I continued, "It's a hard thing, Mr. Secretary, for a descendant of two of the Signers of the Declaration of Independence to be refused a safe transit to any portion of her Country so long as she has not proved herself disloyal."

"Oh," he replied, "It is for the sake of her loyal Ancestors, I wish to retain her on the right side." "Well," I said, saucily, "if you won't let me go by fair means, I will foul." "Then," said he, "if we catch you, we'll put you in prison."

"All right," said I, "catching is before hanging" and made my exit. Oh, no, just here, I said, "I'll go to President Lincoln." "No use, Miss Horner, he can't help you." Then I said, "The country is in a bad way when the President of it is powerless to help a citizen," and left him, no doubt leaving the impression that Miss Horner was a saucy little woman for her age.

We did go to the White House and I was always so glad I did, for like all Southerners, I was deeply prejudiced against Abraham Lincoln. As we approached the house, an elegant carriage drove up. Mrs. Lincoln came out (we knew her from her pictures) and got in. We had rung the bell just as the President came out. He passed us but must have seen the anxiety expressed in my face, for he retraced his steps, saying, "Who do you wish to see, Miss."

I told him my story briefly. I can never forget the benign expression on his face or his kindness of manner. Putting his hand on my shoulder like a father, he said, "My child, I would give you a pass directly, but they have taken from me the power of giving a pass."

Every feeling of prejudice vanished, and when his cruel death overtook him, no one in all our land mourned his dreadful end more than Henrietta Horner. It being the custom to bow one's window-shutters when a friend died, I bowed mine with my own hands for fear some one opposite might think Mr. Wyeth had it done, and told a friend who said it was deceitful in me to do it, that no one in our city mourned President Lincoln's death more truly than I did.

After this fifth unsuccessful effort to return home was over, I returned to Philadelphia, and after getting a letter through "the lines" to my dear parents, asking their advice and sanction to our marriage, waited their answer, meanwhile making a visit to Baltimore to my dear friends, the Lowrays, and to see Rev. John R. Hoff, our old pastor in Virginia, and he and Mrs. Lowray both urged my marriage under the circumstances; Mr. Hoff promising to go to Philadelphia at any time to perform the ceremony.

At last my dear parents conveyed to me their full consent to our marriage, which took place February 20th, 1862 (my dear mother's 58th birthday) at 10 A. M. in Holy Trinity Church, Mr. Hoff officiating and Cousin Alfred Horner acting in my dear father's place.

Time rolled on, and the third year of the War was passing. Hearing at last from my dear ones that my only sister, Elizabeth M. Horner, whom I had left a bright young girl, was seriously ill, I determined to make another attempt to go home. Mr. Wyeth hearing that persons could pass "the lines" by Point of Rocks, Maryland, went to Baltimore, secured a pass for me and companion, the latter being an old acquaintance from Warrenton, Miss Queen Ward.

I was charmed, and set out with high hopes, taking only a satchel. Miss Ward telling Mr. Wyeth no baggage was allowed, yet when I reached Baltimore she asked me to claim one of her large trunks, which request I declined, reminding her of the message sent me of "no baggage" and I added, "I won't go with you until you get a clearance for both trunks from the authorities." This she did with my endorsement, and we started by rail, reaching Point of Rocks at noon. On our arrival, we found the Commandant's office filled with women trying either to go North or South.

I waited my turn for examination quietly (but it being my first real War experience) with beating heart. I showed my pass to Col. Schley, then in Command, advising him that neither Miss Ward or myself carried a line of writing or papers of any kind. He said he would send us across the Potomac safely later on.

When I went upstairs, I found the rest of the families greatly excited, having heard we were to be searched personally. Very well, said I, then Col. Schley superintends my search. I find him to be a gentleman and feel he will allow no insult to be offered me.

Just at this moment, I turned and saw Miss Ward taking from her bosom a package of papers, handing them to a colored girl to burn. I stepped up to her saying, "No! Hand me every paper. When I told Col. Schley neither of us carried a paper, I thought I was telling the truth. You knew I was not. These papers are his, let the consequences be what they may to both of us." And down I went again, finding Col. Schley alone in his office. Oh, how I trembled and how my heart beat, but a sharp, quick prayer for strength held me up.

Approaching the Colonel, I said, "Sir, a few moments ago when I told you neither myself or the young lady under my charge carried papers of any kind, I thought I was telling the truth." Then I related what had happened upstairs. "Now," I said, "I do not know what this package contains but I do know they are yours, even though their contents sends us to prison."

He looked me full in the face all the while, and I always thanked God I stood his searching gaze unflinchingly; he took the package, saying, "Madame, any woman who could act as you have deserves to be trusted," walked to the open fire and tossed the parcel in, and together we stood and saw it burn to ashes.

Even after more than thirty years have elapsed, I can't recall the incident without my face flushing with honest pride, and my heart thanking God for the fulfilment of the promise, "As thy days so shall thy strength be".

The Colonel handed me his card, saying, "Should you need a friend on the other side, send me a special notice and I will go or send for you."

Among the women trying to get North was a very handsome one, Mrs. Cook, from one of the Gulf States, wishing to visit her father, Dr. Humphrey of Washington City. When Col. Schley was questioning her, she forgot herself as a lady and petitioner so far as to be so abusive and ultra in expressing her views. I soon saw the Colonel was simply amusing himself with her, but when we went upstairs, I could not resist saying to her, kindly, "I am a Southerner born and bred in every feeling of my heart, but I have lived North two years and I have learned that it is best to keep one's opinion to themselves, unless you do you will get into trouble."

She laughed, thanking me; result was she was sent to Baltimore under arrest; kept there three weeks and when I returned, Col. Schley told me he had put the handsome widow across the Potomac a few days before when it was boiling, and he would not have cared had she landed in the Atlantic Ocean or sailed there.

Col. Schley courteously saw us on the "Skiff" (think of crossing the Potomac River in a skiff) which bore us, nine women in all, safely across, where two stages awaited us. Miss Ward and myself, among others, were comfortably fixed in one stage. Then literally began the "tug of War" for such roads few would attempt to pass over. Conversation became brisk, as it usually does when six or more females are shut up together; all had a word to say about the Country and Armies. I sat silent. At last, a rather coarse woman addressed me, saying, "What is your opinion, Madame; you seem to have nothing to say." I replied politely, as to my opinion, in these troubled times it is best kept to myself, and I never talk unless I know to whom I am talking.

Just here our team stopped and we were asked to get out, in mud, too, more than ankle deep. After doing so, I discovered the loss of a handsome fur muff of mine. Search was made outside very kindly by the driver. I then bethought me of the inside and found my treasure between the feet of my inquiring friend who had not left the stage. I soon relieved her of the care of it. February and bitter cold was no time to lose so valuable an article.

Very little conversation took place, and we finally drew up at the best, but far from comfortable, hotel in Leesburg. As we made our way in, I saw many rather rough looking men congregated to see the arrival, two of whom I saw at a glance knew my young lady, though no word was spoken.

We soon secured lodging and retired to our room. Shortly after there was a timid knock at my door, which Miss Ward answered, greeting the comer most cordially. Being busy writing a few hasty lines to Mr. Wyeth by a "tallow dip", I did not look up, but on hearing the young gent say, "I knew you as soon as you got out and was rejoiced, knowing you'd tell us all we want to know, who commands on the other side and what numbers."

I sprang to my feet, saying, "Before she answers, excuse me, young man, but Miss Ward can answer no questions. We are under the bond of a lady's word not to divulge anything relative to the condition of 'things on the other side' and let me add, you are jeopardizing your freedom and safety by asking such questions, for you know not who I am."

Quizzically, he replied, "Don't I though! Think you I have forgotten Miss Henrietta Horner, my sister's dear friend?" "Very well," said I, "You have the advantage of me in that particular, but not in prudence." I was very uneasy, this being my first experience "between the lines".

Not sleeping, I arose early and left my companion to do the same. I somehow mistrusted her. Very shortly after breakfast (a light one), I sallied forth to hunt old friends, among them, Mr. Henry Harrison, my father's friend, a wealthy man in my day there (married General Walter Jones' daughter of Washington). They all greeted me most kindly though I had married a Yankee. Mr. Harrison hired me his team (wagon and mules) to take me home the following—25 dollars for 25 miles—and should the mules and wagon be confiscated, I was to pay value. He escorted me to the hotel, telling me much of the trials and losses they had met with in one short year and nine months.

On reaching the hotel, I went to my room to rest, encountering en route my young friend of the eve before, who was no other than John Randolph of Warrenton, one of our country beaux. He introduced me to a very nice fellow, another "Muselyite", both shabby in old clothes (no uniform). After a short chat, I went on. I had scarcely gotten in my room when a loud rap came and an order to open immediately, which I did, this time to find myself confronted by three soldiers in U. S. uniform.

My heart gave one big thud, as a mental vision brought me to immediate imprisonment, but I stood my ground (no Virginian could do otherwise) and said, "What do you wish, Gentlemen?" (Mental reservation there certain.)

"Your name, Madame, and the lady with you; where you are from and where going." "By whose orders or authority do you question me, sir?" I replied, getting a little mad, but taking out my pass, well signed and endorsed, I said, "Where are you from and to whose command do you belong?" ignoring his Captain's toggery or feigning ignorance of same and seeing he was no gentleman.

He replied, "I am Captain Leech, of such and such command (I can't recall it now)." "What state?" I asked. "Philadelphia, Pennsylvania," he said.

"Indeed," said I, "then I am all right. Do you know the drug firm of John Wyeth & Brothers?" "Quite well, Madam." getting respectful.

"My husband is the 'Brother' in that firm and told me if in difficulty or danger to appeal to any Union Soldier for protection or aid in his name, especially any Philadelphian; do I ask too much of you, Captain, now?" He was a resident of Arch Street, a little beyond the pale of Philadelphia's four hundred, still in U. S. uniform looked formidable.

Asked if I had any papers or contraband articles, I showed him my bag. Then he said, "This young lady has two large trunks downstairs. I'll take a look into them." "Very well," I replied, a little dubious as to what these trunks might contain, but descended.

Twelve men were posted around us, trunks and Miss Ward in the middle. The search began. Chancing upon a Doll Baby, the soldier held it up, saucily saying, "We'll pass this; Baby's not being contraband of War," I tell you, old Virginia in me was up in a moment and I turned to Captain Leech with very red cheeks. "Sir," I said, "I told you I'd submit to search, but never to insult. Call your men to order and decency or I demand you to take me to this officer. (showing him Col. Schley's card asking me to call on him if in need of protection)."

I had seen Mr. Harrison, Randolph and friend outside our circle and felt safe, but you should have seen the fellow's face change. I knew I had the upper hand. However, their punishment came quickly; at this moment a picket came in hurriedly, the trunks were deserted and my friends (enemies) were about beating a retreat when I stepped out.

"Captain, my keys and pass before you go," and to my joy, he paused just long enough to hand me both. Word had come that Confederate forces were surrounding the town and my friends in blue literally flew; a fight took place outside the town and several were killed, my insulting friend among them. He was formerly a blacksmith or horseshoer in Leesburg.

I must not forget to say that my stage interrogator was no other than a "Yankee Spy" and she had informed Leech of "these Southern women with quantities of contraband goods going South". I bet if we could have found her, she wouldn't have gone North or South for a while.

The following day, bright and early, we set forth in a strong wagon and well it was strong, for in the snowdrift we were as often on the fence top as in the bed of the road. However, father, mother, sister, and I hoped, brothers were ahead, after a long and cruel separation of two years of war.

I cannot describe my feelings in passing along my old familiar haunts and villages, devastated and destroyed by the relentless hand of the foe. It was my first realization of what War meant, and I assure you it was heartrending. My companion was used to it, having been absent only for a few weeks. It was all new to me. I must not fail to make grateful mention of the Negro man who drove our wagon and who evidently considered himself our protector, for whenever we passed village or house, and were halted with the inquiry, "Where did you come from and how did you keep your mules?" our spokesman would say, "De'se my mules and I'se taking these ladies where de wants to go. I ain't fraid of the Yankees," having been told these latter gentlemen had just passed through taking horses, cows, chickens, everything with them.

On we journeyed until at last in the dusk we stopped at my father's gate. The dear old gentleman came to it, seeing only ladies, he said, "What can I do for you, Madame?" with all that innate politeness of the old Virginia gentlemen, always ready to aid and protect a lady under any circumstances.

I had made Miss Ward my mouthpiece, fearing to trust myself to speak, or making the shock to them too great in declaring my identity at once. I can't express what I felt as Miss Ward said. "We want to beg a night's lodging for ourselves, man and mules." Instantly, he replied, "We will give you the best we have, ladies, but in these war times, the best is very poor."

I could stand it no longer and said, "Oh, my father, don't you know me?" Such rejoicing as followed cannot be expressed. The sad changes in my idolized parents, home and place almost broke my heart. My dear sister's youth had saved her from change, altho a recent severe illness had greatly prostrated her in strength for the time.

Oh, how I did enjoy myself my three weeks there. We managed to get news of my arrival to my brother, Richard, whose division of the Confederate Army was then lying near Winchester, Virginia. We succeeded, and as we sat together one evening, a tap on the windowpane came as though a small switch had just touched it with the wind.

Father said quietly, "Richard is here," and went out. The tap was their signal, if not answered by father, Richard would know the enemy were around and would ride off as fast as possible, but they both soon came in and I was supremely happy.

The dear boy (only twenty-two) did not dare sleep in the house, but in a secluded spot in the grounds, while our faithful true servant, Abram Brown, hid his horse in the woods and watched near my brother till daylight, and let me here say a word of this same Negro. He had been my father's foreman before the war and when my brother, Richard, joined the Army, Abram promised him to stand by our aged parents and sister and faithfully did he do it until the war closed and Richard returned.

I can't express the genuine pleasure it gives me to put on record for my children and grandchildren to remember the true devotion and faithfulness of a Southern Negro to his master and family. He could read well, and when "The Emancipation Proclamation" was issued, my father told him of it and that he was a free man, and he was not able to pay wages. "Well," said the faithful old servant, "I promised Mars Richard to stay till he come and I'm going to do it and take care of things." And he did it! After the war, he bought a nice little house and lived to a good old age, surrounded by his children and grandchildren.

I must add that long before the War in my girlhood, I taught all of our servants to read and was always opposed to slavery, telling my father not to leave me (should I out-live him) Negroes for I should certainly set them free. My brother and sister had no such scruples and would be kind to them though they held them in slavery. My oldest brother, Robert L. Horner, was at this time a U. S. prisoner at Johnston's island. My second brother was in the U. S. Navy but I did not tell old Seward this when I interviewed him.

I had a truly happy three weeks at my dear old home, at the end of which time I prepared to return to my "Groom" of one year, the first anniversary of our wedding day occurring during my visit. My sister, Elizabeth M. Horner, seemed to be such a sick girl, I prevailed on the dear old people to let her return with me, however, before telling of our journey North, let me mention one or two more items connected with the journey South.

I wanted to get home to my groom, and started, reaching Leesburg. Again the news greeted me, "No one is allowed to cross the Potomac."

I said, "I can't help that order; my pass calls for permission to go to Virginia, remain three weeks and return," so down to the Potomac I went and crossed it in a small skiff, altho it was high and muddy from recent heavy rains. I was wretched about my sister, her cough was so troublesome. I wrapped her in my furs and shielded her all I could.

When we reached the other side, we were all (two other ladies and ourselves) taken into custody and shown in the Colonel's office; having been there before I wasn't scared. I found in command an upstart of a lieutenant. Seeing at a glance that he was too little of a gentleman to know how to treat a lady courteously, I asked if Col. Schley was still in command of the Port. He said he was, had gone to Harper's Ferry in the morning and was expected back every moment. Then said I, "Knowing the Colonel, I will wait his return."

He then began examining the two scared females, who contradicted themselves so often I felt sorry for them. They were nieces of Admiral or Commodore Otis, trying to get to relatives in New Jersey, both handsome women, but they didn't get through, so I heard afterwards, but I am anticipating as they were our companions to Baltimore.

While their catechism was going on, in came Col. Schley. You may believe I was glad to see him. At first he failed to place me. I handed him his own card and signature and promise to go over with me if I got into trouble in Virginia. In the most courteous manner he welcomed me back, was introduced to my sister and gave the order, "Take Mrs. Wyeth's things to the hotel. She and her sister are under my care."

. . . Col. Schley went on the train with us, bidding us a courteous farewell, but evidently had an eye to the brother-in-law and his two females, and twitted me with being so stingy with my brandy in going over, where-upon I promised to send him a box, but before I could do it, my good thoughtful husband had sent him a box of choice wines.

During this journey to Baltimore, not knowing whether Mr. Wyeth had been notified of our coming, my fears and anxieties were great. I saw we two were under the surveillance of the officer in charge, nor did his watchfulness cease when we were joyfully met at the station-gate in Baltimore by my dear husband.

We had to drive with the other party to the Provost's office and deliver up my papers. When that was done, we bid our military friend adieu and his two companions, hoping they'd get through all right.

It is useless for me to attenpt any description of the joy of feeling myself at home and in my dear one's care.

'I Had Heard of War . . .'

SUSAN Q. CURLETTE

Excerpts from the letters to a son in Missouri from Susan Q. Curlette of Waverley, near Piedmont Station, now Delaplane.

Piedmont Station
May 9th 1861

. . . things at Washington have assumed such a horrible aspect all previous things have died away. Truly these are sad times. I could have had no idea of it without being a witness—sad faces everywhere. I was at Cool Spring on Sunday, as usual. It was more like a burial than church. I thought of Mr. DaShield's exclamation, "My God, what is to become of the people?"

. . . it would be useless for me to attempt a detail of all the war news all over the State. There is intense Commotion here—many have been called and volunteered to join the troops—amongst them F. L. Marshall, Thos. Marshall, O. H. Williams, Nim Rust, Singleton Rust, Hugh Green and Robert L. A. Washington, Dr. Adams and Co., Turner Ashby and Co. and a great many about Salem and Warrenton—Col. Scruggs of the number—and almost everybody. Cars running all times of the night. Oh, it is heart rending indeed. Very truly our troubles have come upon us. I very much fear Virginia is to be the battleground. The sufferings here must be intense. What will we do in Civil War—the worst of all kinds? My heart sickens at the prospect, and my hand drops nerveless. Some say "Hope" but I cannot see anything to build hope upon. Oh, My country I loved so much: I fear she is doomed for ruin.

I send you a couple of Gazettes, which will give you considerable news, and that may be stopped shortly. Then we shall be all in the dark. Many families are leaving Alexandria and Washington.

A great deal of rain—farming retarded—garden I keep up and the Box and everything looking very pretty now, but I find my strength and energy failing as I grow old—

Mrs. Thomas Marshall, Oak Hill, is dead—she died in March.

Piedmont Station
Sept. 15th 1861

. . . the great battle at Manassas Junction on the 21st of July—the greatest that has ever been in America. I have had descriptions of it—accounts are various. I have not seen an official statement, but persons and papers say about fifteen thousand Yankees were slain and taken prisoners, Three to four thousand Southern, amidst horses and a general wreck of everything. But the Northerners were entirely routed amidst the greatest confusion and alarm, leaving all the grand equipage designed for their victorious entry into Richmond City—estimated at about one and a half million dollars.

Among the captured articles were 30,000 handcuffs, we were left to infer the design of these. Johnston's army (between fifteen and twenty thousand which had been stationed at Winchester) on a forced march came to Piedmont Station on the 19th of July and remained to be carried as fast as the cars could convey them to Manassas, which took three days. They were left without provisions or cooking implements, and a great many dispersed through the neighborhood. I certainly had my share—my cooking stove performing to its utmost capacity—and still they came—a continuous stream for three days, but I have a fine garden which helped me very much. I did not see a face that I knew from Friday until Sunday night. . .

I must narrate an incident showing an especial protecting Providence. Among the first to come on Friday morning were the Culpeper Cavalry—Capt. Thompson's Co. and in a few moments up rode a fine, tall man—Finely mounted—arms glittering, who introduced himself as Col. Boone of Mississippi. I asked if a relative of the famous pioneer of Kentucky. "Yes", he said "a brother of my grandfather", and the family still bears a remarkable resemblance. He said he was unwell and asked to remain and rest a while. I told him I considered myself favored in having him as my guest. He remained until the next day, and was my friend at once. He told me how to proceed in giving the soldiers something to eat, which aided me very much— all was so new and unexpected to me. I hope never again to be placed in so exciting a situation as long as I live. . . .

I had heard of war and thought of it, but I had never formed an adequate idea of it until now. Oh that it was ended. . .our most estimable citizen, John Q. Marr, was the first to fall at Fairfax C. H. in a little skirmish with the enemy. Berkely Ward, Richard Ashby (Mrs. D. A.'s son) He was killed fighting bravely in Western Virginia, also Dr. Thos. Marshall (J.H.M.'s son) from disease contracted in the army in his medical capacity. . .

A great many from this neighborhood are now in the field—L. and Thos. Marshall, G. Carroll, A. Chunn, B. Blackmore and all the young men—everything pressed into service—wagons and whole teams on all sides to the disadvantage of farming operations . . . We are in the midst of war and have to make the best we can of it. And when and where it will end no human being can tell. Maryland, Virginia and Missouri are doomed states. War at a distance is not to be compared to one in our midst—sick, soldiers, hospitals, and everything pertaining to it is horrible! horrible!

. . . I know one thing, without a change, destruction will sweep over the land like a torrent, and I know not what will become of us.

. . . I have not told you how much we miss good old Alexandria, now in Federal possession—no communication, except sometimes a person gets out by stratagem. No Gazette since the 23rd of May. I had taken the paper 30 years and paid in advance.

Alexandria bank notes not current—no goods—no salt—selling at $7.00 per sack in Richmond and $12.00 in our Salem—great scarcity of money. I do not know how we are to live and pay our taxes—and our taxes extra—50 cents on the hundred $. No credit for anything, cash system entirely.

P.S. The Southern army commanded by Beauregard and Johnston are within two miles of Arlington Heights. Their flag is waving in sight of the Capitol—a battle has been expected for the last fifteen days but has not taken place yet.

Nov. 30 1861.

. . . We have had an awful battle at Leesburg—said to be the most brilliant achievement of the South—General Evans, our commander, in which the notorious General Baker was killed by young Hatcher of Loudoun, an only child, but poor fellow, it cost him his brave young life. The Federals now have possession of Romney, and General Jackson's command is stationed at Winchester. There is a battle daily expected between the two armies and also another at Manassas. There is nothing to subsist on from Alexandria to Manassas and the people who were able have fled and have left the poorer ones and the army to pick up their leavings. We have a good many refugees in this immediate neighborhood.

Old Billy Wooden's son Billy had 11 servants stolen in one night. Similar cases too numerous to mention. I fear our farming operations in another year will be considerably lessened, owing to so many horses & having been forced into the State service. For instance, Mrs. George Carter, 16 horses in the army at one time. G. H. Harrison, two wagons and teams and so, according to circumstances. **

I am very sorry to record the death of several more of your acquaintances—John A. Washington (of Cleveland) Nathan Loughborough (Mrs. Morgan's nephew) in battle in Western N. C. Mr. Jones (of Salem) of disease contracted in the army. Wash Shacklett at the depot, and Mrs. Rose Rogers of typhoid fever. There has been a great deal of sickness throughout the country, which I believe is always the case where armies are stationed.

I procured my salt at $3 per bushel. They say it is selling for $10 in Winchester now.

Oct. 1864 . . . A list containing articles taken by Yankees.

2 horses. . 2 oxen. . 2 heifers . 7 killing hogs
30 chickens . 6 turkeys.
30 yards cotton. leather
1 1-2 bu. calt . . . 50 lbs. flour
1 tin pan. . . 1 large stove pan
1 scarlet damask table cover . . 1 plaid gingham handerchief
1 gold pen and extension. . Silver pencil case
1 black alpaca satin bordered handerchief

1 pr. fine new pillow cases. . . 1 nice new head brush
1 book (Inquire Within). . . 1 black worsted head net
1 pr. fur topped gloves
1 Red Morocco Case containing all my Sewing needles—10 or 15 doz.
2 books and Walker's large sized Dictionary.

Waverly, Fauquier County Va.
Near Piedmont Station., M. G. R. R.
Nov. 6th, 1862

Capt. Hall
Sir:

I regret the necessity of asking your attention to depredations committed by soldiers whilst camped near my farm the last two days—5th and 6th.—namely: sheep killed 8 certainly and perhaps more; 3 stacks of hay, 2 of oats; about 15 acres of corn standing in the field, which renders me nearly destitute of provisions.

I most respectfully ask compensation from you to procure subsistence. Your attention will confer a living favor on an unprotected widow.

Very respectfully
Susan Q. Curlette.

Capt. Hall
Chief Quartermaster
General Burnside's Corps.

'Go Fight!'

(Continuing the recollections of Fielding Lewis Marshall, of Ivanhoe, near Delaplane.)

At Shacklett's Tavern, a roadside inn of before the Revolution on the main road from Winchester to Fredericksburg via Warrenton, Miss Kitty Shacklett and her brother 'Kiah—an old maid and an old bachelor—lived and died. Here you may see the room Lord Fairfax occupied.

(Here) on the day of First Manassas, Johnson's rear guard were on the march and stopped near this ancient and famed hostelry to refresh their dry and hungry throats. All day Miss Kitty cooked for them, officers and men alike. When, refreshed, they offered her gold in pay, her reply was "Go fight! I won't have your gold!"

Her brother 'Kiah suffered severe treatment from the Yankees when he refused to take the Oath of Allegiance to the United States. They took him out with a rope around his neck and drew him to a tree.

He resisted, and they desisted, but poor 'Kiah never rallied from the shock and died a few years thereafter.

His brother Washington, called "Dosh", was treated worse still. His house at Piedmont Station was taken, and he, his wife and all his children were confined in the basement of his house and not allowed for any purpose to leave their prison. Dosh was in weak health, and died soon. What became of his widow and orphans I know not, but I am confident they have not been deserted by the God they served so faithfully.

Christmas at Salem, 1864

Letter from Amanda Klipstein to her husband, Philip Augustus Klipstein. Mr. Klipstein, farmer and storekeeper at Salem (Marshall), was advanced in years when he was conscripted for military service. But he served until the end of the conflict and was present at the surrender at Appomattox.

Salem Dec. 25, 1864.

My very dear Husband

Today is Christmas day and how ardently we all did wish and was in high hopes you would be with us but was sorely dissapointed. Yesterday evening your second letter was handed to me brought by Mr. Moore, it made my heart ache to read what you had to pass through and my feeling(s) were such that I could not read it aloud to the children till I was composed. I imagined what your feelings were knowing how backward you were and how sensitive too, and I have thought for sometime past, if you had not been so much so, and when Mosby called and asked you what Regt. you intended joining, if you had only answered him the 6th you would have been spared all you have passed thro' but it is past now and all my hope is, that it may prove all for the best, at the same time it is heart-rendering to think of the long separation I feel so lonely and have no one that I can confide in or look up to for advice. You were everything to me that this world could give. I feel willing and hope I shall be able to look up to a higher Power for council and to show me the true way to guide our house hold and teach my children the right way. I know I have a willing mind but since you left, the multiplicity of cares I feel at times is more than I can bear, but then I look at others that are in a worse condition and I feel grateful that it is no worse, if we all keep well and you are spared to us, I feel that everything else will be as feathers in the air. I do not know how you have done for a change of shirts, it has been a month today since you left and what a long month it has been. Mr. Sanders returned yesterday from Charlottesville and brought our three sacks of salt and 38 3-4 yrds. cotton, there was no Government cotton there. He paid 7$ yd and gave 90$ for salt and sacks. I sent by him 9 3-4 yrds. calico, 12 lbs candles, 14 lbs. soap and 7 pair of socks which paid for the salt and cotton he brought 1¾ $ in change back. The prices are not so high there as in Richmond, he says he will go again so soon as the roads get better he proposed to me to go to Loudoun with him. I have not been over since you left. The blockade has been shut down. I have some idea of going this week and taking my bunch cotton and trade it for Lard and other things. I did not get 1 gal out of our hogs, I have $40 in money with the tobacco I can get the bill of goods. The day the boys went to mill, the yankees came in a large force and tried to catch Dolly but she out ran them. Did not one come in the house, asked me if you were in the service and I told them you were, they wanted to know your age and how long you had been in service, they took only two hens. They were coming through our gate with pistols cocked before I knew they were in 20 miles, stole in the place, went out to Rectortown—met Mr. Cochran had been to Phillipses to trade a horse, had a good deal of money on his person mostly in gold, captured him and carried him on and the family have not heard from him, they got Willie Cocke, Dick Buckner and Mr. McElhany, and when they got to old Lud Lakes, Mosby was eating his dinner, they surrounded the house and shot him through the window and would not go in till one of the ladies handed out his arms. Then they came in, he was badly wounded and pretended he was dead—but pulled off his coat and one lady hid it under the bed and cut the stars off, they took that, his hat, boots, all his papers, and yanked him over three times, and left him as they thought dead, but did not know who he was, passed for a Lt. Tommy Love was with him, he was taken.

I was very uneasy about Ernest but they did not go to Dawsons and he heard they were coming and got out of the way but they did not get home till the next evening, so you may know I was uneasy. They got the flour and bran and I let Dr. Harry have 40 lbs. I have made up a few cakes and pies but they do not do us half the good they would if you could help us to eat them. Kitty has been saving the pumpkins to make pies for you, but I am afraid they will all be gone. Nannie Newman staid last night and witnessed the filling of the childrens stocking and their glee this morning. O how my thoughts ran to you, comparing the different Christmas'es we have spent together and Ernest birth night. I did not make his cake but promised he should have it when you came home, which I hope and trust will not be long. How the children wished Pappy could help to eat their good things. Ernest reads the Bible nearly every night and morning, poor fellow has his hands full, feeding and cutting wood and he has had a rising under his arm which was very painful I put a blistering plaster on it and it is now well. My fingers are now tired, I will rest a while. . .

Advise Against Exposure

Salem Fauquier Cty., Va. Jany 18, 1865

This is to certify that I have visited several time P. A. Klipstine, a private in Comp. D, Capt. Berkeley, 8th Va. Regt. Inty. since his return home on furlough—and found him suffering with Influenza. He was unfit for military duty from the time & before his furlough expired until the time he started back.

John W. Newman, M. D.

Mr. Klipstine is still suffering with Bronchial Cough, induced by Influenza, and I would advise avoiding of exposure until it is removed.

John W. Newman, M. D.

Get A Furlough for 30 Days

(Letter from P. A. Klipstein to his wife Amanda)

(Sunday) Charlottesville, Va. Jany. 22nd, 1865

My Dear Wife I thought I would spend a few moments in writing. I am for to night very comfortably fixed in the house of Mr. Flannagan, who is connected with the Monticello Bank as an officer—he formerly was associated for a short time with the firm of Ball, Criss & Co. Yesterday was a dreadful day, but I was compelled to do what I could in disposing of my horse in the midst of the rain I at last had to let horse saddle & Bridle go for 17 Bunches of No. 10 Cotton—worth here now 100$ a bunch and they may well in a few days bring 150$. I will try to make the amount 20 bunches which ought to bring you in trade to the amount of 250$ in Yankee or 100$ in gold. Smith says there is very little chance of our getting the cotton from the state—it has gone up to 10 to 12$ you can get from 20 to 25$ for Sugar here and 50$ for Coffee, since the fall of Fort Fisher at Wilmington. Tell Dr. Newman that my Cough has troubled me a good deal at night though I feel tolerably well. Joe Button and wife sent their love to you. Mr. Eckloff sent his respects. Mr. Johnson & your Cous. Emily Lee who married Mr. Mitchell (one of Mosby's Men) sent much love to you they were very kind—I spent two night with them—Poor Buff, the cow I sold Eckloff died last September, from swelling in her throat—she was a great loss to them as she was a fine cow—Eckloff is now in the army, if you see any chance send some one of my Regt. by to get the Canteen of Molasses from Eckloff's house. I expect to get to Richmond Monday night and at Camp Tuesday morning. This day one week ago I was with my dear wife and children. Now I am far away with but poor prospects of seeing them soon, but I am now writing this as comfortably fixed as I could be. I am in a very comfortable room and writing at this time by a splendid gaslight. Mr. Flannigan is the Proprietor of a cotton factory also—I sold my horse to him and he invited me to spend the night which I accepted. I was assured before I left Salem that if proper steps were taken I could be gotten out of the army. Get Dr. Newman to write a strong memorial, stating that I was the head of a large helpless family, with all our means of living cut off or destroyed, get several signatures to it, then let it be carried before the board of Exemption and their recommendation for my exemption and I feel sure I would, by handling that document rightly at Richmond or your getting Lieut. Scott to handle it right, get a furlough for thirty days—which would be renewed according to circumstances and I would then prepare to raise a crop—Smith, Foster & Rixey I understood compose the Board, at any rate it will not be much trouble for you to make the attempt, if you wish. Urge Mr. Saunders to come to Charlottesville, with any kind of trade. The cotton weighs about 850 & which he can carry in the place of one box of Tobacco—if you can spare any coffee two pounds will get you a bunch of cotton or 4 lbs. of Sugar. I have not yet opened either of the Haversacks and I have not spent or given away more than two or three Dollars, if Mr. Saunders comes be sure to send me a box of eatables & beans—potatoes—Socks—Cups—haversacks—Emory paper—plates &c &c &c direct to me, Co. D 8th Va. Regt. Hunton Brigade—Picketts Division, Care of Pay Heze. Bishop as quick as you can. Get him immediately to send the certificate about the sale of the horse and forward it to Anderson Smith—that he got the horse from one of Mosby's men—let him acknowledge it before a Magistrate—Be sure to write me by every opportunity—write a little each day so as to have a letter ready by every opportunity—any one coming to Culpeper or Charlottesville can bring a letter and drop it in the office. Calico sells here for 35$ a yard your piece of goods ought to bring at least 50$ a yard. Your own devoted Husband, Augustus. I have paid 3$ gold for 3 bunch No. 6 cotton making 20 Bunches. I am offered 10 lbs fair Tobacco for your Varnish.

Try To Keep Warm

(Letter from Amanda Klipstein to her husband, P. A. Klipstein.)

Salem 3 Feb. 1865

My dear Husband

Cud Rogers has just called and I have not a letter ready to send but Ernest has. I have been waiting to hear from you and never had an opportunity before. I have sent for Hez Bishop to come in and will attend to that matter immediately and also the petition you said if I wished it, now. My dear you know, or ought to know my feeling on that subject, how lonely we all feel without you, I intend

trying my best but it will take some time. I have been very busy making up the boys clothes. Neally left two days after you did. Mr. Eastham sent for her. I have not been to Loudoun yet the weather had been too cold. I think it was the coldest I ever felt. I thought of you all the time, how you must have suffered if you had to stand picket, (crease in paper, not legible) 5 or 6 dollars since you left, he has not been well and has not been hauling constantly. I have been waiting an opportunity to write a long letter went up town yesterday to find out if any person was going to Culpepper. Ernest wrote last night and I intended writing tonight. Now my dear don't you think hard of it, it has been so cold that it has been nothing else much done but try to keep warm. Dr. Adams I understand will be in Charlottesville this week. I will expect a letter by him. There is always someone passing but I do not know it they do not come by here (unreadable) In haste your devoted wife, Amanda.
My love to R. Sanders.

'A Thundering Poor & Piney Place'

PRIVATE JOHN W. CUMMINS

To all whom it may concern.

The bearer Private John W. Cummins, Co. A 9th Va. Cavalry. Twenty two years of age 5 feet 8 inches high, light complexion, blue eyes, light brown hair and by profession a Farmer born in the County of Fauquier and enlisted at Jumping Hollow in the County of Stafford on the 19th day of March 1862 and is to serve for the period of three years, is hereby permitted to go to his home in the county of Stafford, State of Virginia, to remain for fifteen days at the expiration of which time he will return to his company or Regiment whichever it may then be or be considered a deserter. Subsistence has been furnished to the said Cummins to the 22nd day of September 1863 and pay to the first day of July both inclusive. He has not been absent from his company without leave

Ed. M. Henry
Capt. comdg. C. A, 9th Va. Cav.

Private John W. Cummins bears the character of a good soldier prompt and attentive to his duties, deserves a furlough for the purpose of getting a horse & clothing for himself.

Ed. M. Henry
Capt. comdg. Co. A, 9th Va. Cav.

(Among the endorsements on the back is one that reads):
Approved
By order of Genl. Lee.

June 1st 1863.

Dearest Sister

I received your letter of the 20th which gave me great pleasure to hear that you all are well and that the Yankees have not taken everything from you as yet. I am well and heartier than I have been since I have been in the service. I could come home in a days ride if it were not for that great gulf between us. Everything is quiet along the line today. The Yankee pickets and ours talk across the river to each other and some times they meet on the railroad and trade with each other. Cousin John and the rest of the neighborhood boys are well. We had a hard time during the Chancellorsville fight. We had to march and watch day and night. We were in some severe charges but our company was greatly blest—we never lost a man and but one wounded—R. Ashby slightly in the arm. Our Quartermaster James Forbes was killed—on A. P. Hill's Staff. We are camped close to Culpeper Court House. I could write you a good deal if I had the time. I was glad to hear the Pa was well of the Gaders I would be glad above all to see him. I was glad to hear that he was planting a crop of corn. From your brother

John W. Cummins

Camp near Raccoon Ford, Sept. 25th 1863

Dear Father: As I have a chance to write you a letter I will. I have not heard anything direct from home since I left there. I think you might send me a letter by some of the scouts that are constantly coming over if you would try. We have fallen back across the Rapidan River and are camped near Raccoon Ford. We are looking for a battle every day. Our squadron has been made Sharpshooters and as we fell back on the 13th we had to dismount and fight them as infantry. We had two wounded and one missing from our company. J. Brown and W. Tolson. We had to leave Brown on the field. He was shot through the thigh with a grape shot. I helped to bring him about a hundred yards but they graped us so from two batteries that we had to leave him. How any of us got out safe I cannot tell. I had my gun shot from out of my hand but picked it up and trotted back to my horse which was back in the rear and I tell you I was glad to see him. Cousin John is well but not in the fight on account of his horse which was lame. J. E. Barber is well and sends his love. . . I wish you would try to have me a pair of boots made as it is impossible to get them over here. Write every chance you get. In a hurry, from your affectionate son,

J. W. Cummins.

Camp near Orange C. H. Nov. 14th '63.

Dear Pa, I was sorry to hear that you had been sick for I know it threw you back in your fall work. I hope you all are not troubled much with the Yankees through that neighborhood as we have fallen back out of Culpeper and they have taken our place but I do not believe they will stay long for Lee told the infantry since we fell back over the Rapidan not to go building winter quarters for they had built them in Culpeper and they should occupy them. The enemy advanced on our infantry that we had over the river last Saturday and captured two of our redoubts and a good many prisoners and four pieces of artillery. It was a badly managed thing for our officers to let so few men stay over there. Our men stayed in their rifle pits until the Yankees got within one hundred yards of them before they started to fall back across the river. Our infantry fell back during the night and our cavalry had to cover their retreat. We were under fire of their guns all day but none of us were hurt during the day. I tell you we had a cold time of it. We have to stay in nothing but our gum cloth shelters yet but I hope that we will soon go into winter quarters somewhere but I have no idea where it will be but as we cannot stay in Fauquier I do not care where they winter. The paper of the thirteenth states that all is quiet in Tennessee. . .

I wish that I had brought that Colt of Mr. McCoy's out with me and had left my horse home for he has got the distemper most awfully bad. Tell Stephen to feed Kit and get her fat for I expect to get a detail and come home before long, for her or some Yankee horse. You must write every chance you can. . . P. S. John N. Stuart is elected our third Lieutenant

From your son, John W. Cummins.

. . . You wrote that you had plenty of Sweet Potatoes and Cider. I wish that I could get home about this time for cider we never see and sweet potatoes is $32.00 a Bu. Winter is coming on very fast and I am quite bare for under clothing such as drawers and shirts. You mentioned in your letter about sending me some clothes so I will let you know what I stand in need of most: I wish you would try in the first place and get me two over shirts if you have the cloth make them and send them to me by the first chance. Try and dye them some color: also two (2) pair of flannel drawers and my net shirts. Send me my net shirts as soon as you can if you have them and the rest just when ever you can. Some six or seven of the boys are coming home and you can send some of the articles by them—John Cooper and John Taylor. You said in your letter that you would be glad to hear how my finger has gotten so I will let you know for I had almost forgotten that it had ever been sore. It is a little stiff in the first joint but otherwise it is quite well. I think I had better quit for today.

October 12th

Today finds me well but not at the same camp. We have moved our camp about six miles nearer Petersburg to a place I do not know anything about only it is a thundering poor and piney place but how long we will stay here I do not know but I hope it will not be long. . .

All is quiet along the line today only the shelling of Petersburg which is every day business and some times all night. It seems like this cruel war is never going to end but I hope it will. I send you five dollars in greenbacks to get me a hat if you can and keep it until I write for it. Save all the food you can for I will have to come home soon to recruit my old horse. J. W. C.

Jack Frost Camp near Bellfield Station

Dear Sister,

I told you in my last letter that I wrote every chance——for I judge that you are as anxious to hear from me as I am to hear from you. I have no news to write only that we have moved to Bellfield Station on the Weedon Railroad 75 miles from Richmond and we have been all day at work putting up winter quarters. I have just finished my hut. I thought some time ago that I would take my winter quarters at home but I think we will have an active campaign down here all the winter. You have no idea how warm it is here to what it is in old Fauquier at this time. We have been losing ground lately and I am getting very much down hearted but I think it will work all right after a while. . . I send this by Stephen Arrington and you must send me a letter out by him. If you cannot send my boots by Mr. Eustace try him and if you do not succeed in sending them by either of them you must try to send them by some one else that is coming out. If you got my hat try to send it by some one for I am in need of it. Write soon.

From your brother, J. W. C.

P. S. Cousin John is well and is acting courier for General Lee. John Barbee is well and as pretty as ever. December 20th, 1865.

Camp at Bellfield Station January 29th

Dear Pa,

I do with regret for the first time write you since the war but I have bad news to write . . It may not be bad to you but it is to me, and that is I have lost my horse by the Grubs and I am a foot and a long way from home and expect to be so the balance of the war but I hope that will not be long . . . I expect to get a detail before long and I would like very much to come home on it but I will have to sell it to help get a horse for I have no other way to get one . . . You all may say I never tended to my horse as I should but that will not be so for I had him in better plight than he was when I left home with him last summer. He was taken sick and died in less than an hour and men that were good judges said he died with the grubs. Whether he died with the grubs or not he is dead. Cousin John and B. are well.

J. W. Cummins.

Near Center Cross March 15th 1864

Dear Sister,

As I have a chance to send this by a friend who got shot through the hand accidentally and has a furlough to go to his home I will do so. I am well at present but very tired as we have been harassed by the Yankees for the last week and have been running after them or from them, and have just got back to camp. I don't know which is nearer broken down—me or my horse but I hope that we will have a little rest now. (Illegible sentence) for parts unknown across the Rapidan river and started for Richmond but have not gotten there yet. They got to our breast works and charged them but were repulsed with great loss. Our loss was one killed and two or three wounded. We heard that they had gone down the James river and started after them but they had been defeated and we met them at Old Church in Hanover County and had a little fight but they soon got out of our way by crossing the Paumunkey River and burning the last boat. We had to come up the river here to cross and by that time they had a day's start on us again. Our horses being very tired we went into camp for a few days but we soon had to get up and get. The next day they started to charge our camp but we were too soon for them and soon had them on the run. Our force was too weak to rush on them so they got out of our way. That day being the tenth of March you ought to know what a day it was for it was raining all day and we had to charge them some two or three times in the mud and rain. You can judge how muddy and wet we were but they were on the run and we could hardly keep up with them. We ran them all day and then that night marched back to our camp—the distance of twenty miles and it was almost day when we got back. I was so cold and wet I could hardly get off my horse. We made up a fire and thought to dry ourselves but orders came for ten of us to go on picket and I had to go wet and cold as I was. I did not mind it myself but I did for my horse but we went on picket where we got plenty for our horses and ourselves. We stood picket on the Dragon Creek in Middlesex and I never saw kinder people in my life. We stood 48 hours and had nothing from the government but we got more than we could destroy. We would go to one house and eat our breakfast and to another to eat our dinner and to another to eat our supper. The ladies would play the pianos for us and we would not have cared if peaches had never gotten ripe. John Barbee and the rest of the neighborhood boys are well. Believe me to be ever your sincere brother,

John W. Cummins

P.S. P. N. Patton is the man that got shot—a member of our company.

Sept 18th, 1864

Camp near Stony Creek Dinwiddie Co.

Dear Pa,

I am anxious to hear from you as I have not heard since I left home. I am well but very much worsted from a raid that we have just returned from. We have been riding for five days and nights more or less: all the time in dust 4 or 5 inches deep. We went around in the rear of the Yankees and made a very good capture. We got between 5 and 6 hundred head of beef cattle and 11 wagons, 7 Ambulances, 3 or 400 horses and upwards of 500 prisoners. The wagons were loaded with provisions. We got out with them safe. We had to fight a little before we made the capture and a little after we got halfway back to our lines by them getting ahead of us and getting possession of the road that we had to come back on but we soon threshed them out with slight loss. It is the finest beef and the largest drove that I ever saw. Cousin John is well and Tom C. and send their love to you. We can not get anything down here but what the Government gives us for love or money without giving double price. I wish I could get home and get some of the sweet cider that I think you all have.

Jno. W. Cummins

Camp near Stoney Creek, October 8th 1864

Dear Sister,

I received your letter of the 18th and was glad to hear that you all are well for I do appreciate health beyond anything that we can be blessed with in this poor troublesome world. We started from this camp 28th of last month on a review as we thought but when we got out on the field news came that the Yankees were advancing and we had to go to meet them. We had a good many ladies out to see us but when that news came they were taken with the leavings for parts unknown, while we poor dirty Dogs had to march to defend their homes and yet if we were to go to their homes and ask for a canteen of milk they would not know when to stop charging for it and say they had rather see the devil than a grey back Rebel. I will give you a little history of the fight that we have just returned from although you may know more about it by the time you get this, if you ever do. We were marching day and night but not far at a time until the 30th before we got in a fight. We fought all day until about an hour before sundown when they broke and ran pell mell to their fortifications. We were dismounted but we charged them for a mile and a half, our brigade capturing 500 prisoners. Dark came on and we fell back and went into camp but before day the next morning the horn blew to saddle up, being the first day of this month, if you remember it was a very rainy day but we were out all day fighting, but I think we got the worst of the bargain. We whipped their advance and drove them back to their fortifications but we had to charge their fortifications twice and then could not take them. The first time we charged our line broke and fell back some distance but was halted by our commanding General to about face and take the works which we did. But we could not take them. I have been in a good many places that I thought were very bilious but I was very much mistaken for I have seen nothing in comparison. Capt. Henry and Charlie Briggs were wounded. Cousin John is acting courier, yet he was there but not in danger. John E. was holding horses. The fight is over and we return to camp with our plunder. I was not as lucky as some of the boys and this is generally the case with those that do their duty. I got a very good overcoat, and othei little things. I kept a lookout for a chance to get a hat but could not meet with one for 2-3 of them had no hats for they were taken off by the boys that took them and what few our company took had caps, 45 in number.

George James and myself found a Yankee officer that was not quite dead. I do not think he had been robbed but we could not find any greenbacks but we stripped him of his outer clothes which came in very well as we stood in need of some articles that we got. I tried to get a pair of over shirts but could not. I wish you would send me a pair of home made if you have the flannel. Dye them some color.

October 10th. I received your letter of the 1st yesterday. We have just returned from inspection. It was reported last Saturday that the Yankees were coming again and we all started to meet them about dark. Although it was very cold we marched until midnight and then camped for the night. But they went back and we came back to our old camp and remain here under marching order. It is reported here that we will cross the James if we do leave here to meet the party that is coming down by Culpeper but I hope it is not so . . . (Balance of letter missing).

A Most Bloody Battle

MILTON ROBINSON

(The originals of these letters of Milton Robinson to his mother Mrs. John Garner Robinson of Paris, Virginia, are now the property of Mrs. Marie B. Gibson of Upperville.)

Camp Pickens July 23 1861
Manassas Junction

Dear Mother:

Through the benevolence of a just and merciful God, I am spared to communicate to you this morning in brief the particulars of one of the most bloody battles ever fought upon the continent of America; On last Sunday morning we were drawn up in a line of battle

& ammunition distributed to the Company and as soon as that was done, we marched to the field of battle, where we witnessed a conflict that the bloody pages of past history does not furnish a parallel.

The first shot was fired by the enemy. But the gallant and brave sons of Virginia returned the fire immediately after the first shot & then we could not hear anything but bombs whishing during the day.

Our Company was reserved to the last moment when three of the Regiments were cut to pieces, And exhausted, some running to the woods and branches, some with one leg, one arm, one eye and some with no legs, when we saw them it was enough to discourage any one. But General Beauregard called on the 8th Virginia Regiment, and led them through grape and bombs and in the charge, General Beauregard had his horse shot from under him and all his staff killed. He dismounted and loaded the cannon himself and made a lane through them at every shot. They then retreated a mile off. Then the Loudoun Company charged on them. Welby Carter was in the battle & his men were cut all to pieces. Robert Fletcher had his arm shot badly, John deButts had two fingers shot off and several others I could not learn their names were wounded.

We have just received orders to hold ourselves in readiness to march at any moments warning, we know not where. Write soon and give me all the news at home.

Your affectionate son
Milton Robinson

I KILLED A YANKEE, I'M SORRY

Camp Burk
3 'miles from Leesburg Va.

Dear Mother:

I suppose Robert gave you a discription of the fight on the 21st, As he was there to witness the bloody scene. It was a much harder fight than that at Manassas, It lasted about four hours, the last charge was made just about dark, when we took the battery and drove the Yanks in the river, some of them stripped off naked and attempted to swim across but failed.

They were two or three hundred drowned in attempting to swim across. We got a wagon load of clothes and seven or eight hundred stacks of guns. Yesterday one of the Mississippians went out in a skiff and saw a Yankee floating on the water. He pulled him in the boat and got a gold watch and chain and 50.00 in gold out of his pocket. The watch was worth 150.00. There are Yankees from Edwards Ferry to Georgetown floating down the river, I am sorry to tell you that I killed a Yankee. He jumped up out of the bushes in about 30 yards from me and I drew on the gentleman he ran I shot him in the head and the ball came out of his nose.

We expect to fight at the same place every day. We have been out in the rain for two days and two nights. I have gotten a cold and can hardly breathe. We are going to fall back to Mrs. Callet's Mill and let the yanks take possession of Leesburg. Old Gen. Evans has been drunk for a month & every time he hears of a yank being on this side, he sends a dispatch to Hunton to pack up, so we have had to sleep on the ground without tents for a week.

Received a letter from Aunt Alice yesterday saying that Mel was sick, but is getting better, You come down to Cousin Lem's and come down any time & I will try to get off to go home with you. You can send the socks, & pants. I have enough other clothes. What is Jack doing? Write soon. Mr. McArter is waiting for me and I will have to close.

Your affectionate son
Milton Robinson

THE FATIGUE OF A SOLDIER

One mile from Waterford
August the 20th 1861

Dear Mother:

We are still undergoing the fatigue of a soldier's life but hope it will not continue very long. From the reports of the paper, We learn from that they are holding Peace meetings through out the North & I sincerely hope peace will be made before winter sets in.

You cannot imagine the fatigue a soldier has to undergo, I never knew how to appreciate home until now. But since I have experienced the life of a wayward youth not accustomed to leaving home only a day or a week & now it has been three months since I have been home & Now can not get permission to go.

I think it very hard we have to submit to every thing imposed upon us. General Evans says that no man shall go home if he is sick, or if his parents are sick, on account of there being so many sick at the present time. Some of our Company are now sick.

You need not look for me until the time I volunteered my services is expired & and before that time is expired I may be a corpse lying under the green turf with all its verdure of beauty; But I trust in the Supreme being who giveth and taketh all things; Christ died upon the cross for his people, Why should I not die in defence of my country?

Sunday July 21st many a brave man was cut down in the prime of life, who left their beloved homes with the expectation of whipping the Rebels, will never return to enjoy the sweet comforts of home. I trust that I may enjoy good health through out the War and return home once more to the ones I long to mingle my voice.

I was never so glad to see Mel in my life than I was when he came down with C. Adams, I never enjoyed my food more than those, I hope to see such a Mothers box in a day or so but would much rather see some of you, it is only about six hours ride you could start early in the morning and get here by twelve o'clock.

Write soon

Your devoted son
Milton Robinson.

Our Enemies Triumph Over Us

LUCY JOHNSTON AMBLER

Excerpts from the diary of Lucy Johnston Ambler of Morven, February 1862—August 1863. Mrs. Ambler (1800-1888) was the daughter of Charles Johnston and Letitia Pickett and the granddaughter of Peter Johnston who was born in Edinburgh in 1710 and came to Virginia in 1726. She was married on April 15, 1819, to Major Thomas Marshall Ambler. Their children were Lucy Letitia, John, Elizabeth Steptoe, Frances Langhorne, Charles Edward, Thomas Marshall, Richard Jaquelin, Ann Pickett, Mary Cary, and James Markham Marshall Ambler.

Friday evening, February 21, 1862—

I bought a book from Dangerfield for which I paid twenty cents. It is a very large blank book for the price, that is to say, Danger is generally very good at a bargain, but I got the better of him that time.

I intend to get Mr. Downs to show me how to shoot tomorrow, and how to load.

We heard yesterday that 15,000 men were taken prisoners at Fort Donaldson with a good many officers, but it is untrue from beginning to end—there were only 150 instead of 15,000. There were no officers of rank taken prisoners that we know of at all.

July 15, 1863—We have had another tremendous rain today. There is great danger of our losing our wheat crop by the continual rain. It has cleared off so that we can see the sun, but the weather is by no means settled. Our house is wet over the floors by the continued rain. Four of our rooms leak, and if the rain continues I know not what we shall do as we cannot procure nails. Our fields are covered with verdure, but we can procure no cattle to graze. Heard of the death of our Friend Mr. Barton a few days ago, and again today heard of the death of Mrs. Barton. No doubt they both fell victims to the horrid war. Their sons were all in the army, six in number, and two of the six fell fighting for our liberties. May God bless and preserve those that are left and bring them all to his fold through Christ their Redeemer.

July 16-19—We have all been very much cast down by the fall of Vicksburg. Our army has also returned from Pennsylvania without doing great things as we had hoped. Let us not be discouraged by these reverses for I feel that God intends us to separate, or why this entire difference of opinion? The North eager to coerce us, and we striving to establish our independence. I fear we have trusted more in our generals and soldiers than we have in the help of God. Therefore he sees fit to punish us by allowing our enemies to triumph over us for a season.

July 21—Last night a body of cavalry camped within three miles of us and I hope we shall not see them, as they were probably on a raid or scout. All the horses and cows have been driven out of sight as we always fear their killing or taking them. We hear distressing accounts of how our people are killed in battle. Lord, wilt thou not stay the war? Cause the people to cease from strife.

July 27—Since the 22nd we have been in constant excitement. Some Yankey cavalry came here the 22nd and behaved very well doing us no damage in any way. The 23rd the Yankey army commenced passing by. They annoyed us in every possible way. They commenced killing our fowls. The next day they finished every fowl but one hen who was sitting. The 3rd day they killed her. They shot our sheep down, cut what they wanted off, and left the rest in the field. They killed half our hogs. They took every horse and all the cattle except my milch cows, two of which they took. Yesterday two of the steers returned home and the cows. The Yankeys did not leave any place but two rooms unsearched. They broke open the smoke-house, took half my bacon. I then implored an officer to make them come away. He let a man carry four pieces off, and drove the rest away. As soon as they were out of sight I got two men to carry my meat into the house. I then left the door wide open for them to see there was no meat in the house, but most of them went and examined for themselves. They then went to the back part of the house and forced the door. I sent for an officer and unlocked the door of the room they were in. The officer came and drove them off. They had taken wearing apparel part of which they dropped. The horrid brutes came into my chamber stole a pair of shoes and two of Mr. Ambler's shirts. They took every hen the negroes had but one. They pulled open the press and took a little money they found in it. They took the little milk we had in the refrigerator. They broke the yeast jug and destroyed the milk bucket. They carried off three nice buckets. I am told they did all this and more to some of our neighbors. They destroyed the mills. They burnt down our stacks of wheat and also burnt Dr. Stribling's wheat. They drove all Mrs. Stribling's cows away although they had put a guard to protect her. They took the negroes' clothes and any little thing belonging to them that they wanted. The officers heard the firing of the guns as they were killing the sheep, but let it go on.

The officers pretended to stop the slaughter of the fowls by cursing and brandishing their swords and threatening to run the soldiers through. I verily believe the officers connived at all this destruction of our property. I had to keep guard at the doors of the rooms in the brick entry by sitting there all day. Although they would break into the house, yet they did not care about being seen while doing it. They went to my son's house and behaved as far as they could in the same thievish and dastardly manner. Is there a man among them? They seem like demons from the lower regions. I saw a Northern paper and find that the same kind of thing is going on at home on a smaller scale. The miserable wretches took off the wheels of the carriage and laid them in the middle of the road for the wagons to pass over, but one of our servants laid the wheels in the weeds. They went into the garden, took all the potatoes, and commenced pulling up large tomato vines with green tomatoes upon them. They took all my beets and beans and pulled the fence down in every direction. They cut off the tops of the green corn in the field, and I suppose if they had not been obliged to retreat would have destroyed the whole corn-field. Finally as a crowning act they burnt down one of our stock yards and took all our corn except little more than a barrel that Mr. Downs managed to conceal. The corn they fed to their horses. God only knows how we are to get along. It must be terrible. They have taken, as far as I can learn, every grain of corn out of the neighborhood. They came into this neighborhood about ten o'clock and did all this mischief, and had they remained I do not suppose they would have left us anything. They went off in such a hurry that they left four slaughtered beeves on their camp ground. Every one we see tells the same tale of the Yankeys destroying every thing they could lay their hands upon. I do not like to think of the prospect before us. No fowls of any description, no eggs nor anything comfortable. How long, O Lord, are we to groan under the heel of the oppressor? They searched every bush and every weed, peered into every nook, and stole every thing without compunction. Things that they did not want they took from one person and gave to another. They regarded no remonstrance but went ahead with all their might destroying every thing before them. All sense of shame and decency seems to have deserted them and they stalk abroad and take everything before our eyes, cursing and swearing in the most Godless manner.

July 27—Our dear little grandson Mark Ambler was taken sick about the time the Yankeys commenced passing, and is now exceedingly ill of dysentery. This has added very much to our affliction. Our grandson Claude Marshall was taken today with the dysentery, and is now quite sick with it. Two negro children also have the same disease.

July 28—We have heard from several of our neighbors and they all fared very much as we have done. We have now been rid of our enemies for three days and I trust we shall see them no more. On the morning of the 29th our dear little Mark was taken to God and delivered from all the trouble that flesh is heir to. It is a sore grief to us all. May God sanctify it to us and may we all trust in him. I feel now as if I had very little in this world to interest me. I took a great deal of pleasure in attending to my fowls, but that occupation is gone as the Yankeys took all my fowls. A dozen men would run after a hen and never rest until they had cut her down. The Yankeys went to one of our neighbors and met with a lady and demanded her wedding ring, and put a pistol to her head and threatened to shoot her if she did not give them the ring. The lady told the wretch that unless he shot her he would not get the ring. He then let her alone. The officers connive at such atrocities as these as they are elected by the soldiers and fear to lose their places. They tell us it is part of their strategy to starve us out, and they will do it if our Heavenly Father does not provide for us more abundantly than we are able to ask or think.

While passing they all begged for bread. As I said, we lived upon hoe-cakes for four days baked early in the morning. The first day they came we had bread and I put away some rolls for us and thought I would give the scamps the two loaves of bread. I went to the bread and found only one loaf. I brought this up when a Yankey begged for bread. I told him this was all the bread I had and that I had a family of children and no way to feed them. (We could cook no food except early in the morning before they began to move. They would take it as fast as it was cooked.) This wretch expressed the greatest pity for us all, but took the loaf of bread out of my hand and put it in his haversack. It would take a large volume to write all their atrocities. No shame, no decency, uttering all the while most blasphemous oaths. They took the leather bands off the wheat machinery wherever they went. They took our axes, spades, and it is useless for me to enumerate what they took, for they took everything. They went to the Rectory and destroyed everything our pastor had. The rich and the poor fared alike. They would take all the corn, flour, and meal that they could find from the poorest person and their last piece of meat. Surely these people who have acted in this inhuman manner will receive their recompense. Amidst all this war the poor negro seems as indifferent as possible. They actually seem cheerful. They literally take no thought for the morrow. Their only idea is to be supported in idleness. While the Yankeys were about us they did nothing, but took their rest in the sun before their cabins, and, I suppose, enjoyed their occupation—*idleness.* Whether they waited on the Yankeys willingly I do not know, but they certainly cooked for them.

I heard from one of our relations who lives six miles away. Treating them as badly as possible, they, among other little Yankey notions, put some beautiful dessert china in a bag, put it on their horse, and rode off rattling it as they went. One of the demons tied a beautiful tea cup around his horse's neck and exhibited it as a trophy. They certainly conquer old men, women, and children. Lord, how long are our enemies to overrun us?

August 2—Upon seeing some of our neighbors I find that the

Yankeys have cut up the harness and injured all the carriages as far as I can learn so as to make them unfit for use. Wherever anyone had a good wagon or cart they took it off. While the Yankeys were at our house as they were throwing their sabres into the fowls, I asked them if they thought the blessing of God would follow them. One man who seemed to be decent and pretended to restrain them (for it was only pretense) upon my saying this, called to the men, "You can do as you choose now. You may take everything." There was a poor woman whom they were stealing from, and she cursed them and struck them and kicked and cuffed them from her house, and they jumped out of the windows and ran from her fury. This woman told me she feared the Lord would never forgive her for the manner in which she had cursed these wicked wretches. The Yankeys cut up the bellows and took off the tools from the blacksmith's shop. They stopped short of nothing and the officers *saw nothing*. I trust this army will never pass us again. Sometimes I thought it was mocking in them to beg us for something to eat. I sat and guarded four outside doors (our house has eleven), and when one set of hungry beggars went out, another came in. My answer invariably was "you have taken everything from us and we can give you nothing to eat." I think they must have come in to mock us and see our distress. One of these generals asked at one of our neighbors for a private room which was prepared for him. In a short time this same *gallant general* was at the negro cabins with his shirt sleeves rolled up prepared to work, and conversing with the ladies of color. In no face among our enemies did we see an expression of sympathy, whatever they may have felt. When they have been among us before they did not go upon the mountains, but now they have searched every mountain so as to let us have no horses. In a few instances they have given broken down horses to negroes. We have to send to mill by a man carrying the wheat on his back.

August 3—I feel very low spirited to-day. My husband's shirts want patching. The Yankeys came in and took two, one a very good one. I have nothing to patch his shirts with. Indeed, everything looks very gloomy. From having a confortable table, I am reduced to a bacon bone. The Yankeys have overrun my garden and injured what they did not take away, so I have nothing but potatoes and snaps, and not many potatoes. I have a very sick grandchild and several servants sick with no suitable medicine. May God give me grace and strength to bear my burden knowing that . . . .

August 8—Last night we had another grandson born into this world of sin. May this child be a child of God and an inheritor of the Kingdom of Heaven. This boy is much larger than a little granddaughter seven weeks old. May both these children be made partakers of grace. We had a heavy shower last night so that we can haul no wheat today. The Yankeys tried very hard to set fire to a crop of wheat in the shock, but I suppose it was too green to burn. We received most unexpectedly some sugar last night, and if our foes do not come and take it from us, it will last some time. We hear constantly of rumors of intervention by European powers to procure us peace, but apparently there seems to be not the least probability of it.

August 9—We hear of riots at the North for recruiting the draft. They say in their newspapers that they have lost from disease, battle, and various other causes 600,000 men, and the rebellion still goes on. I suppose the people begin to think that while they are putting down the rebellion they are destroying themselves. God grant that they may let us alone even if they should fight each other. Lincoln has called out 300,000 more men, and if they can only hurt us they care not how much their own people are destroyed. May God turn all the counsels of our enemies to utter confusion. They seem perfectly blind and perfectly furious. The Yankeys all talk as if they wished a Union with the South by utterly exterminating us off the face of the earth.

August 10—Again there seems to be apprehension of the negroes going off. At Leeds, Mrs. J. K. Marshall's farm, 29 went off with the Yankey army reducing their numbers very much. They still think more are going. There is a body of Yankey cavalry within five miles of us and it is probable they are there for the purpose of helping off the blacks. Poor creatures! They seem doomed to utter extirpation. Some of the Yankeys advise them to go, and others tell them they had better stay where they are.

We hear nothing of our army that is at all reliable, but trust that God will be with them and give them a signal victory over our enemies. We hear a good deal of riots at the North resisting the draft, but I fear Lincoln has placed his foot too firmly on the necks of the people for them to offer resistance, unless the hand of God interfere.

When Beloved Ties Are Broken

MARY AMBLER STRIBLING

Excerpts from The Journal of Mary Cary Ambler Stribling, wife of Robert Mackey Stribling, commenced at Morven April 22, 1862. She was born at Morven September 9, 1835, died at Mountain View February 9, 1868. (Her children: Letitia Ambler Stribling, b. near Markham May 22, 1861; d. Oct. 4, 1861; Caroline Stribling, b. Morven June 17, 1863; d. Mountain View; Thomas Ambler Stribling, b. Feb. 6, 1866; d. Feb. 8, 1866; Robert Cary Stribling, b. Oct. 5, 1867; d. April 4, 1901.)

April 22, 1862. Mamma (Lucy Johnston Ambler, wife of Thomas Marshall Ambler) came running in this morning and said that Dick and Phillis were gone. I had unbolted the door some time before thinking Phillis would be in for the bread, then when it began to be light Ann came in. Sister Bet (Elizabeth Ambler) asked me why Phillis had not come.

"Has she not been in yet?" she exclaimed with well feigned surprise.

"No, go and call her," said Sister Bet.

She took the basket of bread in her hand and walked out.

"Isn't it strange, Sister Bet," said I. "I wonder if she has gone to the Yankees."

"Oh, no" she replied. "I reckon not."

Just then Mamma came in and said Dick and Phillis were gone, we were quite excited, and then Mamma went out again and soon returned to say that they had taken all their clothes with them. Mamma went out again and soon returned to say that Sam and George had gone too. She had been to see Mr. Downs and asked him if any of the field hands were missing. We all commenced dressing fast and talking about the poor creatures.

Papa says that Mr. Iden was at Markham this morning and some one asked him if he was not afraid to come there for fear the Yankees might catch him. "Oh, no," he said, "if they catch me they can only kill me and I have got nine lives like a cat."

And he said that once while he was away the Yankees had gone to his house and pressed his horses and had them with ropes around their necks to lead away. Mrs. Iden was very much terrified but a poor hired girl (white) who was staying there went out and offered the men ten dollars if they would leave the horses and they said they would so she went in the house and brought out the money saying I am a poor girl and this is all that I have but I will freely give it if you will let the horses alone. They said they were very sorry for her but they took her money and left the horses. I suppose they took the money themselves. The horses would have been for their Government.

23rd. Mamma put her head in the door again this morning. Levi, old Charles and Jacob gone, it seems young and old are going. Mary Ann does not say she is not going. I asked Papa to let me go to Mountain View with him and he said he had to go by Mr. Ben Feigan's to see him so I said I could go by there. Before I went I gave out my washing to Martha. I told her that I wanted to get some clothes for her before she went to the Yankees and then went on to tell her that I heard they had no work and the negroes stole and were put in jail. Also I told her that I told her these things not because I expected her to believe or mind me but that when she went away if she got into trouble she could remember that I had not been careless of her fate but had warned her. She said, if she did go she would not steal. I told her if she found herself starving she might. Well, I hope if she goes she will better her condition. If I thought she would I would bid her Godspeed.

Well, it was a beautiful ride to Mr. Feigan's. I never was there before and we had to ride so far up the mountain. The road was very steep. About a mile from the place it joined the public road (it) terminated abruptly in the stable yard through which we had to get to the house, but after we left it the way to the house was only a narrow path which wound through an orchard. The house was built of logs. It was two stories high and had a porch. There was something soothing in the quiet that reigned around. The house was situated in a little hollow in the highest part of the mountain, and though so high up was still surrounded by higher hills.

Mr. Feigan and Papa talked while I sat on my horse and admired the quiet beauty of that homely and secluded spot. Just behind the house were the negro cabins filled with little negro children. Mr. Feigan said none of his had left him. It may seem strange to some how sad I feel at the breaking of a tie which I have felt from childhood for I do feel an attachment for the servants, but deep down in my heart there is a heavier care and anxiety—which I am trying to keep down. I have had to trust in God. Gradually has He taught the lesson.

One by one those things to which I looked and trusted have been exposed. I have seen the folly of trusting to any thing on this earth, and when every earthly trust had gone I was found to have what I love and value most in his hand. I feel my utter helplessness. Father seemed very much concerned at the departure of Papa's servants. I told him that Papa wanted to go and tell the women that if they did not go too and take their children he would have to sell them for he could not support so many useless ones when all the men who helped to support them had gone, but we begged him not to do that for that would be forcing them to go and leave the washing, milking, cooking, and cleaning the house to us and we were not quite ready to begin. I am sure if they stay he will change his mind before a chance comes to sell them.

While I told it I laughed and Father was very indignant and reproved me for laughing. Sister Milly spoke up and said "Indeed, Papa, we have so much greater things to trouble us that these seem light in comparison."

"And those are the things that ought to keep us from laughing," he said.

Sister Milly told me that she heard that as soon as the servants got to Alexandria they were sent off in a ship, where is not known. Some think to Cuba, some to Jamaica.

Such is my opinion of the Lincoln Government that I believe they are sent to Cuba to pay off the national debt. I hope it may not be so for that will enable them to keep up the war longer and I grieve to think of the poor creatures, though I believe slavery is their best condition. The Yankees want to make us pay their debts for this war and they may take that way, but I hope the United States has not fallen so low.

Papa says he is sure the Yankee nation would not tolerate such a thing, but I am not sure they will not smooth it over to their consciences in some way and get rid of the heavy debt.

Willie Dennis dined here. He is going to try to go to Alexandria in the cars but the Bull Run Bridge has been washed away by the storm and is not yet ready for the cars to pass. This evening Annie and I went out for a walk. We went into the shop field to try the Mont Blanc Road but the water was so high we could not pass so we determined to go by Joanna's house. She has moved up to her mother's house since Edward left her and the house looked lonely. As we came round to the front of the house I saw William standing in the door. He went off to his wife's Saturday and this was Wednesday.

"Why, William," said I. "I thought you had gone. Why have you been away so long?"

"The high water kept me, Miss" said he, stammering and looking very much confused. He always stutters dreadfully, but I thought he looked much confused and he professed entire ignorance of the others having gone. I think Mamma was very glad to hear of his return. She seems to take the departure of the other servants very much to heart.

After tea Miss Fanny (sister Fanny Ambler, born 1825; married James Keith Marshall) read Howett's "Rural Life of England" aloud. It is a refreshing kind of book, so animated, and treats of such peaceful times. I am amused at Miss Fanny's feelings. She seems to be wondering all the time how we will do without servants. Asked Sister Bet how she would manage to kill the veals. She seems to think we will all have to go to plowing and that every kind of work will fall on us. Mamma says that two free men have run away. It only shows how demented the poor darkeys are.

One of these men is living on Papa's farm and Papa hires him when he is busy. Mamma saw his wife and asked her what her husband ran away for. She said that they had been told that the cavalry were going to drive all the negroes south and sell them. My heart is very sad. Father's reproof to me for laughing sunk into my heart.

April 26th. Mamma came to tell us that Jacob, Charles, and Levi had returned last night. Papa seemed dreadfully annoyed at it. He thinks they have come back for some mischief and went to tell them that they should not go backwards and forwards but if they go once more they shall stay. Poor Annie was in very great trouble. A hired servant of hers, Jack, came to Mamma and insisted that Papa should give him his clothes and says his master says that if Annie does not give them to him he is going to buy them and charge them to her.

They all seem deranged, and it is not surprising as they think that this tremendous war is on their account. It is not to be supposed that they should know that there is a natural repugnance between Northerners and Southerners, and they would have separated on one ground if not on another. Papa had been to Markham and came in but had no news. He only told us that he had heard the Yankees were only going to finish the railroad as far as the river and it was said to be built entirely for the purpose of carrying off negroes. If they have done it for that purpose, I feel very sure the Yankees are not going to such expense entirely for the benefit of the servants. Lincoln and Seward will profess not to know anything about it, but they surely will help to pay their debts if they go to any expense. Papa says the servants who ran away told him they did it because they were told our cavalry were going to drive them all south to be sold. Papa told them they might go away if they chose but must not return again. After dinner Annie, Miss Fanny, and I walked out the Mont Blanc road though it was dropping rain. We had a pleasant walk. Went in sight of Mont Blanc and Carrington, near which place we heard the Yankees have a camp.

* * * *

Five years ago, twenty-one and twenty-six: the contrast struck me with mournful vividness.

Five years ago I was engaged. I had just returned from a visit to Norfolk and I remembered how often I had sat in that same window then with Robert by my side. I compared him then with what he is now. The merry boyish lover who I so little knew or understood, though we had been I may almost say intimate all our lives. The clouds and trials of my youth had passed away. For my youth, happy as it was, had not been unclouded, and I still felt young and fresh and lighthearted.

Four years ago! I was married, and went with Mother in the carriage to Stafford to see Anne Eliza, and Robert accompanied us on horseback. I remember he made me fill the trunk with summer and winter clothes for him, taking a great many more than he could have used because he said he liked always to have a plenty; and now, he can only have a change. That visit to Stafford was very pleasant. We stopped at little wayside old fashioned taverns, and the hostess would always come in and entertain us with an account of the neighboring gentry. Stafford is on the river, is beautiful, and I took many delightful walks on the sandy beach and saw the seine hauled in.

Three years ago! Sister Milly, Robert, and I went to Alexandria together. Sister Milly went to Stafford. Robert wanted to go to Philadelphia to visit his old haunts and I staid in Alexandria with Sister Fanny and Sister Bet. It was a pleasant visit and when Robert and I came home we found a cousin of Mother's paying her a visit. I forget her name but she was from Detroit, Michigan, and professed to be so delighted with Virginia, did not at all object to the peculiar institution. I wonder what she thinks now!

Two years ago! Robert and I went to Alexandria again, and he went on to Stafford and I again staid with my sisters. Sister Bet and I went to Washington one day and Brother John met us and took us first to see the Equestrian Statue of Washington. I hardly know what I thought of it for I am no judge of such things. Then we walked over the Capitol and we admired the beautiful marble stairways and the frescoing, but I felt really ashamed of the tawdry gaudiness of the House of Representatives. It was however good enough for the disgraceful scenes which were enacted on its floors.

That was my last visit to Washington except when the Prince of Wales was there. I want to write of that some day before I forget it, but not now. I brought back many lovely flowers from Alexandria when I came home. Robert liked me to cultivate flowers and they gave me many moments of very pure happiness.

One year ago. The war had just begun. I cannot write of those times so full of exciting events crowding so fast on each other. How changed Robert is since then even. He did not leave me for several months. I was not well enough and he staid till my confinement was over. His thoughts were so much taken up with passing events that now when I look back, it almost seems that our separation began then. He was so eager to take his part in the defense of our dear old state, so sanguine and hopeful. I came home because Papa thought the excitement too great for me to be where I could see the cars passing filled with soldiers and hear the thousand exciting rumors every day, but Robert came here every night and told us the sober truths as he could get them.

* * * *

25th. I commenced this journal with a view of self-examination as well to record things as they happen, or rather as they seem to me. Situated as we are here now I certainly have a very poor chance of the latter, for we are cut off from hearing anything either side, except the rumors one day which are contradicted the next.

For all that my self examination seems to progress very slowly. This morning at breakfast I was wondering about the movements of the army, and Papa and Sister Betsy laughed at me as they always do and said it was such a pity the General did not have me to advise them.

Then we began talking about the coffee and Mamma said it had improved greatly lately.

Annie said "I do not believe Sister Betsy has ever told Mother that I taught her how she ought to make the coffee."

Sister Betsy had only a day or two ago announced at the table that Annie had taught her, so we all laughed at her and said she was hard to satisfy.

I laughed and said "You must be put on a pinnacle and all of us bow before you."

I said it in the purest fun and never thought she would be offended but she looked very much displeased and said "I do not see where I have done wrong yet."

"No one said you had done wrong," said I. "Or done anything ridiculous," she said and then she looked hurt and did not speak for a long time.

Papa said he was tired of not knowing any thing that was going on and he wished he could even see some Yankee papers. "Indeed," I said, "I do not want to see any of their stories."

"I wonder, Mary," said Miss Fanny, "that you should mind what you do not believe."

"Still", said I, "I would not like to see them because I would not know how much to believe so they would make me unhappy."

"Prejudice, my daughter" said Papa. "Prejudice. You will have to be more submissive to Yankees."

My heart revolted at the idea, but there came a misgiving that it might be so for I have learned now that what my pride revolts against most is not always impossible.

"I wonder what Papa meant" said I when he left the room. "I am glad he said it to you. I wish he had said more" said Annie, rising to leave the room.

I felt sure then that I had given her no cause to be offended with me, I did not see then that she had just the same reason to be displeased that I had had a moment before. I tried not to say anything, but I spoke before I knew it.

"Why do you say so, Annie" said I. "You often say you are glad when unpleasant things are said to me" and I reminded her of the *only* other occasion on which she had said so.

"Because you said I ought to be set up on a pinnacle."

"But I was only joking" said I, seeing what a very poor joke it was.

"Well, I was joking, too", and then we went into a discussion about it and I believe parted very well satisfied with each other. At least I saw that she and I were just about alike.

After we came upstairs, Miss Fanny and I came in the parlour and talked about joking, how misunderstandings may arise, and how differently the same thing appears from the opposite side. She says, as I have been told before, that I have too grave a face for a joke. I look as if I too honestly meant what I said. All the time I was talking I was looking out at the damp dreary looking sky and debating whether I ought to go to the cabins to hear the children say their catechism, as if there could be any doubt. I persuaded myself that it might be wrong for me to take all the children into Susan's house as it might disturb her sick baby, but my conscience told me that I had taken them there yesterday and they did not disturb the child then, so I knew there could be no harm in my going to see the child and if I saw it was likely to disturb her then I need not call the children, so I went, found the child better and asleep, and called the children. I told them about Abraham and Isaac and they seemed interested, then I read to Susan and Martha.

Susan asked me "Miss Mary, what did Master Tom say in his letter about Barbara?"

"He did not speak of her" said I. "You know we hear from him very seldom now and I suppose he forgot to mention her."

"I spect dey done kill Barbara" said she. She had said the same thing to me several times before.

"How can you be so foolish, Susan? You know you never heard of such a thing being done."

"This war is all about there" said she.

"Well, there has been no war in Williamsburg, and you know Barbara is hired out so Brother Tom forgot to mention her, but if any thing had happened to her he would not have forgotten."

I might have told her that I had never heard of any negroes being killed in this war except some the Yankees shot at Harper's Ferry for disobedience. But I am glad I did not for I do not know whether it is true, and I might have given Susan an opportunity to be impertinent, and she seldom loses one. I came in and played with Jackey. He is so lovely and pure in the morning when he is first dressed, and he prefers me next to his mother.

Annie, Miss Fanny, and I walked up the Mont Blanc road today though it had not cleared off at all. We took the driest road, but had great difficulty in getting over the stream, so Annie and I set to work and carried some flat stones and with some rails made ourselves quite a respectable crossing. Wet as it was and damp as we got our feet, we had a beautiful walk. Surely no land is more beautiful than ours.

When we came home Papa had come in from Markham. He says some men from Charlottesville have just been at Mr. Bradford's. They say that the victory in Tennessee was very decided, that Beauregard was not hurt. They also say Jackson has left the Valley for parts unknown and Banks is in Staunton with 40,000. Freemont with thirty thousand is marching in through Southwestern Virginia and McClellan is still in the Peninsula with 250,000. General Johnston's whereabouts is a mystery, but wherever he is he has an immense army too in the finest spirits, confident of victory whenever they meet the enemy. The public archives and everything which is very valuable has been sent from Richmond in case our army is defeated, but the inhabitants are all confident still of victory. I hope all look to the God of Battles for help and do not trust in their own strength. The evacuation by Jackson of the Valley has left Charlottesville exposed, and our poor refugees are again in Yankee land. The Masons I suppose will again get behind the Confederate lines, but it seems to me the Leeds people and Sister Anna might return home. I see now that Robert was right in leaving me with my own family. It seemed very hard at first to be cut off from hearing from him, but if I had gone to Charlottesville I would still have been cut off from him and away from all my friends without any chance of getting back to them.

I am reminded of what Alice told me Mr. Carroll said of Robert. "Alice, I would not change my captain for any in the Army. He has the best judgment of any man I know. I often see him do things that seem wrong to me at the time, but afterwards I see he was right."

It has not cleared off yet. Uncle Jim who is I think quite a poor judge of weather, says it will not clear today. Annie thought it will, but the Cobbler and the Rattlesnake were both covered with clouds and that is a bad sign.

26th. Brother James came over to breakfast and spoke of starting to Charlottesville for his mother Monday but afterward concluded that it would not be necessary as his father might come. I went to the cabins but did not have Martha to hear me read for Mamma had her busy making soap.

I had returned and was sitting by the window writing when I happened to look out at the front gate and there was poor Papa escorted by some Yankee cavalry. He called Uncle Jim to send him to Mr. Downs for the corn house key and away rode Uncle Jim with a very finely dressed officer. They put a picket on each hill around and then came pouring in the yard over the fences and around in every direction. I could not make out how many there were, but we suppose about thirty. They ran to Mamma's hen house but saw us looking at them, so they went behind and ripped the shingles off, but the officers rode up to them and it seemed to change the current of their thoughts and they ran down the hill as fast as they could to the dairy where they tried to get in, but where they found the door locked so they ran around to the window and peeped in, then went back to the door and pushed it till they pushed it open. Tommy followed them and watched every thing they did, then came up and told us.

"Grandma, the Yankees done butt your springhouse door open." But we had seen the whole performance from the window.

By this time Uncle Jim and the Yankee who went for the key to the corn house returned without having found Mr. Downs and the corn house door had to be broken open. But first the wagon had to be brought up to the smoke house door to be filled with meat. Ham after ham and shoulders and middlings were taken down and thrown into the wagon. Oh, it was sickening to see them taking the hams that poor Mamma had smoked and to know that we were helping to feed those who were invading our beautiful land while our own exiles were perhaps suffering for the very things with which we have supplied *them.*

The Yankee who went for the key was quite a goodlooking man, very well mounted, and quite a good rider. He would not let Papa stay while they were loading the wagons but kept drawing him away to talk to him, and finally came stalking into the house, slighting the eleven out doors. He found his way into a queer little opening (unlike any that a house ever had before) into the brick entry. He stalked across the passage into the parlour and began writing just before the open door.

In the meantime we were watching the loading of the wagon from the window, but Mamma could not stand it. She went out and told the men they had taken enough of the meat, please not to take any more. But they began cursing and continued to throw the meat down so Mamma came back and told the officer who had gone on writing very coolly in spite of the remarks which we were making very freely and which he certainly heard. (I am sorry we said anything for it would have been more dignified and ladylike not to have had anything to say.)

But Mamma and Annie both of whom were losing meat very fast could not stand it any longer, so they walked off to the parlour door and told the officer his men were taking all the meat.

"Oh, no, madam", he said, with the regular down east pronunciation, "they are not going to take all your meat."

"Are you going to bring it back?" asked Annie.

"Oh, no," he said. "We are not going to take it away."

"Are you going to have it taken out of the wagon?" asked Annie.

"Oh, no, we are not going to put it all in, only a portion."

"Well" said Annie, "you ought to take the servants away too for we will have nothing for them to eat."

"Yes" said Mamma, "You may take them all away behind you if you choose."

I could not help stepping to where I could see the Yankee while this conversation was going on. He sat smiling at the ladies all the time but I am sure he was angry, and I think he deserved credit for keeping his temper so well, for I must say I think Annie and Mamma were quite provoking to him. For my part I am rather mortified that I should have gone there, but curiosity overcame my dignity. Miss Fanny called Annie and told her she was surprised at her so Annie came away.

"We are not going to disturb you again," the Yankee said, and Sister Bet said "Well, I am glad to hear that anyhow."

I believe he heard that too, but he did not see her. I saw a man coming towards the little opening in the brick entry, I went to the door and met him. "What do you want? asked I.

"Have you any butter for sale?"

"For sale indeed!" thought I, but I asked Mamma and she said she had only two or three pats. I told the man and he laughed in my face and went off to tell the others who kicked up and went through several evolutions with the swords, laughing. Three or four more came and I went out and met them. I could not bear that the creatures should come into the house.

"Butter," they said half laughing.

"There are only three pats in the house."

"Well, whiskey, then."

"I know nothing about whiskey," said I.

They went out and threatened to go into the cellar. I followed them to the door to watch them. One man stopped and said "The lieutenant will pour out every d- - - drop."

I felt so sorry for the poor fowls. The soldiers ran after them with their swords, and cut off their heads. They peeped into the houses and then crept into the door. They soon came out, a headless hen in each hand. They killed all Uncle Randolph's hens and many of Joanna's. There is a poor gander I saw from the window after they left with a gash in its poor throat. They went to the cabins too.

It was funny and still right sad to see the poor negroes, so smiling and pleased. Aunt Cinthea put on a cap with such wide frills that we saw it at the house. Papa saw Mary Ann take her baby out to show them. On the whole it rather made me feel less kindly to see how pleased the servants were to see the Enemies of their masters who have always been kind to them and taken care of them. Poor creatures! They do not believe one word we say though we have never deceived them, and they must take the consequences, though it is something like leaving children to have their own way and bear the consequences. I never tell them any thing. I cannot let my word be doubted, nor allow them to think that I would beg them to stay. In fact, I begin to feel rather in the spirit of working for myself, and in the humor for them to go, since they are so friendly with the Yankees. However, I cannot bear for poor Martha to go among the Yankees. I cannot bear after having had her with me for so many years and became really fond of her and having had her show me so much affection. I will not be angry with her for she has not gone yet and has been as respectful as she has always been.

Just as the Yankees left all the farm horses passed to the stable to be fed. They each had a little darkey mounted on it and Tommy had gotten up behind one of them. The Yankee who had so much writing to do was not a lieutenant but a Quartermaster. He gave Papa his card and I think Papa was decidedly pleased with him.

He told Papa that he (the Yankee) was a gentleman born and bred. Most gentlemen leave that to be found out of them.

He gave Papa a Yankee paper, but there is very little in it except that they have had a little battle in the Peninsula, which they say was a second edition of Ball's Bluff. I was very glad of that anyhow. The rest of the paper was glorifying themselves and abusing the "Rebels". On the whole I am not satisfied with our treatment of them. We had too much curiosity, but if they come again I do not think I should be so curious.

30th. We are more and more cut off from those we love, and the Yankees seem to draw closer and closer around us, and now that I hear the Yankee cars whistle the very air seems laden with oppression. For the first time I breathe our fresh pure air and feel that we are no longer a free people.

Papa did not even go to Markham yesterday and objects to our walking except in the fields back of the house. It is all in our Father's hands, we have been too proud. If it is his will to humble us, we must feel submissive. I went to Leeds from Church Sunday. I intended to go to Mr. Duncan's on Monday and call on them there, but Charles came over and told me that the Yankees had been here again and given a great deal of trouble and I could not feel like seeing Mrs. Duncan after hearing it. Charles came for my horse so I thought it best to ride it home. I came and soon afterward Mr. Duncan brought his mother and his sister Fanny in. They are going to stay with us several days. It is very sad to think of dear Mr. Duncan, his wife being a Northern woman, her sympathies are entirely northern, and he is so warmly southern. Old Mrs. Duncan and Fanny both seem to feel it very much. Yesterday Papa told me that he had heard that Frank Brooks had just returned from the army and he hoped to hear from brother Jack and Robert but I suppose he had nothing for us for he sent a letter this morning and it was for some one else not for us.

Papa says that he heard Frank had said that McClellan was fortifying himself where he could use his gunboats if we attacked him and

Johnston was fortifying himself out of the reach of gunboats and there they are likely to stay.

God help our poor soldiers if they have to stay all the summer in that unhealthy climate. It seems to me the Yankees do not care how many of their men die. It is nothing when they have only the dregs of society and those foreigners whose lives are not valuable to the Yankees.

Papa says poor cousin Rebecca Marshall is dead. She must have died of a broken heart or a weary spirit. She leaves ten little children and her husband is only an orderly sergeant in a cavalry company and their servants have sold every thing out of the house for the family had all gone away.

Twelve men went out to Markham and ordered supper for themselves and then sat before the family talking of our affairs in the most disrespectful way, saying how badly we were getting on. This lovely day I sit and look on the old familiar scenes and try to wait patiently on the Lord for there are many promises in the Bible to those who wait, but it is a hard lesson. May God help me to learn it.

I asked Susan's two little twins this morning when they were going to the Yankees.

"We won't see you no more," said little Hannah gravely. "Who said so?" asked I.

They are nice little children, but I cannot help feeling sorry to think of the suffering they may have to bear. Mamma says they will not let us send to the mill to get meal. Well, I trust God will give us each day our daily bread. Mr. Duncan came in today. He brought us news that discouraged me very much. When we were evacuating Island No. 10 we were cut off by the Yankees and two thousand prisoners taken and then he says they have attacked New Orleans and Savannah and several other places so it seems they are advancing all around. God help us, we are in his hands and must trust to Him.

Mr. Duncan went to Markham and had a prayer meeting. We were a little afraid he might be detained, but he says he went there and returned without any difficulty. He brought a Yankee paper and read it to us and it depressed me very much, though it ought not. I heard of a chance to write to Robert and wrote him a very sad letter which I regret very much now for it is too bad when he is away from home that I should write such letters which must depress his spirits.

May 1st. I had a cold and did not go to the cabins because it was very damp. I feel more cheerful than I did yesterday. I hope in the Lord. He is my trust, may I never be brought to confusion. All yesterday I was struggling to get more submission to His will. I do not know that I have succeeded, it is only that my spirits are elastic and rose after such depression. It takes very long for a proud heart to bend in submission to misfortunes and I fear I do not feel as a Christian should about our enemies. I cannot but think it right to pray that they may be driven back but still I feel far more angry and vindictive against them than a Christian should. I know that if it was not God's will they could do nothing to us, so I ought to take these trials as coming from His hand, but I do not always remember to take it in this way. I sat in the Parlour a long time after breakfast with Mrs. Duncan and Fanny. They talk of Mrs. Duncan's Northern sympathies more than they ought to for she is our Pastor's wife and it is very wrong to prejudice us against her, and we ought to be charitable to her for she has no sympathy in the parish from any one.

May 2nd. It has been a beautiful day though there was a shower at dinner time and it rained very hard for a few minutes. We took a walk in the morning on the hills back of the house. Miss Fanny Willis, Fanny Duncan, Annie, and I. In spite of my low spirits the beauty of the scenery made me glad. The whole country is dotted with the full blooming cherry trees and peach trees, and at our feet the earth seemed carpeted with violets springing up in the soft young turf. We have still a great deal to be thankful for, and we were all very much refreshed. Not long before dinner Mr. Duncan came to carry his mother and sister home. He was going to Markham and would return after dinner for them.

While Mr. Duncan was here we looked out the window and saw an ox wagon driven by a black boy. My mind misgave me when I saw something in the wagon, just the colour of the US uniform great coat. It was not Papa's wagon but still it seemed full. Some one looked out and said, "That is Jim Dade," and we saw walking with the wagon a coloured man very finely dressed in the US uniform. Papa went out to speak to him. Jim Dade is a free negro who has been living on the farm for several years. Papa was warned against him by many persons, but in spite of every thing we heard which was very much against him Papa took compassion on him and he has been living here ever since, Papa often hiring him in busy season. Last spring when the war broke out, he was employed by two of the Lieutenants in Robert's company. They soon dismissed him for stealing and he got employment on the fortifications every week I hear sending trunks full of plunder, stolen it is supposed. He came back home in the winter and when our servants ran away he went too. He had contrived to give offense to some of the neighbors about here and they threatened that if he ever came here again he would be shot. Papa went out to tell Jim that he had heard that some persons had threatened to shoot him and moreover he told him that he did not intend to let him live here any longer. Mr. Duncan was afraid that Jim might be impertinent to Papa so he went out and when they came in, they said that he was carrying some supplies home to his wife in a wagon of Cousin Edward Marshall's which the officer pressed for the purpose.

When we heard this we were afraid Papa had gotten himself into trouble though he only told Jim of the threats against his life because he thought it might save him. Mr. Duncan said he would mention it to the officer who he expected to see that evening. Well, Jim left the wagon at our gate and went off to see he said what could be done, and he returned in a much shorter time than I could have believed possible and he gave Papa a note from the Captain saying, that if any one injured Jim Dade, Papa would be held responsible and that he had been sent by the officer of the U S service. It was a dreadful thing to see how they could tyrannize over us, but I trust God will enable us to bear what He sees fit to put upon us.

I hope no one will hurt Jim Dade as I believe that our neighbors have too much consideration for Papa to do anything which would subject him to annoyance. Indeed, I do not believe that Papa could get into trouble for anything of the kind, but the impertinence of the man who wrote the note was what we all felt that we would have to submit to.

After we had been talking affairs over for some time Mr. Duncan came back and said he had spoken to the Officer about Jim and told him his character and that some of Papa's neighbors upon whom he had been depredating had threatened to shoot him and Papa had warned him. Mr. Duncan went on to say that now we had no laws to appeal to and that it was very likely some one would shoot him if he continued his thieving. He said the Officer said he had not understood the circumstances. If he had, his course would have been different and that under the circumstances he would not blame any one for shooting him. He went on to say that the officer said that if he had belonged to brother John they would not have taken it. They knew he was quartermaster of a Division and they intended to have taken his whiskey.

Now, that seems very strange. Papa told them that he did not know that his son to whom the whiskey belonged was in the Army at all, that he left he believed to join the army but he had not heard from him and did not know whether he had done so, but they refused to pay for the whiskey, and I do not see why they should not pay for it now if they have made a mistake, though I do not see why they should not take the property of one as well as that of the other.

Another thing that he told Mr. Duncan was that the Quartermaster who came here last Saturday and took so much meat was not sent here but ordered somewhere else, so it seems every one does wrong according to the next man you hear talk. But we never can have any redress.

Mr. Duncan seemed to think it was very uncharitable in Annie and I to think that he ought not to put confidence in what they say. They are always so plausible in what they say and their actions are always so different.

I may be uncharitable, but it seems to me very strange in him to say that he would think it right if some one would shoot Jim Dade. It certainly would not be the right way to get redress and it seems very strange that he should have said such a thing.

I have so little confidence in them that I almost think he said it just to get some one into trouble, but this may be uncharitable in me, and as Papa said to Mr. Duncan, "Do you expect these ladies to be reasonable?"

I will try not to give place to such suspicions.

I was sitting in the parlour when Mr. Duncan came this morning and he told us about the capture of New Orleans and after he left we were speaking about it and I was in the depths of despair as I always am when I first hear bad news for I supposed if they have New Orleans they will get Memphis and all the Mississippi and so cut off all communication with Missouri, Arkansas, Texas, and nearly all of Louisiana. This may all be true now, but I hope it may not be.

Sister Bet looked really sad, more so than I have ever seen her about the war for she is generally very hopeful.

She said sadly, "Well, we have been very vainglorious."

"Yes," said Annie, "we have always boasted entirely too much. I have always thought them the greatest boasters I ever saw."

"Indeed, they do not boast more than the Yankees have," said I.

"Do you call it boasting when they say they are going to do a thing and then go and do it?" said Miss Fanny very calmly.

Her very calmness made me angry. "Well," said I, "if you are going to take up for the Yankees in every thing they do I will have to hush."

I was irritated at her constantly saying such things for if any thing is said against the South she seems to agree, but if it is said against the North she argues the point. I know it is only for the sake of argument with us who are probably too violent.

She condemns the course of the South in the whole affair, while we do not know that the South could have done but as the South has done it. I know she wishes us to succeed but still I cannot help being provoked very often when she blames the South and vindicates the North and she always is very indignant if she is accused of being union. She was very angry with me for saying what I did and I knew when I said it she would be and yet I said it and it was long before I could bring myself to feel right about it. I told her that I was wrong to say it and Annie thought I was going to be very humble. Annie and Miss Fanny said I could not bear a difference of opinion. I did not care for their saying so for I knew I was too little accustomed to have my opinion very much respected to mind a difference of opinion and I have to change it too often to respect it much myself.

Miss Fanny did not say much but later after I had cooled down and told her that I was very sorry, her face flushed up and she said "Mary, I cannot bear to be called a Yankee."

"I never called you a Yankee" said I, "or thought you a Yankee."

She has forgiven me now I believe and I shall try hereafter to restrain my temper.

3rd. I was afraid that Jim Dade's triumph over Papa would make the servants here presumptious, but I am thankful to say that their manner was more respectful and pleasant than it generally is. I believe they rather sympathized with us. Uncle Randal is the only exception, and I do not suppose his impertinence was anything more than bad temper.

Papa was walking up and down by the fence near the kitchen and Uncle Randal was standing in the kitchen door as I came from the cabins and he was looking in my face and said, "Go and ask Mistiss for some more meal."

"She ain't going to give me no more," said Joanna who was standing by.

"Well, I had better go and work for somebody else if I cannot get as much bread as I can eat". I stopped, looked at him, and walked on without speaking and he came out of the kitchen door and walked towards Papa.

"Did not that boy bring meal?" asked Papa.

"I do not know," he replied. "I cannot get as much bread as I can eat. I got some meat and some milk but I want some more bread."

"Well, I cannot get any meal," said Papa meekly and sadly.

We all took a lovely walk. My spirit seems calmer now. I know that we are all in God's hands and we must submit for He has given us many mercies and blessings and we must be thankful and trust in Him. Mr. Duncan came this evening. He says he will have a prayer meeting here tomorrow evening. I am thankful for that.

Papa complained yesterday morning that we talked so much that we did not let him hear all he wanted so we determined to let him have a chance.

Mr. Duncan had been to Mont Blanc and Papa says he told him that the Yankees who went to Mont Blanc took nearly every thing from them and told them if they would go down to the camp they might get the money, telling Cousin John they would write the receipt in his name, so Cousin John went down in the hopes of getting the money but of course there was something wrong. When he looked he found that it was in Mrs. Marshall's name, so he had his ride for nothing and besides that they stole a pair of shoes and a pair of boots. In these days when they are so hard to get. They also stole some forks from Minnie and some jewelry which were in an open box.

It was careless in Cousin John not to read his bill before he took it. Well, I hope I will not wish for their punishment.

5th. Yesterday was a calm lovely Sabbath morning. We read and walked about the yard some but did not walk out. Mr. Duncan has so few persons to hear him preach now that he is going about to the different houses instead of preaching at Church. He passed here in the morning on his way to Markham where he had service. He told us that Minnie had promised to come here in the evening to a prayer meeting he would have. He seemed very anxious that we should all know that he had not told the Yankee Captain that his wife was a sister of George Morris and had friends on McClellan's staff. He says Cousin Jaquelin Marshall told him. I told him that we had not, but supposed some servant had told him.

Minnie came soon after dinner. She walked over with a servant and little Elizabeth. She says the Yankees took only 25 wagon loads from Mont Blanc, most of it was hay. She told us of long conversations she had with the Captain who was there. At first she refused to answer his questions, but he promised her if she would talk to them she might say what she pleased. She says she was right glad of a chance to say what she chose, so she talked very plainly to them, but in the most good natured way so they could not take offense.

One man wanted to kiss little Susy. She could not stand that but pulled Susy away and said, "Stand back, Susy."

"What is the matter?" said the man, "She is not afraid."

"Oh, no, sir, but her father is in the Confederate Army."

"You are right, ma'am," said the Captain. "I would not give a cent for a child who was kissed by her father's enemy."

They said the war would soon be over and peace restored now that there was very little more to be done before the Union was restored. She smiled and the Captain said "You do not believe me."

"No, I do not think it will be over so soon."

"Yes, it will be over in four months," said he, "either one way or the other for it must stop soon."

"Oh, well, if that is the case it may stop," said Minnie. He asked her in a very triumphant tone if she had heard the last news from York and she said no and she did not care to hear it for she says she was sure he would tell her a story so she would not let him tell her.

We walked home part the way with Minnie and she was telling us all the way of the things that he said and did. We were gone right long and Papa became uneasy about us and came to meet us and scolded us for walking so far when hostile soldiers were about. Sister Betsy told me after supper last night that Brother James' woman Katy came down from the farm and took her son Billy who was at Miss Ruth Garrot's and carried him off to the Yankees. Carey says that Billy cried and the Miss Garrots cried. Poor Billy, I am very sorry for him. I expect he will never have such good friends again. Katy says she is going to take possession of Sister Fanny's house in Alexandria. Poor thing!

We took a lovely walk this morning. I felt all day that probably there would be a battle at York. Mr. Duncan said yesterday that the officer at Markham told him he had had no mail for several days, and some Yankees who were at Miss Ruth Garrots yesterday told her that they were fighting at York but they could give no account of the battle. This evening Papa came in and said he had heard that we had gained a great victory there and McClellan was killed. We do not know whether to believe it or not, but somehow I have faith in it though we heard the same thing several weeks ago and it was not true.

Papa brought another very sad report that Cousin Robert Scott was in the mountain near Warrenton with some of Munford's cavalry and he was killed and thirty of Munford's men taken prisoner. It is very sad to think of his poor wife and children and then he was such a loss to the country for the place of so talented a man cannot easily be supplied.

But his poor old mother, what must her sufferings be. I believe she is more than eighty and so proud as she was of him, but the saddest part is that she has not the comfort of religion. She has spent her long life with every thing good to be thankful for without acknowledging from whose hand it came and now in her old age every thing which makes life valuable is taken from her and she has nothing left unless it is the hope that she may live to see her remaining children after the war is over. With such a portion of talents, wealth, beauty, and all the honors of this world, what did they lack. Only religion, and now we can see that wanting that they wanted all. May God in his infinite mercy bring the lesson home to their hearts and give them the rich blessings of His Spirit to comfort them.

6th. A Yankee pickett came here this morning just as we finished breakfast to ask for some food. I went on without seeing him except in passing upstairs and I repeated to myself, "If thine enemy hunger, feed him."

If it was heaping coals of fire on his head he did not feel them for he told Papa that the war would be over in two months now for McClellan had 100,000 men on the Peninsula and Burnside and McDowell had 100,000 at Fredericksburg to cut off the retreat from Richmond. It is clear he did not exactly understand things. After breakfast I saw some one out in the yard. It turned out to be Mr. Chancellor and his son who were in search of servants who had run off and taken all their horses. They want to recover their horses.

They had heard the report about York from several sources but seemed to doubt it, and they knew all about Cousin Robert's death. He and some other gentlemen were trying to catch two Yankee soldiers who were stealing in the neighborhood and he was shot and another gentleman wounded and they killed one of the Yankees.

I have written to Robert. I hope I may find some way to send the letter. I wrote more cheerfully than I did the last time. Mr. Chancellor came back with his horses and he says the captain says he will drive out his servants from his camp and Mr. Chancellor hopes they may go back home but I suspect he will be disappointed.

7th. This morning after I had returned from the cabins I was sitting by the window reading and Annie called me to look out of the window. I looked, and there were two Yankees fastening their horses. I went into the side porch and they came walking up the walk with the front door staring in their faces, they were coming around to the side door, but I said, "You had better come in at the front door" so I went and opened it.

"Is Mr. Duncan in?"

"He does not live here. He lives several miles further on."

"A misarrangement." said the one behind.

They were both dressed quite handsomely and I saw they were officers, and I expected them to go but they stood still and just then

Mamma came in. She looked very pale and said "I heard that there was a ship at Alexandria waiting to carry off the negroes and they refused to go and fifty of them were shot. Is that true?"

"I have heard nothing of it," said Captain Hamner (for we found out his name) "but I believe there are great efforts being made to get them out of the United States."

There is a bill in Congress" said Captain M, "to keep them in the United States. I believe they are going to colonize Georgia and Florida with them."

"You will have to get them first," said Mamma." "Oh," said Captain Hamner, "We have no doubt of getting it." "And we have no doubt the other way," said I.

I did not intend to have talked with them, but I could not help saying that.

"I have no doubt of that" said the Captain, "but we will certainly have it." His eyes gleamed vehemently. "We will bring down five hundred thousand more and bring on our men till they have all spilt their blood."

"Do you not think it would be better to spare" asked I. I did not mean spare our men but their own. He misunderstood me and replied violently, "Spare, no".

Mamma was going to tell him how they had treated us, but I begged her not to do that. Captain Hamner's eyes gleamed angrily.

"Do you think we are not going to take what we want to eat? You have brought on the war and must pay for it. We think we are in an enemy's country."

"And you are right about that" said I.

"But we can find plenty of union men around here."

"Indeed" said I, "I know everybody about here and I do not know any union men."

"There are plenty who would take the oath."

"That may be" said I. "You could hardly find the whole population of a country to be honest, but if you trust those men you will be sorry for it. They may take the oath to protect their property."

They remarked that more than half of Virginia was union and shortly after said that all our men were in the army now and when they were beaten we would have no more.

"If they are all in the army" asked I, "how can you say they are union?"

"They were forced in," said he.

"I know of no one who was forced in," said I.

"The militia was called out but there were so few men left that they could not make a draught."

They then told me a good deal about Capt. Anderson and his company of militia, to which I paid no attention.

Annie asked, "After you have subdued the South what are you going to do then?" and then she went on, "Mary I asked that question, let them answer it."

"Why we will have the old union."

"Never" said I. "We will have to be held down then,"

"Ah, you need not be uneasy about that" said M, "we will leave regiments in all your cities."

I laughed. Indeed, I said every thing in the most smiling way. And I laughed still more when Captain M said that the last dispatch from York was that Yorktown was evacuated and Gen. Johnston with twenty thousand men had been taken.

"I expect they intended to evacuate York," said I, "but do not think you have taken Gen. Johnston. He is rather too cute an old fox to catch in that way."

"Yes, he is very cute" said Capt. M.

"He is a relation of ours, he is my mother's first cousin, and we are very proud of him."

"Well, you might be" said he, "but McClellan is a very fine general."

"I expect he is," replied I, "but he has never been tried as Gen. Johnston."

"That is true," said Captain M.

Speaking of union men, they seemed to think Papa was a union man.

"Oh, no," said I. "He is not a union man now. He was opposed to Sumter being fired upon, but he is a Southern man and Lincoln's proclamation changed him."

"'And what was it in that to change him?" exclaimed Captain Hamner angrily. "They took our forts, ammunition, and guns, and what were we to do, to let them do all the fighting, I suppose?"

"Oh, well" said I. "You know we did the same in the Revolution."

"Yes" said M. "Oh, yes. I do not blame them so much for that. But that was a foreign power."

"Not now."

"Well," said Hamner, "I do not think we will go there. I have been a union man."

I believe he meant to frighten me but I knew that Papa was known not to be a union man now, so I know I have not hurt Papa.

He said that he thought ladies ought to have nothing to do with this but to talk of it. "If they do they would be just like men to me."

That was another threat, but I did not care. I was not afraid of him though he was so fierce. He walked towards the side porch and I began to think it time they should go, so I said "You can see Mr. Duncan's house from there." "They can find the way," said Annie.

"Well," said Hamner, "I do not think we will go there. I have been gone too long from camp now. You have a pretty country here. I cannot help thinking how many Yankees will come here to live when all this is over."

"That is the only reason that we object to having this for a free state" said Annie.

"Now I want to ask you a question just as I would ask a lady at

Notes On The Plates

COMPILED BY JOHN K. GOTT

(Sketches are from Harper's Weekly or Leslie's Illustrated Weekly)

Plate A (Top): Warrenton, Virginia. This town is the capital of Fauquier County and has three or four thousand inhabitants. It has for many years been a fashionable resort during the summer on account of the mineral springs in its neighborhood. It is noted for its healthfulness and its beautiful scenery near the Blue Ridge mountains. Warrenton has been for a whole year in the miserable plight of a border town held alternately by friends and foes. After the evacuation of Manassas and all that section of Virginia by the Confederate army, it was held by the Federals. For a time its beautiful residences became hospitals and soldiers' quarters; and its fields and gardens were laid waste. Then, again, Confederate successes drove the Northern forces from the neighborhood. The whole of Fauquier County is now almost cleared of provisions, the land has remained uncultivated, those of the inhabitants who could afford to seek other homes have long since done so, while the poor have been compelled to remain, and to suffer all the miserable privations of war. . . It has six or seven small churches, the handsomest of which is the Episcopal church, seen in the centre of our Engraving. To the right, the flag is waving from the cupola of the Courthouse. . . (The town) boasted a large and handsome new college, where the education of young ladies was conducted by professors of acknowledged ability. To the left of the Engraving is the railroad, which terminates about 100 yards beyond the little wooden bridge, one of those slight structures so much more easily burned or destroyed than replaced in these troublous times.

Plate B (Bottom): From Harper's Weekly, 19 September 1863. "Our artist, Mr. Waud, is enjoying the rest which has been vouchsafed to the Army of the Potomac." He writes, "Warrenton Sulphur Springs. This famous resort of bogus aristocracy was laid in ruins by Sigel's division at the time when Pope made his brilliant backward movement upon Washington. (Note: What the artist meant was 'retreat'. He did not mention how Pope was so thoroughly outmaneuvered by Gen. Jackson and routed at Bristoe Station.—J.K.G.).) The Hotel proper is entirely destroyed; but the building known as 'Rowdy Hall' and the dwelling in the grounds remain—the former occupied as a hospital. In the grounds, under the grateful shadow of the trees, some of which show the marks of shell or shot, are the First Division Headquarters of the Third Corps, forcibly reminding the spectator of an Arab encampment at the foot of some ancient ruin. This is especially the case at night, when the moon, lighting up the shattered columns and white tents, gives a ghostly and mysterious effect to the scene, the flickering shadows falling with softening influence on the harsh outlines of the ruin. The Springs attract a great number of officers and men by their supposed beneficial effect on the blood. The water is cold and clear, but not pleasant, tasting strongly and smelling worse of sulphurated hydrogen. It has occasionally been taken mixed with Old Rye; but it is justly remarked that, though the water might be improved in this way, the whisky is certainly spoiled."

Plate C (Top): Thoroughfare Gap, Va. From Frank Leslie's Illustrated Weekly, 7 June 1862. "This famous break in. . . Bull Run Mountain is about nine miles N.E. of Warrenton. . . The Gap. . . has been called the Virginia Thermopylae since a few determined men might hold it against thousands. The rocks lie scattered around in such wild confusion as to suggest the idea of being the result of some convulsion of Nature. . . Many a regiment and brigade, loyal and rebel, has tramped through that dark, gloomy cleft in the mountains."

Plate D (Bottom): "Warrenton, Va. A little street scene, garnished with wagons, forage, soldiers, etc., the inhabitants remaining mostly out of sight." Harpers Weekly, 13 December 1862.

Plate E (Top): "Catlett Station, Va. From Warrenton the army moved toward Catlett's Station, near which place they encamped for the night. The iron wheels and other indestructible portions of railroad cars, as well as the charred remains of various things burned up by the rebels, show traces of Stuart's visitation while Pope was falling back upon Washington. . . Not much farther on is the junction of the Warrenton branch with the main line of railroad. This was quite a busy spot while the army lay to the west of it, and when the sketch was made was occupied by the 11th Massachusetts and other regiments, part of General Sickle's division." Harpers Weekly, 13 December 1862.

Plate F (Bottom): Bealeton Station from a sketch by E. Forbes.

THE WAR IN VIRGINIA—BEALTON STATION.—FROM A SKETCH BY E. FORBES

Plate G (Top): "Crossing the Manassas Gap Railroad and the Alexandria and Warrington Turnpike. Arrival of reinforcements for Beauregard at the camp of the Tiger Zouaves of Louisiana."

Plate H (Bottom): Recapture of a Wagon Train from Mosby's Guerrillas. Sketched by Edwin Forbes in Leslie's Illustrated Weekly.

Plate I (Top): THE BATTLE NEAR UPPERVILLE, Ashby's Gap in the distance, Harpers Weekly, 11 July 1863. "The square inclosure is called the vineyard; on the right on the rise is a stone wall; against this a charge was made, the men returning to form again a little to the left. On the extreme left five rebel regiments came out with their large flags to charge our men before they could form, but the First and Sixth regulars, sweeping round the hill, charged upon them while the band played Hail Columbia. Captain Tidball and two of his guns are in the foreground." Harpers Weekly, 11 July 1863.

Plate J (Bottom): Harpers Weekly, 18 July 1863. "Arriving at Upperville, two squadrons of the 1st Maine were ordered to charge through the town, which they did in the most gallant manner. The rest of the 1st Maine and the 4th N. Y. acted as supports. Just beyond the town considerable force of the enemy was massed. The 1st Maine, 6th Ohio, 10th N. Y., 2nd N. Y. and 4th Penna. charged upon them furiously. The resistance was greater here than at any other point. Two of our regiments were in the road, and one on each side. They charged and were repulsed; the enemy charged and were likewise repulsed. Several charges were made with like results, until the two forces became jammed in together, and a regular hand-to-hand conflict took place, lasting more than 20 minutes. The enemy placed sharp-shooters along the stone walls at the side of the road, and our troops suffered from their fire. The officers and men on both sides fought like fiends, and in the excitement many of the enemy were killed who might have been taken prisoners. Gen. Kilpatrick nearly lost his own life in attempting to save the life of the Colonel of a N. C. regiment. . ."

Plate K: There were actions at Kellys Ford on March 17 and March 29. The sketches by A. R. Waud from Harpers Weekly, 5 December 1863, depict another action of 7 November 1863. "The Recent Fighting at Kellys Ford. While General Sedgwick, with the right wing of the army, was advancing upon Rappahannock Station, General French, with a command of three corps, moved for a crossing at Kellysville. Here he found the ford protected by some rifle-pits upon the opposite bank, and beyond by other fieldworks, for guns as well as men. Upon these our guns opened with effect, Randolph's battery giving them shell, canister and case in front, while Sleeper's battery enfiladed them from a height to the left, near Mount Holly Church, General French's headquarters. . . After a short action the accuracy of our fire caused the rebels to take to the woods in confusion, leaving a number of men in the rifle-pits. At these, wading middle-deep through the cold river, General Hobart Ward directed one of his regiments to charge. Once on the opposite shore, the advance dashed up the low ridge of earth which formed the defense, and the garrison was captured. The sketch presents a view from the island, after the deepest portion of the river was crossed. . . The more extended picture. . . shows the houses, mill, etc. called Kellyville, beyond the ford; still further, the rifle-pits and pine woods where the enemy found refuge. Sleeper's battery, on the authority of some prisoners, is said to have taken off the legs of some of the rebel staff officers. Their horses were killed, and left upon the ground. . ."

Plate L (Above): THE LAST REVIEW. Col. John S. Mosby bids farewel to his troops at Salem (Marshall) in 1865. Sketch is from Scott's "Partisa Life With Col. John S. Mosby", New York, 1867.

Plate M (Top): Soldiers of Pope's Army Crossing The Rappahannock near Warrenton.

Plate N (Bottom): Kellys Ford on The Rappahannock, the scene of the battle of the 17th March, 1863, and of Gen. Stoneman's Reconnaissance of the 21st April. Sketches by Edwin Forbes.

Plate O (Above): MELROSE CASTLE near Auburn. "In the fall of 1863, the headquarters of the Army of the Potomac were pitched for some days on the Warrenton Railroad near Auburn. Nearby lay Dr. Murray's house, called The Castle, a picturesque gray stone edifice. . .green ivy had partly overgrown it, and situated in a grove on an eminence known as Rockhill. Here General Pleasanton, commanding the cavalry, has his camp. . ."

Plate T (Top left): The photograph of Dr. Thomas Lee Settle is reproduced through the courtesy of John K. Gott and the U.D.C. Museum, Front Royal, Va.

Plate U (Bottom): The sketch of General Turner Ashby is from the Southern Illustrated News, Richmond, Va., 18 October, 1862.

Strasburg [1862]
March 14th, 1862.

My dear Colonel,

It gives me great pleasure to forward your well earned appointment as Colonel of Cavalry.

Very truly your friend
T. J. Jackson

Colonel Turner Ashby.

Confederate States of America,
WAR DEPARTMENT,
Richmond, Feby [illegible] 1862

Sir:

You are hereby informed that the President has appointed you Colonel of Cavalry under act No 356 approved Jany 22/62 In the Provisional Army in the service of the Confederate States. You are requested to signify your acceptance or non-acceptance of said appointment: and should you accept you will sign before a magistrate the oath of office herewith, and forward the same with your letter of acceptance to this Department.

J. P. Benjamin
Secretary of War.

Col. Turner Ashby
&c, &c,

TURNER ASHBY IS APPOINTED COLONEL IN THE CAVALRY
From Original in Flowers Collection, Duke University

DR. THOMAS LEE SETTLE

COLONEL JOHN SINGLETON MOSBY

GENERAL TURNER ASHBY

Lexington 6 Nov '65 —

Mr Channing M. Smith served in the Cav. of the Confederate Army, & was one of Genl J. E. B. Stuart's most trusted scouts. He was frequently sent in charge of detached parties, to watch the enemy gain information of his movements, &c, & always acquitted himself well. He sometimes acted under my special directions, & I found him active, bold, faithful & intelligent in the discharge of his duties. & very reliable

R E Lee

A CITATION FROM GENERAL LEE

Channing M. Smith, of Delaplane, was a scout for General J. E. B. Stuart and was later transferred to Mosby's command. This citation inscribed by General Robert E. Lee is now the property of his daughter-in-law, Mrs. Harry L. Smith, of Delaplane.

GENERAL EPPA HUNTON
Led a Brigade in Pickett's Charge

WILLIAM H. PAYNE
Leader of The Black Horse Cavalry

ROBERT EDEN SCOTT

LT. COL. JOHN QUINCY MARR

Plate X: From Harpers Weekly, 10 August 1861. "The Fire Zouaves and The Black Horse Cavalry in the "terrible conflict which took place at the battle of Bull Run. The Zouaves rushed out of the woods only to find themselves the target for another body of infantry beyond, while the Black Horse Cavalry were seen charging full upon them. They formed hastily in line, kneeling, semi-kneeling, and standing, that they might receive their enemies with successive volleys. Although some were killed, they waited patiently until the enemy was almost upon them, when, in quick succession, the three ranks fired, each man doing his best for the good cause. The shock to the rebels was great, but they rallied, behaving splendidly, and attempted a renewal of the charge, for which, however, the excited firemen were prepared. They (the Black Horse Cavalry) were completely shattered, broken up, and swept away. Not more than a hundred of them (six or seven hundred) rode off. As they went their rebellious ears were saluted with 'one, two, three, four, five, six, seven, tigah, Zouave!' "

From a private letter: "It was a splendid corps of cavalry, all the horses of which were coal black". Attacking, "they bore an American flag, and a part of the Zouaves supposed for an instant that they were friends. . . The flag was quickly thrown down, however, the horses dashed upon the regiment, the ruse was discovered, and the slaughter commenced. No quarter, no halting, no flinching now, marked the rapid and death-dealing blows of our men as they closed in upon the foe, in their madness and desperation. . . The sabres, bowie-knives, and bayonets glistened in the sunlight, horse after horse went down, platoon after platoon disappeared. . . the yells of the wounded and crushed belligerents filled the air, and a terrible carnage succeeded. The gallant Zouaves fought to the death and were sadly cut up; but of those hundreds of Black Horse Guard not many left that bloody rencounter!"

W. Morton Brown
1st Lt. Breckinridge Artillery
Brownsburg Va.

J. F. Withers
Capt. Partizan Rangers
Address Army of N. Virginia
Warrenton Va.
Captured on Raid in Fauquier Co. Va.
Sept 23 1864.

J T Latimer Lt
Co "K" 55th Ga Vol
Grantville Ga

A PRISONER'S SIGNATURE

This is a photostatic copy of a portion of a page from a notebook of autographs of fellow prisoners of Captain John Thomas Howe, CSA, collected by him while he was incarcerated in the Union prison at Johnston's Island, Lake Erie.

Captain Howe was wounded and captured at Gettysburg, July 3, 1863, in the final stages of the battle—Pickett's charge. He was in the Union prison about a year before he was released on an exchange of prisoners. His, pasteboard-bound well-worn notebook contains among other notes a dozen or more pages of autographs of his fellow prisoners. Some were those captured at Gettysburg but many others were taken by the Yankees in battles, skirmishes and raids on other fronts.

Of the many autographs only one gave a home address in Fauquier County.

—DAN HOWE

Plate Y (Top): GENERAL PATRICK'S HEADQUARTERS. "During General Patrick's absence from camp (at Warrenton Sulphur Springs) this pretty bower was raised, as a token of esteem, by two companies of the Twentieth New York Volunteers. These men had been misled by the officers who enlisted them as to the length of time they were to serve. Being left behind, they refused to do duty, and were tried and sentenced. Gen. Patrick, Provost Marshal of the Army, feeling they were harshly used, procured their pardon and dismissal from service. These poor Germans had not the means to offer any costly present, but their humble offering was as acceptable to the General as if it had cost thousands. . ." Harpers Weekly, 19 September 1863.

Plate Z (Bottom): Another view of Catlett's Station on the Orange and Alexandria Railroad "now held by the Excelsior Brigade". Harpers Weekly, 13 December 1862.

Plate AA: Virginia Troops crossing the Blue Ridge at daybreak, en route for Manassas Junction.

HENRIETTA BRAXTON HORNER WYETH.

Order reprieving John Washington Fletcher, Union spy, from the sentence of hanging in the murder of Ernest G. Hunton, 22 October 1867 at New Baltimore.

HEADQUARTERS FIRST MILITARY DISTRICT,
STATE OF VIRGINIA,
Richmond, Va., March 4, 1869.

SPECIAL ORDERS
No. 42.

(*Extract.*)

* * * * *

5. In the case of *J. Washington Fletcher*, (citizen,) indicted for murder, who was sentenced by the circuit court of Fauquier county, Virginia, at its April term, 1868, which sentence was commuted to imprisonment for five years in the Penitentiary of the Commonwealth of Virginia, by paragraph 1, of Special Orders No. 82, from these Headquarters, dated April 29, 1868, the unexecuted portion of the commuted sentence is hereby remitted, and the said *J. Washington Fletcher* will be at once released from custody.

* * * * *

BY COMMAND OF BREVET MAJOR-GENERAL STONEMAN:

S. F. CHALFIN,
Assistant Adjutant General.

OFFICIAL:

S. F. Chalfin

Assistant Adjutant General.

Clerk of the Circuit Court of Fauquier County
Through Military Commissioner
1st Division of Virginia.

home," asked Captain Hamner. "Do you not believe there are any gentlemen at the North?" "Yes," we both said "I have known Northern gentlemen," I added.

"Well, what makes you hate us so?" "Because" said Annie "you are trespassing on us."

"But before the war, why did you hate us?"

"We did not hate you so then," said Annie.

"And I want to ask you one question" said I. "If we beat you at York, how long do you think the war will last then?"

"Indefinitely" said Captain Hamner.

Papa had come in some time before and asked them to sit down. I had been expecting them to leave and had not asked them to sit down. Papa listened to me and was uneasy all the time and I was annoyed with myself for beginning such a conversation; but I did not know how to stop it. I could not let those Yankees talk as if they had us under their feet without showing them that we had some hope left.

Papa spoke to Capt. Hamner about Jim Dade and he said he thought Papa knew that he had sent him and he was mad at his disputing his authority. I was indignant that a young man like him could speak to Papa so, but we had to accept the apology poor as it was.

In one of his vehement moods Captain Hamner said "We are not Lincoln's hirelings. We are men and will fight." Capt. M said he hoped he would meet us when we were one people.

"That will never be. If you will let me leave here, I will go away." They called me "Miss" all the time and I did not tell them that I was married.

I do not think I would have talked to them if I had not been married, but it was entirely an unexpected thing, my talking anyhow. Sister Bet and Miss Fanny retired and were more dignified. I am very much dissatisfied with myself and Robert will not be pleased when he hears I talked to them.

This evening Cousin John of Mont Blanc came over. I told him about the visit we had this morning and he listened to all I had to say with some interest and then said very quietly, "I think the proper way to do is to listen to them and hear all they have to say and not talk to them at all." I could not help laughing at his quiet criticism of my performance and I agree with him, but I have such a quantity to say always that I cannot hold my tongue. Capt. Hamner told us that he liked to talk to persons who were well educated, that he did not profess to be very highly educated himself, but he enjoyed the society of those who were.

He was candid and truthful about his education for both he and Capt. M. betrayed a want of it in the grammar that they used.

Conversations as they really occur are not so convenient to relate as they can be made in a book. Sometimes there are two conversations going on at once, and then they flow into each other and a narrator in attempting to give a truthful account finds it very hard to do justice to what was said.

There are several remarks which were made by our visitors which I remember and wish to mention and yet cannot remember the exact connexions. One thing Capt. M. said which I wish to record here because I want to see if there will ever be any truth in it. "Never since we have been on the 'sacred soil' of Virginia has any one lost any thing by us. We have always paid for every thing."

I made no reply to that for though I had never heard of any person who had been paid except for some things which officers bought on their own account. I was afraid to tell them so. I can but contrast Captain Hamner's cold cruel looking eyes with those of our own men, so gentle and kind, so clear and frank and free from all malice and hatred, but I know how much they would do and dare sooner than submit to such as he.

10th. The visit of the Yankee captains has disturbed the "even tenor of my way" very much! I have found it hard to read or think, the recollection of how confident they were that they would soon have us all at their feet to do as they pleased makes me so indignant and things that I might have said if I had not been afraid will come back to me. Then I am so dissatisfied with myself that I should have broken all my resolutions and spoken to them. I am afraid to make any more resolutions. We are almost afraid to walk since they come about here so much, but yesterday evening Sister Bet, Annie, and I went to Clifton by the back way. It is a beautiful walk. Miss Ruth and Miss Eliza amused us telling different threats and boasts that Yankees had made to them. They seemed to have a great horror of guerillas and told the Misses Garrott that if any thing of the kind was attempted by the Confederates they would burn every house before them.

As we came back and passed through the meadow I felt peculiarly calm and placid passing through the scenes I used to love in childhood and I almost went back to those times and felt as I did then till the shrill whistle of the Yankee cars reminded me that we were no longer a free people. Oh, what a chill the sound of that whistle sends through me now. I cannot help recalling the times when our own cars came up and we expected to hear news from those we love. Well, I trust those times will come again.

Minnie walked over here Thursday evening. She came with her sister Lizzie and says there is not the least danger. She told us that her father had heard from Cousin James Jones that he was a lieutenant of ordinance and that Mr. Carroll is to be his clerk, and he has had another letter from some one who told him that brother Jack was at York with Robert. We were glad to hear even that. This morning Mrs. Pinsen, the mother of one of Roberts company, came here and said she had heard that the company were dreadfully cut up in a battle. God grant that there may be no truth in it. The poor woman sat a long time telling us of how the Yankees had treated her and her neighbors. It is very sad to hear of the troubles that have come upon our poor people. God relieve us in his good time. Papa went to Mountain View this morning for the first time for more than a week. Dr. Stribling is very unwell and they are all distressed at the departure of Albert, one of the servants who they trusted.

13th. I have not written for several days. Saturday evening Cousin Henry Marshall passed here. He had been to Markham to try to get his horses which were stolen by some runaways, but he could hear nothing of them. He rode up here and told us that Richmond was taken and Gen. Johnston's army with 75 thousand taken too. I did not believe at all that the army was taken, but there seemed to be no doubt that Richmond was taken. They said it was taken by gunboats going up to the city.

I never suffered greater distress of mind in my life than while I believed that. If the army had been taken I believed the war would soon be over for if 100,000 men surrendered I could not see what we could expect from the others. I was miserably mortified at the idea of such a thing and yet the thoughts of their all being driven in the heat of summer into the mountains and swamps of North and South Carolina seemed too miserable to think of, Papa tried to comfort me and they all seemed to think I gave way, but it seemed to me as if my heart would break. I felt that the war must last indefinitely and I was without any thing to occupy me and no prospect of having any thing. I sometimes almost wished to die, but then the thoughts of seeing Robert come back after the war was over made me still cling to life. I have tried to know what my own feelings were, but I cannot tell. I hope I did not feel rebellious against God. I do not think I did, but I felt then doubtful whether it was His will that we should be happy in this life. I felt that perhaps His will was that those that He loved should suffer in this life and the wicked should enjoy all the happiness in this world. I read differently in my Bible and it was a comfort, and it was a comfort too that "Whom the Lord loveth he chasteneth".

Sunday morning Cousin Jaquelin Marshall came by. He had never been able to get a pass to go to Prospect Hill before and he was obliged to return Monday evening. He stood in the yard and said he thought the war was nearly over, that he had heard the same report that Cousin Henry did the evening before and after he went up to Markham he had heard great rejoicings in the camp and had gone to hear about it. They told him Richmond was taken and Johnston's army captured.

He then went on to tell us that the property of everybody in Virginia who was in the army would be confiscated and that it would be impossible to carry on the war without Virginia because they had no munitions of war and nothing to provision an army. He acknowledged himself completely subjugated, said it seemed to him like months since the Yankees had been at Markham instead of two weeks. On the whole, though we were glad to see him, his visit was not very cheering.

Miss Fanny and I walked in the field in front of the kitchen after dinner, we had a talk about Lincoln. She seemed to think he was very conscientious in everything he had done, but I do not think so.

(While I am writing I look up and there is a poor negro woman toiling along with a baby in her arms followed by a little boy with her carrying her bundle. Well, it is not strange. Freedom I know is sweet. Oh how sweet!) I was saying Miss Fanny thought Lincoln was conscientious. She acknowledged several instances in which he had gone beyond his lawful power.

I read some Sunday but my mind was so distracted that I could not read any thing but the Bible with any interest.

Mr. Duncan had service at Leeds and Papa and Sister Bet went there, but Sister Bet did not come back with Papa. Sunday evening I was sitting with Emily who was making up the bread and I asked if she had ever heard anything from our servants who had run away and she said, well, yes. She had heard some rangled talk about them but knew nothing particularly. I said I heard that Patsy was in Upperville. Mary Ann came in then and said "Patsy and Cousin Phillis is in Washington. Sam, ——, George, and Cousin Felix are gone to Fort Monroe."

"I heard," said I "that Edward and Felix were on the railroad."

"Cousin Edward is, but the others is gone to Fort Monroe."

"And where is Dick?" "He is waiting on some General. I forgot his name, and getting fifteen dollars a month. And, Miss Mary, you know Aunt Ann's Mary. Well, her husband has been with the Yankees and came back for her and is going to stay at Doctor Stribling's tonight and take the cars tomorrow. He has a house near Alexandria and he is going to take her there."

"I wonder whose house it is?" said I.

"Oh, I suppose he rents it. He could not have it without renting it from somebody."

Poor darkeys! There is every thing done to induce them to go. I cannot blame them, but after the way the Yankees associate with them I am rather anxious they should go except on their own account. They will become rather unmanageable after all this.

Yesterday (Monday) morning, Uncle Cary came here. He thought the war was over. He had heard that Davis, Lee, and Johnston were all taken, said he would not have given up but after he was shipped he did not know what else he could do, and he thought the war was over. Well, yesterday was another day of misery to me. I could not recover my spirits. I prayed that God would give me the right spirit of submission. I felt for the first time that if I could see Robert again I would even be willing to submit to the Yankees, but it was only because it was God's will, and after that feeling came the hope that God would still give us our liberty after a long time. And then I thought of the time that it would be, and it seemed impossible for me to feel anything but wretched. In the evening we were all going to walk and as we passed out of the front gate we saw a gentleman passing Joanna's house wave his hat to us and he looked like brother Jack. Annie turned pale with excitement, but my heart died within me. Our army was taken and the prisoners were free on parole, and where was Robert? While we were going to the gate to meet him we were speculating about him, but as he turned the hill we saw it was Cousin Jaquelin and he was waving to us to meet him at the gate.

He told us he had just seen a man who was from Richmond Saturday. It was not taken and vigorous preparations were being made to defend the town. There had been quite a battle at Williamsburg, we claim that we repulsed them, but as it was in a retreat they kept the field and we left our dead and wounded there. So they claim the victory too.

Our account says we killed a great many, but we cannot know as they kept the field and if they had my respect for the truth I should believe their side, but they do seem to have so little regard for the truth that I do not believe them.

Every soldier who has been here (and they come every day sitting in the cabins with the servants and dining at our table) tells us that Richmond was taken and Johnston with part of his army certainly. They told us that Gen. Geary had received a dispatch from McClellan and there has been a universal rejoicing among them. Cousin Jaquelin said that his informant knew nothing of Stribling's company, but he had heard the death of several acquaintances and would he thinks have heard of any thing that happened to any of the Fauquier companies.

Poor Major Payne of Warrenton was killed. His poor wife? My heart feels for her.

Oh, the misery this war brings! He was one of the most violent secessionists in Fauquier and opposed Cousin Robert Scott who was the union candidate for the Convention. Cousin Robert was elected and I heard then that Mr. Payne was very deeply mortified, but when the State seceded and the war broke out he had everything as he wished and was rapidly promoted in the army. He was the Captain of the Blackhorse company at the Battle of Manassas, and soon after he received a pair of silver spurs sent from New York to the Capt. of that company by a gentleman who did not know his name but said he had come from New York on that day to witness the fight and his sympathies were Southern and he was struck by the gallantry of the Captain of the Blackhorse. Well, he was an ambitious man. It seems a singular coincidence that he and Cousin Robert Scott should both have died at nearly the same time. They have been opposed to each other in elections and politics ever since Mr. Payne has been a man nearly. He was not equal to Cousin Robert in any respect and yet he died the most glorious death of the two. How little human judgment is worth when it attempts to judge of the future. Who could ever have known the two men and predicted or dreamed of predicting their end.

We all walked on after we had seen Cousin Jaquelin and our hearts were much lightened. As we returned Papa met us and told us that two Yankees were at the stable and he had been uneasy about us ever since we left. Two had dined here and gone to Susan's house and been sitting there ever since and now two more had come. At supper I said that if I were in Papa's place I would not stand that, but I would ask the Captain if he could not stop that. After supper they all came and told Papa that there was someone in their lines who ought not to be there. A man with a cavalry saddle and a mail bag had passed and they were picqueted here to find out who it was. Papa told them of Cousin Jaquelin Marshall and they agreed that it might be the person they meant. Papa never doubted the story and because we did not believe it, he was quite indignant. He said he would not ask the Captain about it as he had intended because he thought as the men had taken the trouble to come to explain to him just to keep him from being uneasy, it would be very ungrateful in him to ask the Captain anything about it. We told him that it was strange for two of the men had been here before Cousin Jaquelin passed and the other two had met him, but he said we were prejudiced and uncharitable. It is always so with Papa. Every Yankee that comes here tells him some story that he finds out afterwards. Still he believes the next one who comes.

This morning Papa concluded that he would go and see the Captain and ask him if extending the picquets would make it necessary for him to have a pass to go the other way. He invited me to ride with him as far as Dr. Stribling's so I was glad to have a chance of seeing the family there. When we came to the top of the hill that overlooks Dr. Stribling's there stood a little short Dutch man to dispute our passage. He had taken off his shoes and stockings and stood with his bare feet just as dirty!

"You can't go no farder."

Papa told him that he had been allowed to pass yesterday and then went on to explain to the picquet why he wanted to go. I sat by amused that he should waste his breath to such a man, but it had a good effect for he called the Corporal of the Guard and the Corporal let us pass. Sister Milly met me and we stopped at the pit to look at the flowers and she told me how the servants were performing there. She says that the kitchen and cabins were full at all hours of the day with the Yankee soldiers and the servants were all beside themselves all the time. Albert had gone away and returned and established himself with his wife, one of Cousin William's women, in a house of Mr. Green's at Markham Station. The house was one that Mr. Green built to rent and he was very indignant and went to ask the Captain about it and he said that Mr. King, Albert's employer, had a written permission from McClellan to take any house that suited him and he wanted Albert to have the house and it was not to be disputed.

So Caroline, Albert's wife, is established mistress of the house and a pastry cook. The most amusing part (for I can but laugh) is that Mother was so indignant with the Yankees that she would not sell them her butter or eggs, but had distributed what she had to spare among the servants, and Albert's establishment was supplied with those articles in that way. I cannot help thinking of Caroline and Albert. She was one of the most respectful kind servants I ever saw and I cannot help having a curiosity to know how she appears now.

When I came up to the house I found Father sitting in his own room looking better than I expected to see him. Mother seemed greatly excited at what Cousin Jaquelin was telling them.

Cousin John Scott has opened an office for guerillas to avenge Cousin Robert's death he says now; but it was before his death, I believe and they are coming up here and wage what seems to me almost a savage warfare, and Cousin John is such a wild kind of a man I would be very much afraid of what he might do. As soon as he opened his office two hundred names were put down. They receive no pay from the Confederate Government, but get commissions so they may be treated as prisoners of war if they are taken. Cousin Jaquelin Marshall had come over from Markham to see his mother and tell her how things were getting on at Prospect Hill. He said he had gone there very much in favour of going back there with his mother, but after he heard of the guerillas he thought it would be best for all of them to stay where they were, as they would be sure to get into trouble if they went there. He says our men are driving all the cattle from this part of the country to Richmond and he wants them to take his without asking him anything about it, as if he gives his consent the Yankees will be angry. They talked over their concerns for some time and then spoke of other things.

This morning all the young girls who staid in the house at Markham took their departure leaving nine little white children without any nurses and one of the girls left her own baby, a child of nine months. Cousin Jaquelin says he went to Captain Hamner's tent afterwards and found them all seated up around him.

The Captain looked somewhat embarrassed and told him they had come there to ask him to let them go off and he was trying to persuade them to go back home.

Sister Milly told me that Mother went into the yard the other day and saw Eve watering the flowers, and Capt. Hamner who had never been into the house was lying down near her leaning his head on his hands. As soon as he saw mother he jumped up and went away without speaking. Mother asked Eve what he was talking about.

"He came to ask if his men disturbed us any here."

"Did he say nothing of the flowers?" asked Mother who suspected that this was not all.

"Oh, yes, he said they were very pretty and refreshing."

Cousin Jaquelin and all of them began telling me how Capt. Hamner had described his visit to Morven. They all seemed very much amused at it. Cousin Jaquelin said he had made a very good story of it and he had laughed more than he had for a long time.

"Well" said I, "I assure you I am very much mortified that I should have done it, but it seems to me I should not laugh if a Yankee were to come tell me anything of the kind about my cousins making them ridiculous." The whole company looked crestfallen.

"I reckon you would" said Cousin John of Leeds.

"Oh, no, I do not think I would." "Well, you know, Mary, we heard it second hand" said Cousin Eliza apologetically.

"Oh, yes, of course" said I, "you would laugh. I expect that when Cousin Jaquelin tells you, but if I had been in his place I would not have laughed at my cousins with a Yankee."

"You ought never to have spoken to them," said Mother. "One of them came and told me they were going to colonize South Carolina with negroes and I did not say a word."

The whole company then united in advising me not to enter into any such discussion again and I told them I thought I might promise them I would not.

I was tested very soon for Papa came in and told us that Captain Hamner had proposed to ride home with him and he said we must start as he could not keep him waiting. I was again advised to be cautious and we started. Papa introduced me to the Captain and we bowed as if we had never met before. He and Papa talked about the country, the war, and the crops. I only occasionally making some remark to show him I was not afraid of him. He said there was no truth in the reports that Richmond and Norfolk were taken. The men he said were always expecting to hear of victory and they anticipated it. I felt like telling him about the newspapers, but I did not say anything. He said he did not know what would become of the negroes and that he had talked to some girls a half hour that morning to persuade them to return home, but when he was done they said they wanted to go.

When I got home I went into Sister Betsy's room and left him to Papa. We did not see him again.

Sister Milly says the ladies at Markham do not see him when he goes there except by accident. Captain Hamner told Papa that the men who professed to be picquets had no business here at all and if he could find them out they should be punished. There were five men here that night, and if he cannot find who was absent at roll call it seems to me he must keep very poor discipline, but he told Papa the men had no business here and he would be obliged to him if he would ... them from here whenever they came. Soon after he left Papa saw two men and told them that their Captain said they had no business here and they must go away. They told him they would go when they pleased.

"Well" said he, "give me your names and you may do it and I will ask the Captain about it." They refused to give their names and he said "Well, I would know you again."

So they turned and walked away saying "You old Secesh," and they will not come again, he hopes.

After dinner Sister Betsy went to Mont Blanc. She rode and Uncle Jim escorted her. Soon after she left, Mr. Duncan came in. He had been to see Gen. Geary to ask if his mother could go to Washington on the cars. The Gen. was very courteous and commenced talking politics. He told Mr. Duncan that the people about here seemed to know nothing of politics.

He wished to meet them to talk with them. He would illustrate the position of the United States.

"It was like a father," he said "with 32 children, all of whom had been living very harmoniously together till one started up and determined to rebel. The father was going to correct that child (South Carolina) when up springs another child who had hitherto been very dutiful and said, 'Father, you must not do that, if you do I will not submit.' " Such he said was the position of Virginia and he wanted to meet the people. In the language of Scripture, he would say "Come, let us reason together." Mr. Duncan said he did not say anything to the contrary.

I was glad that our people generally were more discreet than I had been but I believe I would be afraid to have talked to Gen. Geary, for it is reported that he seized a lady by the shoulder and shook her for talking what he called treason. . .

Mr. Duncan told me that Robert had been very highly complimented for his conduct at Malvern Hill, that he had fought the enemy with three hundred men and his Battery for four hours while they had three whole divisions of the army. Gen. Tombs said it was the best artillery fight of the war, and Gen. Stewart said the Yankee general had told him that the guns were bravely and skillfully managed and did fearful execution. Gen. Stewart had this conversation when he met them under a flag of truce. I am so thankful that Robert did not lose his guns. I would have been mortified if he had lost them. He had to run very fast to get off after he did begin retreating for they were nearer a wood than he was by three hundred yards and he had to get thru to keep from being surrounded. He lost three men killed and several wounded who were taken prisoners. Martin Marshall was taken prisoner too but not wounded.

25th. Sister Bet and Papa came over to see me this evening. I was well enough to go home but I had no horse so I promised to go tomorrow. Today we heard that Longstreet was at Waterloo so Sister Fanny and I went up to the Cross Roads to see if we could hear anything. One of Robert's Company had just passed and said they were at the Rappahannock River but had not crossed. I suppose Robert will not be able to come home.

26th. Last night I went to bed in Sister Fanny's room with her. About one o'clock I was waked with a confused impression that an army was passing through the yard and more fully roused by hearing someone near the window call out. Sister Fanny sprang from the bed and asked, "Who is there?"

"How are you, Cousin Fanny?" said the voice.

"Robert Stribling?" said Sister Fanny.

"Is Mary Cary here?" was the next question, and I discovered that it really was him. God has brought him safely through every danger and now I hope I shall thank him for his mercy.

Robert is looking very thin. His clothes are very shabby and he is very sad. He had heard of his Father's death and could not bring himself to speak of him at all. He asked many questions about his mother and sister but did not speak of his Father though I never saw him so sad and out of spirits about the war and everything else. He had not received my letter telling him all the particulars about Father's death and I wanted to have told him some things, but I could not make up my mind to introduce so painful a subject during the little time that he had to stay, for he left in an hour or two after breakfast this morning.

'I Wish I Had A Hundred Like Him'

COL. JOHN S. MOSBY AND HIS COMMAND

(From Evans, Gen. C.A.: CONFEDERATE MILITARY HISTORY. Vol. III: "Virginia" by Jed Hotchkiss. (Atlanta, Ga., 1899, 12 vols.)

John Singleton Mosby, one of the greatest scouts of history, was the life of his command, the genius that inspired all its achievements and maintained the organization throughout the changes of its personnel. He was in his twenty-eighth year when the State seceded, had married a daughter of a distinguished Kentuckian, member of congress and diplomat, and was practicing law at Bristol and Abingdon in southwest Virginia.

He went to Harper's Ferry as a private in the cavalry company of William E. Jones, and was first in the field as a member of Stuart's cavalry regiment about Winchester in the Shenandoah valley. He attracted Stuart's attention after the battle of First Manassas by his ability as a scout while the cavalry was on outpost duty before Washington, and during the withdrawal from the Rappahannock line.

While General Jones was colonel of the regiment, Mosby was adjutant, and after that he was detailed as a scout at brigade headquarters. He suggested and led a raid on the enemy's line on the Totpotomoy which circumstances developed into the famous ride around McClellan's peninsular army, and made Stuart a major-general.

It was not until the close of 1862 after a battle of Fredericksburg that Mosby began his career as a partisan leader. At that time Stuart, whom he had accompanied through the Maryland campaign, made a raid into Loudoun county, and the young lieutenant obtained permission to remain for a few days with nine men. Riding into Fairfax county, he attacked the outposts of Col. Percy Wyndham commanding the Federal cavalry brigade in front of Washington, capturing more than his own number of men. In Fairfax he was joined by John Underwood, his trusted scout. Stuart then detailed Mosby fifteen men, with seven of whom he attacked Wyndham and one hundred cavalry at Middleburg.

During the winter "he kept things lively and humming," as he described it in his Reminiscences. "Old men and boys joined my band. Some had run the gauntlet of Yankee pickets and others swam the Potomac to get to me. I mounted, armed and equipped my command at the expense of the United States government." The status of Mosby's command in the Confederate forces at this time is clearly indicated in General Orders No. 27 of Gen. R. E. Lee dated February 28, 1863 in which he says: "Lieutenant Mosby, with his detachment, has done much to harass the enemy, attacking him boldly on several occasions, and capturing many prisoners." The latter were regularly sent in to General Stuart.

The Confederate army at this time was south of the Rappahannock. Mosby and his men were north of it in the Piedmont region of Fauquier and Loudoun counties, thereafter known as "Mosby's Confederacy" to the rear of the main Federal strength, and between that force and the one in the lower Shenandoah valley.

On the east stretched the Federal line of communication, through the plains of Manassas, to Washington, and to the north were the Potomac river and the Baltimore & Ohio railroad. From this point of vantage Mosby could strike with equal freedom toward Washington or Harper's Ferry, and by incessant and worrying attacks compel the enemy greatly to contract his lines or reinforce the guards of his communications, either of which would be to the advantage of the Confederate army.

Mosby's men had no superiors in the saddle, and were expert pistol shots. They were never very numerous but what they lacked in numbers was more than compensated by high individual intelligence, reckless daring and love of adventure. Among them were some who deserve to rank among the heroes of romance.

The captains were heroes of as brilliant forays as those led by Mosby himself. Four men were particularly conspicuous in the earliest operations, Fount Beattie, Dick Moran, John Underwood and "Major" Hibbs, the latter a brawny blacksmith, over fifty years of age. "Around the triumvirate," Mosby afterward wrote, "recruits gathered as iron filings cluster around a magnet. They were the germs from which my command grew and spread like a banyan tree. Beattie, always my Achates, had been captured (at Middleburg), but was soon afterward exchanged." Others notable at this period were Sergeant Ames, a deserter from a New York regiment, Frank Williams, Joe Nelson, and Walter Frankland, afterward quartermaster.

On February 28, 1863, Mosby had the pleasure of reporting to General Stuart that he had 27 men, and that with them on the 26th he had attacked a cavalry outpost of 50, routed them out of log houses near Germantown, killed four and captured five men, and taken 39 horses, without loss to his band. By March he had the rank of captain of partisan rangers, and had become so troublesome that a strong Federal detachment of cavalry was sent into Loudoun county to put an end to his operations. Failing to find any trace of the band, they arrested and started back with a number of old men from Middleburg. Mosby pursued with 17 men and attacked the rear guard of 57 while feeding horses at Aldie, routed them, captured 17 men, including a captain, and released all the prisoners. The Federal commander was cashiered and the fame of Mosby's men spread through the North and South.

But a still more brilliant exploit speedily followed. At Fairfax Court House within fifteen miles of Washington were the headquarters of Brigadier-General Stoughton and Colonels Wyndham and Johnston, cavalry commanders especially charged to attend to Mosby. On Sunday night, March 8, it being dark and rainy, Mosby and his men set out with the audacious plan of capturing these officers. They reached the town early next morning, quietly seized the few guards on duty and then separated, different parties seeking the Federal officers. Unfortunately Wyndham was absent, and Johnston escaped in a state of nudity in the cold night, but Stoughton was found in bed and made a prisoner. The daring raiders came back with two captains and 30 prisoners, besides their brigadier, and 58 horses, on the way passing so close to the Federal entrenchments at Centerville that the sentinels hailed them.

About a week later they attacked a body of cavalry at Herndon Station, Fairfax county, and brought off a major, a captain, 21 men and 26 horses, without loss to themselves.

When pursuit was made the rear guard repulsed it. The report of this exploit was sent to Richmond with commendatory endorsements, including this: "Respectfully forwarded for the information of the department, and as an evidence of the merit and continued success of Captain Mosby. (Signed) R. E. LEE, General."

On March 26, General Stuart transmitted to General Lee another report that caused the great leader to exclaim: "Hurrah for Mosby! I wish I had a hundred like him." He forwarded the intelligence to Adjutant-General Cooper in these words: "On the 25th instant Capt. John S. Mosby attacked and routed a body of the enemy's cavalry on the Little River turnpike, near Chantilly. He reports 10 killed and wounded. and a lieutenant and 30 men, with their horses, arms and equipments, captured. He sustained no loss."

On this raid the company had a new recruit, Captain Hoskins, an English soldier of fortune, who, because he would fight with his sword only, lost his life a few weeks later. In the first set of fours that led the decisive charge were James W. Foster, Thomas W. Richards, and William L. Hunter, who gained commissions by their gallantry and afterwards won honorable positions in civil life.

On April 1 the daring scouts had a memorable experience and narrow escape. They had been ordered to Dranesville by Stuart and finding the enemy had fallen back were early that morning feeding their horses in an enclosure at Miskel's house when six companies of the First Vermont cavalry charged in upon and surrounded them. Mosby ordered an attack and 20 of his men instantly responded while the others joined as rapidly as possible. The countercharge was so fierce and unexpected that the Federals broke in confusion and were driven for seven miles. Their commander and eight others were killed, 15 badly wounded, and besides these 82 were made prisoners.

Mosby had about 65 men in the fight, of whom Private R. A. Hart, Ned Hurst, Keyes and Davis were wounded, the latter fatally. Lt. William H. Chapman, afterward second in command, Sergeant Hunter and Privates Sam Chapman, Wellington, Welt and Harry Hatcher, Tom Turner, Wild, Sowers, Ames and Sibert were commended for gallantry. Mosby's report of this affair was characteristic. The story was told in a matter-of-fact way without rhetoric or exaggeration, and with a frank confession that he had not sufficiently guarded himself against surprise. But it was so evident that victory had been won by his coolness and the splendid audacity of his men that to honor him and further dignify his command Stuart transmitted the report with a recommendation for promotion, and Secretary Seddon indorsed upon it: "ADJUTANT GENERAL: Nominate as major if it has not been previously done."

Soon after this, Major-General Stahel, who according to his own statement, was promoted to that rank in order to take command before Washington and relieve the capital from fear of Mosby's men as well as save the communications of Hooker's army from continual disturbance sent out two brigades of cavalry and a battery of artillery to gather in the raiders as a prelude to the Chancellorsville campaign, but this formidable force did hardly more than capture a few non-combatants at Middleburg.

Quiet followed in the Mosby country until the battle of Chancellorsville. Then, while the guns were booming on the other side of the Rapidan, Mosby with 70 or 80 men looking for a field of usefulness, surprised the First Virginia Cavalry dismounted near Warrenton Junction, drove them into houses, and had taken their surrender when heavy reinforcements arrived and the squadron was compelled to retreat leaving one man, Templeman, killed, and about 20 captured.

Mortified, but not discouraged, Mosby collected 30 or 40 men a few days later, burned two railroad bridges in the Federal rear and rode as far as Dumfries where they had another fight with superior numbers at Frying Pan church and saved themselves as they did at Chantilly by retreating and when the enemy was scattered turning rapidly and attacking as if supported by reinforcements. They never had them, but the effect was the same. It conveyed the idea of "ambush," the suspicion of which had a demoralizing effect upon their antagonists.

Stuart now at Mosby's request sent him a mounted howitzer for more effective work on the railroad. This was turned over to Sam Chapman, an ex-theological student and a reckless fighter and supported by about 40 men, was used on May 30 to capture and burn a train loaded with sutler's goods near Catlett's Station in hearing of the Federal bugles. On the retreat, attacked by De Forest's cavalry brigade, Mosby's men made a desperate fight to save their howitzer, repulsing several charges, but finally lost it with Sam Chapman, Robert P. Mountjoy, and Fontaine Beattie as prisoners and Captain Hoskins killed. This was a disaster to the command, but so demoralizing was the effect upon the Federal transportation that Stuart promptly sent word that they might sell another gun at the same price.

On June 10 the first company of the battalion was organized in regular form with James William Foster as captain and Thomas Turner, William L. Hunter and George Whitescarver lieutenants. On the same day the command started for the Potomac River and crossing into Maryland had a brisk fight at Seneca Creek in which Alfred Glascock was wounded and Lieutenant Whitescarver and Captain Brawner were killed. A number of prisoners and horses were taken. The North was alarmed regarding the possible extent of these forays.

The opposing armies were now maneuvering preparatory to the Gettysburg campaign, and Mosby and his men were indefatigable in the work of procuring information.

Among the many prisoners taken was Hooker's chief signal officer bearing dispatches from which Stuart and Lee learned the strength and plans of the enemy. On the 22nd they varied their work by capturing a wagon train, and Hooker greatly annoyed withdrew Stahel's division from an important movement already ordered against Richmond to break Lee's communications in order to drive Mosby from within the Federal lines. Rejoining Stuart, Mosby found Lee anxious for definite information as to whether the Federals had yet crossed the Potomac and went back into Hooker's lines with two companions, obtained the information, and on his return rode through a Federal column of cavalry with two prisoners, disguised only by a waterproof cloak.

When Stuart started out on his raid into Pennsylvania Mosby and his men were to accompany him but were cut off by Hancock's column and compelled to go north through the Shenandoah Valley. For a time they were obscured by the great events of the Gettysburg campaign. but after the army was back again in Virginia their forays were resumed with the same old daring and success. An expedition of cavalry and infantry was soon sent against them, with the usual result. The story was told in Mosby's report to Stuart, July 28: "GENERAL: I send you, in the charge of Sergt. F. Beattie, 414 prisoners which were captured from the enemy during their march through this county (Fauquier). I also sent you 45 several days ago . . . I also captured 123 horses, 12 wagons, 50 sets of fine harness, arms, etc."

On August 24 with 27 men, Mosby was looking for unguarded brigades near Annandale and had a serious fight at Gooding's Tavern in which he was shot through the side and thigh. At the same time the gallant Lieutenant Shriver and Norman E. Smith were killed. Lieutenant Turner, conspicuous for bravery, during Mosby's absence led attacks upon the outposts near Waterloo and Warrenton. In September Mosby was again in the saddle and conducted raids along the Federal lines of communication near Alexandria capturing Colonel Dulaney, aide to the Federal governor of Virginia. Company B was now organized with William R. Smith of the Black Horse Cavalry as captain and Frank Williams, Abner Wren and Robert Gray, lieutenants; and in December, Company C was organized, with William H. Chapman, captain, and A. E. Richards, Frank Fox and Yager, lieutenants.

Among the later exploits in 1863 was an attack on October 26 with 50 men on a long and heavily guarded wagon train near New Baltimore, bringing off many prisoners, horses and mules. Nearly 300 more prisoners were taken by the end of the year. Captains Smith, Chapman and Turner, commanding detachments, did brilliant service As a result Gregg's entire cavalry division guarded the Federal rear, sentinels were stationed all along the railroad in hailing distance, and the railroad trains were heavily guarded. General Lee, looking out for opportunities for still greater influence for the squadron, advised General Imboden to send a force east of the Blue Ridge to assist Major Mosby in breaking up the railroad north of the Rappahannock in case the Federals should advance.

By the beginning of 1864 Mosby's command was regularly enrolled as the Forty-third Virginia Cavalry Battalion, and on January 21 General Lee recommended his promotion to lieutenant-colonel, which was granted . Company D was organized in May 1864 with Robert P. Mountjoy of Mississippi as captain and Alfred Glascock, Charles E. Grogan and William Trunnell, lieutenants. The company was mainly Marylanders. Company E. was organized July 28 with Sam Chapman as captain and Fount Beattie, Ben Palmer and Martin as lieutenants. Two of the company commanders distinguished themselves early in the year: Capt. William R. Smith on the 1st at Rectortown by an attack with 35 men upon 78 of whom he killed and wounded 57; and Lieut. W. T. Turner by a successful onslaught upon a post near Warrenton. Both these gallant soldiers lost their lives, however, on the 9th of the same month, in a night attack upon Maryland troops on Loudoun Heights. William E. Colston, W. H. Turner and Robertson were also killed in that fight.

At Dranesville on February 22 with 160 men, a spirited and successful little battle was fought in which Mosby's officers, Mountjoy, Chapman, Hunter and Williams won special commendation. Fifteen Federals were killed, 70 prisoners were taken, and some of those who escaped were chased into the Potomac. Mosby's men lost one killed and four wounded.

Lieut. A. E. Richards on March 10 with a detachment of 30 men surprised an outpost near Charlestown, killing the major commanding and bringing off several prisoners thus opening operations in the lower Shenandoah Valley which were maintained throughout the year without neglecting Fairfax County and the Maryland border. When Grant crossed the Rapidan, Mosby with forty men started down the Rappahannock while two other detachments under Richards and Chapman were sent to embarrass Sigel. The latter field of operations was found the most promising for although Mosby was able to capture an ambulance train and 40 prisoners near Belle Plain, the line was so heavily guarded that his efforts were of slight avail. Meanwhile, in the valley, Captains Richards and Chapman had been seriously disturbing the enemy and Mosby repaired to that quarter, captured a cavalry outpost at Front Royal, and on about May 20 with 150 men made a daring attack upon a wagon train guarded by 700 troops. While little was accomplished in the way of captures, large forces of men were kept from the front to guard the trains, and only one more wagon train was sent up the valley to Hunter.

In the latter part of June, after an excursion to Centreville, the battalion took Duffield's Depot, on the Baltimore & Ohio Railroad, capturing 50 prisoners and a large amount of stores. At the same time, Lieutenant Nelson, guarding the flank, routed a Federal expedition from Harper's Ferry, taking 19 prisoners.

General Early was now coming down the valley, Hunter having retreated across West Virginia, and Mosby's command, to cooperate with Early, crossed the Potomac at Point of Rocks. A Federal force was ready to dispute his crossing but this was scattered by artillery. Captain Richards led a charge across the river and under heavy fire from a redoubt drove the enemy from camp . The use of a howitzer on this occasion was the source of greatly magnified reports of Mosby's strength which spread alarm through the North. Early then invaded Maryland, and Mosby crossed lower down the river, and raided towards Frederick City. To interrupt these movements Federal cavalry was sent out from Falls Church which Mosby promptly hastened to meet and completely routed at Mount Zion Church near Aldie on July 7, the Federals losing 40 killed and wounded besides 57 prisoners. Of his own command one was killed and six wounded.

According to the Federal official reports only one officer returned to camp that evening and 33 men out of the party of 150. Major Forbes and two lieutenants were captured. Captain Stone and Lieutenant Schuyler of New York were badly wounded, and 12 killed and 37 wounded were found on the field.

Col. Charles R. Lowell said of the opposing commands, "There was not enough difference to talk about," but Major Forbes made a faulty movement by the right flank, "the rebels saw their chance, gave a yell, and our men, in the confusion of the moment, broke."

Sheridan was soon in the Shenandoah Valley. On August 13 Mosby gave the new commander notice of his presence by attacking a supply train at Berryville guarded by several hundred infantry and cavalry under Brigadier-General Kenly, capturing 200 prisoners, destroying 75 loaded wagons, and taking over 200 beef cattle and 500 mules and horses. This was one of the most brilliant achievements of Mosby's Battalion. It had 300 men engaged and lost but two killed and three wounded.

On the 16th General Grant telegraphed to Sheridan: "The families of most of Mosby's command are known and can be collected. I think they should be taken and kept at Fort McHenry or some secure place as hostages for the good conduct of Mosby and his men. When any of Mosby's men are caught, hang them without trial." This severe order was based on the understanding, prevalent among Northern soldiers and citizens alike, that Mosby and his men were guerrillas. It was followed on the same day by an order to send a division of cavalry through Loudoun County "to destroy and carry off the crops, animals, negroes and all men under fifty years of age capable of bearing arms."

The work of devastation was already begun in the valley and Mosby's men endeavored to prevent it. Captain Chapman, in the language of Colonel Mosby, "coming upon a portion of the enemy's cavalry which was burning houses, attacked and routed them. Such was the indignation of our men at witnessing some of the finest residences in that portion of the state enveloped in flames that no quarter was shown, and about 25 of them were shot to death for their villainy. About 30 horses were brought off, but no prisoners."

Mosby's men were never more active than in this period of deadly struggle. The fortune of war was varying. Capt. Sam Chapman defeated the Sixth New York Cavalry at Berryville but with serious loss to his own command. Lieutenant Glascock with 10 men rode through Sheridan's camps as a provost guard, and brought out 18 mounted prisoners. Capt. A. E. Richards was specially successful in the valley. In Fairfax County, while scouting, Mosby was severely wounded. In the course of his operations Sam Chapman charged into the advance guard of one of General Torbert's brigades, and six of his men were captured. These six prisoners were executed at Front Royal on September 23. In retaliation six Federal prisoners were hanged by Mosby's orders in sight of the Federal camp near Berryville.

In the latter part of September, Merritt's and Custer's divisions were sent around through the Piedmont and every foot of the territory known as "Mosby's Confederacy" was swept by them. From the Blue Ridge Mountains some of Mosby's men watched the work of destruction, and Major Richards has described the scene in these words: "As far as the eye could see the whole country east of the mountains was lit up by the destroying flames, and the glare was reflected from the sky above. It was a sublime sight to the eye, but a sickening one to the heart. Our one battalion of Cavalry was powerless to prevent these two divisions of the enemy from executing their orders."

On September 19, 1864, Gen. R. E. Lee summarized the work of Mosby as follows: "With the loss of little more than 20 men, he has killed, wounded and captured during the period embraced in the report (from March 1st) about 1,200 of the enemy, and taken more than 1,600 horses and mules, 230 beef cattle, and 85 wagons and ambulances, without counting many smaller operations. The services rendered by Colonel Mosby and his command in watching and reporting the enemy's movements have also been of great value. His operations have been highly creditable to himself and his command."

In October, Mosby's battalion performed one of its most notable feats, preventing the rebuilding of the Manassas Gap Railroad, an enterprise intended to furnish a shorter line of communication between Grant and Sheridan. A thousand Federal soldiers went up the road with railroad material, but Mosby's men destroyed their camp at Salem (Marshall), put them in a state of siege at Rectortown and destroyed the communications in their rear. About ten days later, October 14, occurred Mosby's famous "Greenback Raid" in which a Baltimore & Ohio military train was destroyed at Duffield's and two paymasters were captured with $168,000 in currency.

Company F was now organized with Walter Frankland, captain,

and Walter Bowie, Ames and Frank Turner, lieutenants, and the command was divided in two squadrons, Companies A and B under Capt. A. E. Richards and the others under Capt. W. H. Chapman.

Late in December Mosby was promoted to Colonel, Chapman to Lieutenant-Colonel and Richards to Major. Notable among the events toward the close of 1864 were a disastrous fight at Upperville late in October; the defeat and capture of Captain Brasher, a famous and gallant Federal scout, by Captain Richards in November; the death of Captain Mountjoy near Leesburg in the same month; and the desperate wounding and capture of Mosby himself near Rector's Cross-roads, December 21. The wounded colonel gave his captors a false name and they left him at the farm house whence his men 'spirited' him through the country and saved him from recapture although the country was scoured by several thousand Federal cavalry.

Notwithstanding the devastation in "Mosby's Confederacy," the families were not deported and imprisoned, as ordered, and the battalion found shelter during the winter. In February 1865 a Federal force of 224 cavalry was sent into Loudoun County to disturb the men, and the official reports show that a remnant returned with a tale of a mysterious panic, with Mosby's cavalry emptying their cartridges into a mass of disorganized Federal soldiery, and then beating them over the heads with empty pistols, a flight for safety, and the major and 78 men missing. Major Richards led the fight and reported 100 Federals killed, wounded and captured. Thus the battalion held its ground to the last. A new company, H, was organized April 5, 1865, with George Baylor as Captain, and Edward Thompson, James Wiltshire and Franklin Carter as lieutenants. It at once went out and stormed Bolivar Heights, capturing 77 horses and 47 men. On March 21 Mosby had defeated Colonel Reno and the Twelfth Pennsylvania Cavalry at Hamilton and about the time of Appomattox there were active operations in Fairfax, the Valley and Northern Neck.

After the surrender a Federal force was sent up the valley to parole detachments of the Confederates under the terms of the capitulation of the Army of Northern Virginia. Mosby was at first excepted, under orders from the War Department at Washington, but General Grant interfered and directed General Hancock to tender parole to Mosby and his battalion. After considerable negotiation the command was assembled at Salem for the last time on April 21, and Colonel Mosby issued his farewell order in which he said: "I disband your organization in preference to surrendering it to our enemies. I am no longer your commander." The main body under command of Lt. Col. Chapman was paroled and Colonel Mosby himself, as soon as assured of personal security, also availed himself of the tendered parole, and the history of his famous command was at an end.

He Felt John Brown's Pulse

DR. THOMAS LEE SETTLE

By CARLTON STAPLES

Humility, dignity, and the desire to avoid publicity in life have caused one worthy of much recognition to fade through memory to the threshold of the forgotten past. However, those who knew Dr. Thomas Settle will always remember his skill as a physician, his dry humor, and his devotion to people.

Dr. Settle was born February 12, 1836, in Paris (Fauquier County), Virginia, the son of Abner and Isabella Settle. Abner Settle ran a general store in Delaplane and possibly at one time had a store in Paris where he lived.

After attending local schools Dr. Settle attended a school in Vermont and was graduated from a medical college in Louisville, Kentucky, where he also served a short period on the staff of a hospital.

Louisa Hampton O'Rear, who was born in 1833 in the old Ashby home on the western slope of the Blue Ridge Mountain a mile west of Paris, married Dr. Settle in 1861. The marriage took place in the parlor of the present Settle home. They became the parents of eight daughters and two sons. One son at the age of seven and Mrs. Settle died from diphtheria in 1884. Dr. Settle never married again.

For a number of years Dr. Settle had his office in a building in the yard of the Settle home. In addition to patients who came to the office it became the place for the men of the community to assemble after the day's work to spin many tall and humorous tales. In later years his office was moved to a room in the Settle house.

It was Dr. Settle who felt the pulse of John Brown and pronounced him dead at Brown's execution. During the War Between the States, Colonel Charles T. O'Ferrall was so badly wounded near Upperville that he was considered dead by many, but a ray of life was detected by Alfred Ferguson who had him taken to the old Dunbar home northwest of Upperville where Dr. Settle gave medical attention, and is given credit for saving Colonel O'Ferrall's life. Colonel O'Ferrall, who later became governor of Virginia, gave Dr. Settle a plain gold ring with "friendship and gratitude" engraved on the inside. The ring, being endless, was to be symbolic of the duration of the friendship.

Alfred Ferguson was from Winchester, and on December 21, 1893 was appointed postmaster of the Winchester postoffice.

Dr. Settle was imprisoned at Fort McHenry for three months. The story is reliably told of one case where Dr. Settle, treating a patient wounded through the lung, found it necessary to draw a white silk handkerchief through the patient's chest to clean the wound.

After having been paralyzed almost three years earlier Dr. Thomas

Lee Settle died on August 26, 1920, at the age of eighty-four. Dr. Settle was born, lived, practiced medicine, was married, and died in the same house. During his sixty-two years of practice his visits were made by buggy or horseback. Roads and weather were never too bad for him to go to relieve illness and very often cheer a despondent spirit.

Memories of his life are cherished by those who knew him, and his record is a surviving challenge for those who follow.

'First Blood of The War'

JOHN QUINCY MARR

Captain, Warrenton Rifles

John Q. Marr was born in Warrenton, Fauquier County, on the 27th of May, 1825. On his father's side he was principally of French and on his mother's chiefly of English descent.

His father, John Marr, Esq., who died in 1848, was the grandson of a Frenchman, who, after the revocation of the Edict of Nantes, is said to have sought with two brothers a refuge from tyranny in the wilds of America.

The two brothers of this ancestor, soon after their arrival in this country, removed to Carolina. It has been said that at this time of their history the family name was La Mar, the article having been afterwards dropped.

One brother, who remained settled in what afterwards became the county of Fauquier, had two sons, Daniel and Thomas. Thomas was killed at Braddock's defeat, being in the colonial troops under the command of Washington.

Daniel was the father of numerous children, only one of whom survived (Daniel Marr, Esq. of Campbell County, Va.). Daniel Marr, the elder, died in 1826. His eldest son, John Marr, the father of John Q. Marr, was for many years a resident of Warrenton, the county seat of Fauquier. The maiden name of the mother of John Q. Marr was Catherine Inman Horner.

John Q. Marr entered the Virginia Military Institute as a cadet in July, 1843, and graduated in 1846 with the second distinguished honor of his class.

He was afterwards appointed assistant professor of mathematics and tactics at the Institute, and filled this post with great credit until called home by the death of his father.

It was at the election for delegates to the convention which passed the ordinance of secession that the most decided proof was exhibited of the people's confidence in his safe judgment and ability to serve them, when we regard the dangerous crisis, the magnitude of the trust committed to his hands, and the overwhelming vote which manifested the general confidence. Such was the people's trust in his judgment and the purity of his purposes, and the probity which would govern and control it, that they confided the mighty trust to him by a vote much larger than they gave even to his talented and trusted colleague (Robert E. Scott).

After the raid of John Brown, he organized, in his native village, a military company known as the "Warrenton Rifles," and with indefatigable industry drilled and instructed it in the art of war.

John Q. Marr was commissioned as lieutenant-colonel in the active volunteer forces of Virginia, his commission bearing date the 5th of May, 1861. Although he knew of the existence of this commission, he never saw it, it having been sent by mistake to Harper's Ferry. During the war, it was rescued from the letters remaining in the deadletter office at Richmond, and is now in the possession of his family.

The indications of hostile collision with the Federal authorities that immediately followed that ordinance (of secession) caused him to address himself at once to his military duties, and his company was soon marched towards the Potomac River, where the danger seemed most threatening.

On the morning of Saturday, June 1, 1861, the sentinels of the Virginia troops, then in barracks at Fairfax Court-House, were driven in by a company of United States Cavalry, who swiftly followed them into the village. The enemy came by a side road, entering on the north. The Virginia forces consisted of a cavalry company from Prince William, a company of cavalry from Rappahannock, and the Warrenton Rifles, commanded by Captain John Q. Marr. The cavalry, composed entirely of raw levies and imperfectly armed, misinformed as to the force of the enemy, gave way at the onset, and left the Rifles unsupported to deal with the foe. It unfortunately happened that, as his men were being conducted into the inclosure, about one-half of them were cut off by the retreating horsemen, and, thus separated from their companions, the remaining half got into action, so that there were only about forty men engaged in the skirmish.

The assailants, numbering about eighty-six men, under Lieutenant Tompkins, separated. Part of them charged along the road which leads through the village, while the other part, supposed to be under the guidance of the officer in command, passed in pursuit of the fugitives through the inclosure in which the Rifles were stationed. As these passed, Captain Marr was heard to challenge them, asking, "What cavalry is that?" and these were the last words that issued from his lips. Scattering shots were interchanged, and the pursuers passed on. Without their captain, and ignorant of his fate, without their first or second lieutenant, both of whom, at the beginning of the fight, were unfortunately absent, these forty riflemen, who had never before heard the report of an enemy's gun, composed, in part, of youths of seventeen and eighteen years of age, stood unfaltering in their position, while well-trained troopers charged in front and rear. At this moment ex-Governor William Smith, who chanced to be in the village, appeared among them, with Colonel (afterwards General) Ewell, who took the direction of their movements. The enemy, soon desisting from their pursuit, collected together a short distance upon the turnpike road and charged back upon the village. The Rifles, advancing to the roadside, by a well-directed fire drove them back. Again they returned to the attack, when a deadly volley, emptying many saddles, threw them into confusion. They broke through the fencing and fled from the conflict. The loss of the enemy in killed, wounded, and missing was probably not under thirty. The casualties on our side were one killed, one wounded, and four missing. In the beginning of the fight Colonel Ewell received a wound in the shoulder. Until a late hour in the morning the fate of Captain Marr was unknown, and it was hoped that he would reappear with the missing part of his company; but upon search being made in the clover lot, where the challenge was given, his body was found with a shot through the heart.

When the sad intelligence of his death reached his native place the Confederate flag was lowered to half-mast, and a gloom overspread the countenances of all. His remains, which reached Warrenton on Saturday evening between six and seven o'clock, were met and escorted into the town by the Lee Guard, and a large concourse of citizens. On Sunday afternoon, at five o'clock, after a feeling tribute had been paid to his memory by Rev. O. S. Barten, in the Clerk's Office yard, in the presence of at least fifteen hundred persons, he was buried, in full dress uniform, with the honors of war.

In the report of the adjutant-general for the year ending September 30, 1862, we find the following in the memorial list of the eleves of the Virginia Military Institute in the war for independence of the Confederate States of America:

"J. Q. Marr. Graduated July 4, 1846. Member of Virginia Convention. Entered military service as captain of Virginia volunteers, April, 1861. Killed at Fairfax Court-House, May 31, 1861. First blood of the war."

(From: Walker, Charles D.: MEMORIAL, VIRGINIA MILITARY INSTITUTE, BIOGRAPHICAL SKETCHES OF THE GRADUATES AND ELEVES OF THE VIRGINIA MILITARY INSTITUTE WHO FELL DURING THE WAR BETWEEN THE STATES. Philadelphia. Lippincott, 1875.)

Refugee of Ravenscroft

ROBERT HENRY DOWNMAN

Robert Henry Downman, CSA, of Ravenscroft, Fauquier County, Virginia. Born at Layton Stone, Fauquier County, September 9, 1833. Died at Warrenton, October 8, 1891. University of Virginia 1850-53. Black Horse Cavalry. Served in the Confederate Army during the entire Civil War. Major on General Rooney Lee's staff at the surrender of General Lee at Appomattox. Clerk, Fauquier County Court, Warrenton, 1866 until his death in 1891.

In 1817 a bride and groom, Mr. and Mrs. John B. Downman, came to Warrenton, Virginia, from "Belle Isle," Lancaster County, Virginia. They lived there until 1821, while they were building their home, "Layton Stone," one mile north of Remington, Virginia, on 1500 acres which John B. Downman's grandfather had bought from W. William Robinson on March 19, 1773. The house was brick, 40 by 50, with a wing.

They had in time 10 daughters and 3 sons, all three of whom served in the Confederate Army. John B. Downman gave his second son, Robert Henry Downman, some land southeast of Layton Stone where he built a frame house called Ravenscroft.

On April 30th, 1856, he married Frances Scott Horner.

When the war clouds began to gather, he joined the Black Horse Cavalry. At the time of John Brown's Raid at Harpers Ferry, this Cavalry was called out, with other troops to quell the insurrection.

Early in 1862, Union troops under General Pope were moving into lower Fauquier for their spring campaign. Robert Henry Downman's family had to seek refuge. His wife and four children, one of them only three months old, and two servants, left with what few possessions they could take with them, and went to Bremo Bluff. This young wife was not to see her home again for Union troops tore down the house to use the lumber to make a marquee for a ball for General Pope.

On March 12th, 1862, the Yankee troops burned Layton Stone and used the rail fences for camp fires and slaughtered, or drove off, all the cattle and other livestock.

Robert Henry Downman served the Confederacy during the entire war and was a major on General Rooney Lee's staff at the surrender of General Lee at Appomattox.

The terms of the surrender allowed him, as other officers, to return to his home with his horse and arms. He joined his wife and five children at Bremo Bluff and brought them to Warrenton. He became Clerk of the Court at Warrenton, and served in this capacity until his death.

Today on the West Wall of the Clerk's Office, there is a portrait of him wearing his Confederate uniform.

Lincoln Wanted Him in His Cabinet

ROBERT EDEN SCOTT
1808-1862

By JOHN K. GOTT

Robert E. Scott, the son of John and Elizabeth (Pickett) Scott, was born in Fauquier County on 22 April 1808. Mr. Scott was educated at the University of Virginia, studied law and was admitted to the bar of Fauquier County in 1829. He was elected Commonwealth's Attorney and for years served in the Virginia Legislature.

He was a member of the Constitutional Convention of 1850 and of the Convention of 1861 that passed the ordinance of Secession, in which Convention he supported the Union until Virginia seceded. He was a member of the Provisional Congress of the Confederate States, July, 1861 and in September was a candidate for the C. S. Congress.

During the turbulent interval between the election and inauguration of Mr. Lincoln, among the various important matters which had attention was the formation of his Cabinet. (1)

Within a month after the election of November 1860, Senator William H. Seward, who had been his principal competitor for the Republican nomination, was offered and agreed to accept the office of Secretary of State, although later he was inclined to recall his acceptance. Immediately thereafter Lincoln and Seward began thinking about the other Cabinet positions, and in that connection two citizens of Northern Virginia, residing in Fauquier and Culpeper Counties, were considered. The President-elect and his prospective Secretary of State were naturally anxious to discourage the secession movement and believed that a step towards that end might be the selection of one or more Southern men for the Cabinet.

From the beginning there was grave concern as to the course Virginia would take. Everybody recognized the importance of Virginia's relation to the far-flung controversy then raging. More than any other state Virginia had been responsible for the success of the Revolution and the adoption of the Constitution. Historically and geographically her position was pivotal and any decision she made could be expected to exert a powerful influence on the states a little further south; affect the entire trend of events, and bear vitally on the future of the Union.

It is therefore not surprising that Seward in regard to the selection of the Cabinet should have promptly turned to Virginia. In a letter to Lincoln dated December 28th, he said: "I have had my thoughts directed to the Hon. Robert E. Scott of Virginia as a gentleman whose ap-

1. Moore, R. Walton: "Two Virginia Citizens Were Considered for President Lincoln's Cabinet and One of Them Offered an Appointment" in THE NORTHERN VIRGINIAN, Fall 1932, pp. 13f.

pointment to a place in your Cabinet might be exceedingly wise at the present juncture. It strikes me now so favorably that I beg to ask you to take it into consideration. I shall write you again after getting some further information."

Mr. Scott, though he had held no federal office and confined himself pretty closely to his profession as a lawyer and as representative to the state from Fauquier, was recognized as an outstanding leader of the Whig party in Virginia. Lincoln replying to the Seward letter, on January 3, 1861 wrote: "It certainly would be some advantage if you could know who are to be at the heads of the War and Navy Departments; but until I can ascertain definitely whether I can get any suitable man from the South, and who, or how many, I cannot well decide."

On January 15th he wrote Lincoln: "I think Mr. Scott has been terrified into dropping the subject about which I wrote you. He has not come to see me, so we will let him pass if you please."

Seward's assumption was very wide of the truth. Scott was not the kind of man to be swayed by fear, for no one exceeded him in political courage. It is clear from a letter to a friend written January 18th only three days after the date of Seward's last mentioned letter, that Scott knew he was being talked of for the Cabinet; that he had no wish to be appointed; and that he did not believe he should accept an appointment if tendered. He based this view not on any fear of the consequences to himself, but on his opinion that in such a position it would not be possible for him, so to adjust himself to the situation as to render service of real value.

Such was the attitude of affairs when Mr. Scott received at Oakwood, his home in Fauquier, a message from Mr. Seward of Mr. Lincoln's administration, inviting him to a consultation in respect to the public disorders. (2)

Mr. Scott went to Washington hoping that something might be done by the new administration to reunite the States or preserve the general peace. Although the strong bias of his character was towards conservatism in government, he recognized the fact that the Union had worked off its centre and that the balance of sections would have to be restored as a condition of permanent settlement. Therefore when invited by Mr. Seward to state his opinion as to the policy which ought to be pursued to recall the detached States, he answered: (3)

" 'Justice, Mr. Seward, justice! Do the South justice, and I will engage that every State will return to the Union and abide with you forever.'

2. Hayden, Rev. H. E.: VIRGINIA GENEALOGIES. (Washington, 1931) pp. 651f.

3. Conversation reported by Col. John Scott, brother of R. E. Scott, in his book, SELF GOVERNMENT IN AMERICA: AN INSIDE VIEW OF THE GREAT REPUBLIC. (London, 1890)

"If justice be all that the South demands she will assuredly receive that at our hands."

Mr. Scott was a direct man, he was a matter of fact man, and not at all given to the fence of words, so he said to Mr. Seward:

"The kind and measure of justice which the South now demands from you is not such justice as is contained in promises or paper guarantees. She must have a substantial guarantee. She demands to be admitted to equal power with the free soil section in every department of the government—in the legislature, in the judiciary, in the presidential office. The South must have equality in the Union as the condition of its restoration."

This brought the conversation to an abrupt termination, for Mr. Seward responded promptly and with emphasis:

"That cannot be. The North will never consent to part with its supremacy in the Union."

On January 27th Mr. Seward wrote Mr. Lincoln as follows: "I saw Mr. Robert E. Scott today. He is a splendid man and would be a fit and creditable representative of the Southern Union party. Whether he is not too exacting for his section to make a practical minister for you is quite doubtful in my mind. I will think more." He and Mr. Lincoln promptly did more thinking because Scott was actually invited to become a member of the Cabinet as Secretary of the Navy.

On January 14th the Virginia Legislature had ordered the election of a State Convention and Mr. Scott, with his colleague, the Hon. John Quincy Marr, became a candidate for delegate from Fauquier County and did everything in his power to insure deliberate action by preventing public opinion becoming inflamed.

Mr. Scott, too old for military service, while at his home in May 1862 was shot and killed while resisting marauders who were terrorizing the community. The following account of the murder of Mr. Scott is from the NATIONAL INTELLIGENCER, Washington, May 20, 1862:

"Hon. Robert E. Scott of Fauquier Co., Va., was killed on Saturday, the 3rd inst., at Frank Smith's, (4) near Salem, Fauquier Co. A couple of Geary's or Blenker's men, supposed to be deserters, having committed many depredations through the country, among other things violating a woman, Robert E. Scott, with Winter Payne and others, some ten or twelve, made an attempt to capture them at Smith's. On approaching the house Mr. Scott and his overseer, Delaney, were shot dead by the deserters; the others ran, and Scott's double barrel gun was afterwards broken over him by the villains. The deserters escaped. One account says Mr. S. went to the Provost Marshal at Warrenton to have a detail of soldiers to arrest the marauders, and that these soldiers were

4. The home of G. W. F. Smith at Meadowville is still standing on the hill, on Rt. 17, right of the road from Warrenton to Marshall. It is now the property of Mrs. J. W. McIntosh and is called Overlook Farm.

the persons who accompanied Mr. S. to their place of rendezvous when he was shot. The event gives the deepest pain in Washington to all classes, and particularly to the administration, as Mr. Scott was one of the noblest of Virginia's sons, and was seeking the return of his State to the Union."

The murder of Mr. Scott was brought before the U. S. Congress, where immediate action was taken by the passage of a resolution in the House, May 8, 1862, calling upon the Secretary of War for information relative to the homicide. In response to the letter of Secretary Stanton, Gen. Geary made the following report, which will be found in Ex. Doc., 37th U. S. Cong., 2d Sess., No 113, Vol. 9, 1861-2

Headquarters Detached Brigade,
near Rectortown, Va, May 13, 1862

"Sir: Various versions of the recent shooting of Robert E. Scott and John Matthews, citizens of Fauquier Co., Va., having obtained currency, I herewith respectfully beg to submit to you a correct statement of the occurrence, a detailed account of which was furnished by me to Major General Banks. It was reported to me that two deserters from another branch of our army were committing depredations between Salem and Warrenton, when I immediately detailed Lt. Wells, with a detachment of 1st Mich. Cav., to trace them up. Guerrilla cavalry infesting the neighborhood, a squad was sent forward in advance, who returned and reported to the Lt. that Messrs. Scott and Matthews had been killed by the two men in question, when the whole party hurried to the scene of action, which was on the farm of Franklin Smith, about 5 miles from Warrenton. They there found the bodies of the two citizens and that of one of the supposed deserters, and ascertained that the two soldiers had been occupying a house for some time, when upon this day (May 3) Robert E. Scott, dec'd, led a party to capture them, among which were John Matthews, dec'd, Robert Hames, George Riley, Winter Payne, Alfred Perkins, Edward Briggs, J. W. Heflin, and Tibley Page, all residents of Warrenton and vicinity. Mr. Scott was shot while entering the house at the head of the party, gun in hand, and Mr. Matthews in the melee consequent upon the attempted escape of the two soldiers. One of the soldiers was shot by a citizen in attempting to escape; the other escaped to the mountains, where Lt. Wells did not deem it safe to pursue him owing to the presence of bodies of guerrilla cavalry.

"I have since learned that the remaining soldier voluntarily gave himself up to the commanding officer at White Plains. His name is H. H. Bayard, and that of his comrade who was shot was William C. Franklin. He represented that they were both privates in Capt. A. Gordon's Co. of 7th Reg. Wisconsin Vols., Gen. King's Brigade. The initials of the names and their identity with the regiment named, are shown upon the blankets found upon the site of the melee. Bayard stated that they had been taken prisoner by scouts of the enemy, from whom they had escaped, and that they were in search of the command to which they belonged when the attempt was made by the citizens to capture them.

"It appears, however, that they had been guilty of marauding in the section through which they passed.

Very respectfully yr. ob't serv't,
John W. Geary, Brig. Gen. Com'g."

The Rev. Mr. Hayden gives a further account sent to him by a member of the Fauquier bar:

"In the spring of 1862 two deserters from the U. S. Army were plundering the people in lower Carter's (Run) valley, Fauq'r Co., and frightening women and children. The citizens appealed in vain to the Federal Commander for protection or for men to arrest and remove the marauders. The officers replied that they could not risk a small squad of soldiers for such a purpose, and advised the citizens to arrest and take before them the lawless parties for punishment. Accordingly Mr. Scott and some ten other elderly gentlemen of that region went in search of the deserters, and traced them to the Winchester road, opposite G. W. F. Smith's house, where they had been the previous night. In going from Mr. Smith's gate to his house they had to pass that of one of his servants. The tramp of horses brought from the cabin one of the deserters without arms. Mr. Scott, who was at the head of the column, said to him, "You are my prisoner," whereupon he promptly replied, "I surrender, but won't you let me speak with my comrade in the house?" Mr. Scott rejoined, "Yes, but we'll see him first." Whereupon Mr. S. turned to Thomas Digges, familiarly known as Bishop, and said, "Bishop, won't you take charge of this prisoner?" and retaining his position in front, Mr. Matthews and he riding side by side, moved to the cabin, where they immediately dismounted. Without waiting for the others to come up they walked upon the porch, and had scarcely opened the front door sufficiently to show Mr. Scott's form when a shot from within pierced his heart, and he fell back on the porch a dead man, exclaiming as he fell, "I'm shot—fire into the house!" Matthews, who was immediately behind him, stepped forward, but ere his foot touched the sill of the door a second shot entered his brain and he fell dead on the porch. The murderer had his own gun and that of his comrade, both of which he used in his deadly purpose. As soon as the firing began the prisoner bolted and ran into the garden back of the house, when those who had not dismounted pursued him on horseback. At the lower end of the garden a stone fence prevented further pursuit with horses. The prisoner leaped the fence and started up the hill, when one of the party shot and killed him. In the meantime the murderer, reloading his two guns, opened the back door wide enough to admit his gun and fired at the party by the stone wall. Whereupon they put the hill between themselves and the house, and despatched a messenger to the Federal officers in Salem, six miles off, for soldiers to capture the murderer, and one to Warrenton, seven miles away. A troop of 20 cavalry from Salem reached there first, only to find that the murderer had escaped. As soon as he found himself screened from view by the hill, he broke the guns of Messrs. Scott and Matthews, and with his own guns made good his retreat to his command near Thoroughfare. In the death of Mr. Scott was lost to us the wisest, best and most valuable man in the county."

In corroboration of all that has been said of Hon. R. E. Scott's eminent abilities and exalted character, also of the correctness of the accounts of his brutal murder and its effect upon the people at large much will be found in the McDowell Court of Inquiry, Nov., 1862, "Official Records of the Union and Confederate Armies, Series I, Vol. XII, pt. I, Reports," (Serial No. Vol. 15), pp. 47-49, 78, 294, 326.

Chieftains in Gray

By WALLACE D. PHILLIPS

BRIGADIER GENERAL RALEIGH EDWARD COLSTON

1825-July 29, 1896

Although this Confederate brigadier general had quite an exciting life, and a rather lengthy life for a Confederate officer, he has never been mentioned very much.

He was born in Paris, France, in 1825. His mother was a French lady. His father was Raleigh Colston, Jr., the son of Raleigh Colston, who was a brother-in-law of Chief Justice John Marshall and a member of the syndicate that John Marshall organized to purchase the Fairfax Manors after the Revolutionary War.

His father once owned Lot 49, now known as the Gulick House, in Upperville and he also owned Snowden Farm near Paris, Va.

Colston got his early education in Paris, France.

In the fall of 1843 he entered VMI from Hedgesville, Berkley County, Va. (now West Virginia), and graduated fourth in his class in 1846.

After graduation he stayed on to teach French at VMI, starting as lieutenant and assistant professor of French. When he resigned from VMI in 1846 he was a major, and professor of French.

Upon Virginia's seceding from the Union he went to Richmond with a group of officers and students from VMI as instructors for the volunteers that were flocking to the colors.

On May 2, 1861, he was made colonel and mustering officer of the 16th Va. Inf. Volunteers. This regiment was later called the 26th Va. Infantry Volunteers.

December 24, 1861, he was made brigadier general of a brigade and was under Longstreet in the Peninsular Campaign.

In April 1863 he was given the Third Brigade under Jackson. As the Division Commander—General Trimble—was out sick, Jackson placed Colston in Command of the division and picked this division to lead the attack in the opening of the Battle of Chancellorsville. Jackson had implicit confidence in Colston's ability.

After Chancellorsville, and the death of Jackson, Colston was ordered to report to General Beauregard and was placed in command of a brigade of Georgians at Savannah and also in command of defenses of St. Augustine River.

When Union General Butler landed at City Point and threatened Petersburg, General Colston was ordered to Petersburg where he remained in command of the lines south of the Appomattox until General Lee came with the Army of Northern Virginia.

At the war's end we find him in command at Lynchburg.

We next find him at a military school that he established in North Carolina.

He soon accepted a Colonelcy in the Egyptian Army.

On an exploration trip in the Sudan he fell from a camel and was paralyzed from the waist down. In this condition he continued his exploration until quite a while later he met up with a party that sent him back to Alexandria (Egypt) by litter bearers.

He was discharged in 1879 and came home crippled and financially embarrassed.

He was able to get a job as a War Department Clerk which he held until 1894.

The last two years of his life were spent in the Confederate Soldiers Home in Richmond and he died there on July 29, 1896.

Too late I stayed, forgive the crime,
Unheeded passed the hours;
For noiseless falls the foot of time
which only treads on flowers.
—R. B. Sheridan

BRIGADIER GENERAL LEWIS ADDISON ARMISTEAD
1817—July 3, 1863

The subject of this memorial was the son of General Walker Keith Armistead of Ben Lomond Farm between Kerfoot and Paris.

While yet in his teens he entered West Point, from North Carolina, in the Class of 1837. But he did not stay to graduate with his class.

During the Mexican War he won two brevets while serving with the 2nd U. S. Infantry Regiment,

In 1860 he visited his friend Turner Ashby at Markham. In the course of the conversation Ashby told him that John Brown's Raid could only mean that the troublemakers in the North would make another try at invading the South and would force the Southern States to secede. Armistead hadn't believed that such was the case. He told Ashby he didn't believe they would force a dissolution of the Union. He said he couldn't think of such a thing, and that he was all for the Union and that he had given the best years of his life in its military service.

In the spring of 1861 at a little known little town in California called Los Angeles the then Captain Winfield Scott Hancock gave a little party to say goodby to some officer friends who were going to Richmond to offer their services to the Southern cause.

As the party was breaking up, Mrs. Albert Sidney Johnston sat at the piano and played and sang "Kathleen Mavorneen". After the song had ended the then Major Lewis A. Armistead came over and put his hands on Hancock's shoulders, tears streaming down his cheeks, and said: "Hancock, goodby, you can never know what this has cost me."

His resignation from the Union Army became effective on May 26, 1861. However, his Confederate commission as a Major C.S.A. became effective March 16, 1861.

Late in the year he was promoted to colonel and given command of the 57th Va. Infantry Regiment.

On April 1, 1862, he was promoted to brigadier general and given a brigade in Huger's Division in the peninsula campaign. Later on, the division became known as Pickett's Division, Longstreet's Corps (The First Corps). Armistead stayed with this division until he was killed in the Third Day's Battle at Gettysburg, more commonly referred to as "Pickett's Charge". This was the best division in Longstreet's Corps. But President Davis had ordered some units left in middle Virginia as a safeguard against any Union forces getting between Lee and Richmond. Consequently they took the brigades of Jenkins and Corse out of Pickett's division and left them down in middle Virginia, leaving Pickett's Division at only three-fifths strength.

In the Third Day's Battle at Gettysburg, Armistead had the 9th, 14th, 38th, 53rd, and 57th Virginia Infantry Regiments under his command.

Armistead's Brigade was in support of Garnett's and Kemper's Brigades. His brigade was even back of Wilcox's Brigade which was protecting Kemper's right flank. They were to charge in the direction of a little clump of trees near that part of the line known as "The Angle".

Armistead placed his black hat on the end of his saber and held the saber aloft so that the men could see it and keep going in the proper direction.

Armistead's Brigade gained the Union Lines and Armistead led the advance through The Angle.

Alonzo Hersford Cushing, 1st Lieutenant, Battery A, 4th U S Artillery, the only survivor of his battery, and several times severely wounded, succeeded in having his only usable gun rolled down to the wall. By this time he was the only survivor able to stand up, and holding his intestines in his hands. As Armistead's Brigade came up, Cushing alone fired once before he died, point blank into Armistead's brigade and Armistead was one of those mortally wounded by the discharge of the gun. He staggered to the gun and fell over its muzzle.

Some Union officers came around and said something to Armistead and he is alleged to have pointed to his rations and said, "You can't whip men who can live and fight on this parched corn".

As fate would have it, it was Major Gen. Winfield Scott Hancock's II Corps of Meade's Army that Armistead's brigade went up against in this charge—the former Capt. Hancock of the old California Army days. Armistead's sword, spurs, and other personalty went to Hancock, allegedly upon the request of the dying Gen. Armistead.

There is a monument at the spot where General Armistead fell "marking the high tide of the Confederacy".

To every man upon this earth
Death cometh soon or late;
And where can man die better
Than facing fearful odds,
For the ashes of his fathers,
And the temples of his Gods!

—Unknown.

CAPTAIN BOWLES E. ARMISTEAD

Capt. Bowles E. Armistead was a brother of Brig. Gen. Lewis Addison Armistead who went the farthest in Pickett's Charge at Gettysburg and there is a monument there marking the spot where he fell mortally wounded.

Capt. Bowles E. Armistead joined Capt. Richard H. Dulany's company on July 24, 1861, at Union (now Unison), Va. as a 1st Corporal. Shortly after this the company was incorporated under Turner Ashby's command and designated as Company A, 6th Va. Cavalry. Ashby's brigade soon became known as the Laurel Brigade and it kept that designation all through the Civil War.

He was later promoted to 4th Sgt, then 2nd Lieutenant and shortly to 1st Lieutenant.

On May 23, 1862 at the Battle of Cedarville, under the eyes of Lieutenant General "Stonewall" Jackson, he was knighted on the field of battle for especially gallant conduct by a dashing General Officer. Brig. Gen. Wm. H. Payne came up and struck the then 1st Lieutenant Bowles E. Armistead on the shoulder with his saber and said, "I make you a captain upon the field."

However, he stayed with his company as a 1st Lieutenant and when the company commander, Capt. Bruce Gibson, was captured at the Battle of Yellow Tavern on May 11, 1864, Armistead was made acting captain of his company. But he remained at his permanent rank of First Lieutenant and signed his parole as such at Winchester on May 17, 1865.

BRIGADIER GENERAL TURNER ASHBY

Turner Ashby, "The Knight of the Valley", was born at Rose Bank near what is now Markham on October 23, 1828. His father was Col. Turner Ashby of the War of 1812, and his mother was the former Miss Dorothea Farrar Green of Rappahannock County.

Young Turner was delicate in his youth—but he persisted in indulging in outdoors sports with the other boys. Like most boys he soon acquired an animal pet, but his pet happened to be a wolf that he named Lupus. He soon had to get rid of him as everyone was afraid of a wolf for a pet.

His first education was from a hired tutor, a Mr. Underwood from the North, as was customary among the leading families in those days. After young Turner had passed the private tutoring stage his mother sent him off to school. But this he did not like at all. He just wouldn't stay away from the hills and valleys that he loved so well in the northern part of Fauquier County. So his mother sent him to Major Ambler's School which was nearby. He didn't take too well to studies there either.

After leaving school he went into the mill which was "under the hill" below his home. He took in a Mr. Sommerville as a partner and operated the mill until Mrs. Ashby sold her property to Edward C. Marshall who was then President of the Manassas Gap Railroad.

From Rose Bank he went across the railroad up on another hill to what is now called "The Craig".

In the meantime he had become very fond of tournaments, and being an expert horseman he was very successful in the competitions. Once he dressed as an Indian chief and rode in on a horse without bridle or saddle and won the tournament. His dark complexion and small stature made him easy to disguise as an Indian. They say he rode a horse like an Indian.

While the Manassas Gap railroad was being built he had organized a cavalry company of militia to maintain order when the laborers would get into drunken brawls. Every member of the company was an excellent horseman and they named their company "The Mountain Rangers".

In October of 1859, Ashby and his confreres were at the harvest festival (the last tournament of the year) on the banks of Pantherskin Run just below where Green Garden Mill now stands. It was the closest and the most expert competition that they had had. The excitement had gotten so great that the cheering had become something like a yell. A few years later, that same cheer became known as the "Rebel Yell". Later General Stonewall Jackson was wont to remark that it was the sweetest music he ever heard.

While at this harvest festival, word of John Brown's Raid reached the then Capt. Turner Ashby. He immediately told all of his "Mountain Rangers" at the festival to meet him in Harpers Ferry. He then set off for The Craig to get his equipment and notify his other Rangers to go to Harpers Ferry.

It was at Harper's Ferry and Charles Town awaiting John Brown's trial that he met a professor from the Virginia Military Institute named Thomas J. Jackson and a young army lieutenant named James Ewell Brown Stuart, and Ashby made a lasting impression on these two future generals.

After John Brown's trial, Ashby brought his mountain rangers home and dismissed them.

During the winter of 1860, a Maj. Lewis A. Armistead, who was later to leave his imprint in history in one of the most dramatic and spectacular battles of all time, paid a visit to his friend Ashby. The subject of John Brown's Raid came up. Armistead thought it was just a localized operation by a misinformed never-do-well. However, Ashby took a deeper and a more realistic view of the matter and told Armistead there were many behind Brown's attack and that they would keep on until they forced the South to secede.

As soon as Virginia seceded on April 17, 1861, Ashby assembled his little company of Mountain Rangers and proceeded to Harpers Ferry. In the organization of Col. Angus McDonald's regiment, known later as 7th Va. Cavalry, Ashby's company was known as Company "A". Ashby was made lieutenant colonel of the regiment. Ashby's brother as 7th Va. Cavalry, Ashby's company was known as Company "A". 7th Va. Cavalry.

Soon Col. McDonald had to resign due to age and physical disabilities.

Ashby did scouting duty along the Potomac in those early days. His brother Richard was brutally wounded in a skirmish while near Kelly Island and shortly died. This had a very depressing effect on Ashby.

General Patterson was so well covered by Ashby that he never learned that Gen. Johnston had left Winchester until Gen. Johnston was at the First Battle of Manassas. Thus Ashby missed First Manassas. He passed through Upperville that famous July 21, 1861, about the middle of the afternoon and went into camp for the night at Clifton Mill on the Pantherskin Run. This was near the home of Capt. John Fletcher whom Ashby considered his best captain.

On July 22, 1861, Ashby got to Manassas, too late for the battle. He had foxhunted over the Manassas plains, knew every pig path there.

In all his duties he did well and he always amply rewarded his superiors' confidence in him. Danger was no terror to him. But he was a terror to his enemies. While on the Potomac he would sometimes ride a picket line of fifty miles. His regiment was so effective that it was named the Laurel Brigade. When his command grew to twenty-six companies, the whole twenty-six were allowed to be called the Laurel Brigade.

His bravery and ability were invaluable to Jackson when he wanted

Dam 5 on the C&O Canal destroyed. It was Ashby's men who destroyed the dam after so many had failed.

While in Harpers Ferry and Charles Town in the winter of 1861-'62, he became a Master Mason of Equality Lodge 136 at Martinsburg.

Jackson placed great confidence in Ashby's scouting ability. Ashby was in front of the advances and he covered the rear of the retreats.

In February 1862, Judah P. Benjamin, the Confederate Secretary of War, commissioned Ashby to organize units of cavalry, infantry, and artillery to protect the Valley. This was quite an honor for an officer who had no military service prior to the war. No other man of like circumstance in either army had risen so fast.

In Jackson's Valley Campaign, Ashby had twenty-six companies of cavalry. His weakness was that he didn't have any staff and his discipline was lax. One visiting officer remarked that Ashby had the best officers he ever saw. His men knew him and would follow him anywhere. During the Valley Campaign, Ashby sometimes would have pickets from the top of North Mountain to the top of the Blue Ridge Mountain. Ashby would ride this picket line daily, nearly seventy miles. He was tireless and would stay in the saddle day and night sometimes.

His greatest desire was to follow out Jackson's instructions. He would shield Jackson's army from the enemy's observations and at the same time find out all about the enemy for Jackson.

Jackson's retreat up the valley had been very trying on Ashby. His single handed burning of the Mount Jackson bridge and protection of Jackson's rear had completely worn out Ashby and his men. Another unit was thrown in to relieve Ashby, but it failed, and Ashby had to take up the line again.

At Port Republic, Jackson needed time to get his Army across the bridge. Ashby was detailed to maintain a delaying action. He was everywhere in this battle. Soon a brigade of infantry was in a tight place. Ashby took charge and was leading them on when his horse was shot down. He proceeded afoot with his sword over his head encouraging his men to follow—"Forward, my brave men" were his last words. He went about six feet and was pierced by a musket ball and died almost instantly. This was June 6, 1862, just about sundown.

General Jackson said of him: "As a partisan officer, I never knew his superior. His daring was proverbial, his powers of endurance almost incredible, his tone of character heroic, and his sagacity almost intuitive in divining the purposes and movements of the enemy."

Far dearer's the grave or the prison,
Illumined by one Patriot's name,
Than the trophies of all who have risen
On Liberty's ruin to fame.

The Battle of Rectortown

It was a cold and rainy day, that first of January 1864, when Federal Capt. A. N. Hunter with 77 men of the Second Maryland Cavalry from Harpers Ferry rode hard and fast through Hillsboro and Purcellville searching for Mosby's Rangers.

As they had met with no sight of any of the Confederates anywhere, they became overconfident and pushed on into Upperville and everything there seemed to be serene until a rifle blast out of calm stillness left one of their command dead with a bullet hole in his head.

The cautious Capt. Hunter searched the neighborhood but found nothing and then galloped on to Rectortown. There he worked up a good case of "Creeps" as on all the hills around he could see, against the skyline, riders sitting their horses very calmly and very still and in no apparent intention of moving.

The Yankees were baffled, and didn't know what to make of the situation. The detachment stayed in Rectortown most of the day waiting for something to happen, and when nothing happened, decided it best to get out of Rectortown before night.

Capt. Hunter decided to go to Middleburg and struck out across the fields towards that place. About two miles northeast of Rectortown is a crossroads known as Five Points, and all five roads leading from there had stone fences.

As the Yankees were nearing Five Points, Captain William R. Smith with 35 of Mosby's Rangers from the 43rd Battalion of Virginia Cavalry swooped down upon the Yankees, completely demoralizing them. The Rangers got in behind the stone fences and poured deadly fire into the Yankees, completely routing them.

The Official Reports of the engagement were as follows:-

"Major: I have the honor to report that during the month of December there were captured by this command over a hundred horses and mules and about 100 prisoners. A considerable number of the enemy have also been killed and wounded. It would be too tedious to mention the various occasions on which we have met the enemy, but there is one which justice to a brave officer demands to be noticed. On the morning of January 1, I received information that a body of the enemy's cavalry were in Upperville. It being the day on which my command was to assemble, I directed Capt. William R. Smith to take command of the men while I went toward Upperville to ascertain the movements of the enemy. In the mean time the enemy had gone on toward Rectortown, and I pursued, but came up just as Captain Smith with about 35 men had attacked and routed them (78 strong), killing, wounding, and capturing 57.

"Respectfully, your obedient servant.

JNO. S. MOSBY,
Major, Commanding"

"Maj. H. B. McClellan,
Assistant Adjutant-General"

(First indorsement)

HDQRS Cavalry Corps, February 13th, 1864

Respectfully forwarded.

"A subsequent report of subsequent operations has been already sent in, this having been mislaid. Major Mosby continues his distinguished services in the enemy's rear, relieving our people of the depredations of the enemy in a great measure.

J. E. B. STUART
Major-General"

(Second indorsement)

"February 15th 1864

"Adjutant-General:

"A characteristic report from Colonel Mosby, who has become so familiar with brave deeds as to consider them too tedious to treat unless when necessary to reflect glory on his gallant comrades. Captain Smith's was a brilliant and most successful affair."

"J.A.S."

Cure for Rheumatism

It was customary when a soldier was sick or incapacitated for some reason, and wanted to return home, to send along another soldier to see that he got home safely.

One day a Mr. Kerrick from the Markham neighborhood became all crippled up with rheumatism and wasn't able to do military duty and could hardly move about. The captain of the company released a Mr. Payne, from the same neighborhood, to accompany Mr. Kerrick home.

They started out and due to Mr. Kerrick's rheumatism they made slow time. One evening they came upon walnuts some children had hulled and ricked up. Both men decided to sit down and crack enough walnuts to satisfy their hunger. One got at one end of the rick and the other got at the other end of the rick.

But what they didn't notice was that some Yankees were away over on another hill. As soon as the Yankees saw them at the walnut rick they brought up a small cannon and fired at them. The shell struck the rick about middle ways and scattered walnuts everywhere. The two Confederates jumped up and started running to escape capture and Mr. Kerrick outran his escort Mr. Payne. After a few days at home, Mr. Payne took Mr. Kerrick back to the army with him and Mr. Kerrick was never bothered with rheumatism any more.

A Long 100 Yards

One of the Green family from the Paris area was serving in an infantry company. The captain halted the company one evening about sundown in an area where the road was crooked, hilly, and overgrown with trees, bushes, and weeds. The captain had decided to rest his men there for a while and he said to Green, "Private Green, you go down the road about a hundred yards and stand picket." Green immediately spoke up, disregarding all military courtesy, and said, "Look-a here man, you don't know how far down that road a hundred yards is, do you?"

Eating on The Run

In that very hot July of 1861 when Gen. Joseph E. Johnston was quietly and rapidly moving his little army from the Shenandoah Valley to the First Battle of Manassas he was entraining his infantry at Piedmont Station, now Delaplane, to be transported in the cars, as they spoke of passenger coaches in those days.

When two of the trains had been loaded and were ready to go, the engineers, who happened to be Union sympathizers, prearranged to have a train collision, and they ran the trains together, which caused a serious delay in the movement of the balance of the troops.

The road from Paris to what is now Delaplane was soon blocked with infantrymen.

The companies that then came into Paris turned off and came by the way of Upperville at quick step to make sure that they wouldn't be left behind when the cars got to rolling again.

The men that went by Upperville never stopped to eat nor drink water. The children, the servants, and the men along the route who hadn't gone to the colors, took food and water, milk and coffee, out to the soldiers and trotted alongside the soldiers while they marched and ate until the containers were empty. They then would run back to the house and load up again and run back out to the road and give to another company of men that would be passing their particular spot at the time.

Bag Jackson

When Jackson was outmaneuvering the Federal generals in the Valley in the late spring of '62, the Federal authorities in Washington hit upon the idea of sending up some reinforcements composed principally of foreigners who knew only a few words of English. They did learn some way that lots of houses in Upperville had honey in jars. So they raided all the houses poking their hands in the jars and putting their fingers in their mouths, sucking off the honey from their fingers and saying "Hooney goo-oode". They didn't stop at the honey jars.

Some houses had soft soap and they stuck their fingers in the soft soap and ate it just like they did the honey.

When asked what they came over here for they would reply in chorus, "Bag Jackson". "Bag Jackson" was all they seemed to know what they were here for. However, their guides and maps too were inferior and they got good and lost in the woods and hills west of Strasburg and wandered around and nearly starved until they were finally rescued. For some reason Jackson never tried to capture them which he could easily have done. He must have thought he could use his forces better elsewhere.

Execution at Rectortown

On September 22, 1864, Capt. Sam Chapman with 120 men from Co. E, 43rd Battalion, Virginia Cavalry, Mosby's Rangers, left Piedmont Station (now Delaplane) and headed for Chester's Gap to knock over a Federal picket post that the 6th New York Cavalry were reportedly holding in Chester's Gap.

Before they reached their objective Sam Chapman learned that the gap was clear of the enemy. So he bivouacked on the west side of the Blue Ridge Mountains.

Early on the morning of September 23, 1864, Sam Chapman went to a good observation point to find out what was transpiring around the countryside. He soon saw a Federal ambulance train escorted by about 200 men moving towards Front Royal.

After making proper disposition of his men, the order to attack the train was given. Moving to the rear of the train, Sam Chapman saw Merritt's Reserve Cavalry Brigade coming in sight and he realized that he had sent his men into a death trap. He immediately instructed Lieutenant Harry Hatcher to take his portion of the command towards Chester Gap while he set off to try to intercept Capt. Frankland before he attacked. But he was too late. Frankland had charged and run over the escort and was at the ambulances. When Sam Chapman advised Frankland that he was attacking a brigade, Frankland misunderstood him and said, "Sam, we can't stop now, we've got them whipped."

As Blue cavalrymen were closing in from everywhere, Sam Chapman had nothing else left to do but wave his arm in a circle which meant for the Rangers to get out. Their only avenue of escape was to shoot their way out.

After they got away from Merritt's Bluecoats they collided with the 2nd U. S. Cavalry who had gotten lost and had found the Chester Gap road and had doubled back. The Rangers struck the Union Cavalry, pushed them back, and rode through them.

Those who came to clear the field of the losses of the battle found the body of Union Lieutenant McMaster lying prone in the road. The Unionists got the wrong impression that he was killed after he had surrendered. The Rangers contended that he was killed at the head of his detail trying to cut off the retreat of the Rangers.

The fiery and excitable Brigadier George A. Custer could see the situation only one way. He ordered seven Rangers executed. Two were shot at a church after much fanfare by a mob of Union soldiers. One was shot beneath an elm tree after the same riotous actions as at the church. Two Union horsemen rode through the streets dragging, roped to their saddles, a seventeen year old schoolboy, who had borrowed a neighbor's horse hoping to catch a stray horse so that he could join Mosby's Rangers. The borrowed horse had broken down and the rider had been captured. He was shot after the ordeal of being dragged and while still dazed and helpless. The last two were hanged between Front Royal and the Shenandoah River. Later another Ranger was hanged in Rappahannock County by a brigadier named Powell in command of a detachment of West Virginia Unionist troops.

When Mosby recovered from his wound and again assumed command, he apparently took notice of the horrible murder of his seven Rangers. After he had captured 700 or so Union soldiers from Sheridan's Army he kept close tab on the different prisoners that he had captured from Custer's and Powell's Brigades. He explained to General Lee the atrocious acts committed by Generals Custer and Powell and gave his plans for retaliation. General Lee concurred with Mosby's plans.

On November 6, 1864, Mosby had 27 prisoners from Custer's and Powell's Brigades lined up at an old brick storebuilding near where the brick dwelling owned by Mrs. Nannie Ashby now stands in the western edge of Rectortown. They were to draw slips of paper from a hat and seven of the slips were marked and the ones who drew the marked slips were doomed to die as a reprisal for those Rangers bestially executed at Front Royal in the previous September. One of the doomed men happened to be a very young drummer boy. Mosby released the drummer boy and held a second drawing for his substitute.

The condemned prisoners were carried as near to Sheridan's Headquarters as possible and they got just a little west of Berryville on the road to Winchester. The guards proceeded with their assigned task as best as they could, but hanging proved too slow for them that close to Sheridan's forces and they decided to shoot the last three. They were then lined up for the firing squad. However, before the guards pulled the triggers one doomed man, a W. W. Badger, had worked his hands out of the ropes that bound them, and he knocked the gun aside and knocked the Confederate on the head and pushed him aside and ran into the darkness. Another doomed man was shot through the eye and the bullet came out of the back of his head. He kept very still for a long while and eventually gained consciousness and survived.

Sometime later when Mosby was at Richmond with another wound, he was invited to ride down on the prisoner exchange boat. The drummer boy whom he had released from the list of doomed men at Rectortown, was also on the boat. He came up and made himself known to Mosby and embraced him.

Stuart at Atoka—Rector's Crossroads

After successfully keeping Union General Alfred Pleasanton's cavalry out of the mountain gaps and away from the mountain peaks of the Blue Ridge Mountains, Major General Jeb Stuart settled down at Rector's Crossroads, (now Atoka), with part of his cavalry regiments to rest from the effects of the battles of Middleburg, Union (now Unison), and Upperville.

It was June 23, 1863, and Ewell was already tearing up through Pennsylvania, A. P. Hill was in Maryland, and "Bulldog" Longstreet was heading his First Corps northward after leaving Corse's and Jenkins' brigades of Pickett's division in middle Virginia to hold in check any Union outfits that should try to make a run for Richmond while Lee was north of the Potomac.

That evening late it began to rain hard and it was rainy all night. It was the custom of Stuart that all officers should stay out in the weather with the men. Major H. B. McClellan was on the porch of a nearby residence as messengers and scouts were bringing in reports all night and they didn't want the papers to get wet. Major McClellan was the adjutant for Stuart's division.

It was late at night and raining hard when a messenger brought in the order from General Lee to General Stuart's headquarters instructing him on his course to follow on the march of the Army into Pennsylvania. Major McClellan took a lantern and woke the General and read to him Lee's orders. Jeb Stuart already knew the approximate substance of the orders as he had conferred with General Lee when he passed through Paris on June 21 on his way to Pennsylvania through Ashby's Gap.

Before daylight Major McClellan was sending messengers with orders to the various brigades of the command. Thomason wrote, "And here at Rector's Crossroads crop up the first events that lose for the South the Gettysburg Campaign." One officer holding his orders and a candle under the cape of his coat misread his orders and didn't move his cavalrymen to the designated location when it was intended for him to do so.

The night of June 24 we find Jeb Stuart bivouacking at Salem (now Marshall) with the brigades of Wade Hampton, Fitz Lee, and Chambliss. At one a. m. of June 25 Stuart leaves Salem headed through Thoroughfare Gap on a wide swing around Hooker's Army to his assigned destination at Carlisle, Pa.

Stuart left his two largest brigades at Rector's Crossroads to watch for any straggling Federal outfits, and after the Federals were known to have crossed to the north side of the Potomac these units were to keep in touch with the commanding general and to follow close on Longstreet's heels, which they didn't do. They stayed east of the Blue Ridge too long and were late getting to Gettysburg. These two brigades were Beverly H. Robertson's and W. E. "Grumble" Jones' Laurel Brigade. Jones' was the largest brigade, but Robertson was the senior officer so he was in command of the detachment and any failures fell on him.

It was also here at Rector's Crossroads at the home of Clinton Caleb Rector, a staunch Confederate, (the home now owned by Maurice B. Rector) that Ranger Mosby last saw Jeb Stuart alive shortly before the Battle of Yellow Tavern, May 11, 1864.

—WALLACE B. PHILLIPS

General Lee Recommends A Promotion

(J. Stevens Mason lived at Rutledge, near Marshall, and was the grandson of George Mason.)

Hdqrs. 19 July '62

Hon'l G. W. Randolph
Secty of War
Gen'l.

Mr. J. Stevens Mason, at the Commencement of the War, entered the ranks of the Army where he has served faithfully ever since. He is a young Gentleman of good education, impeccable morals & beginning at the battle of Manassas has been engaged in the Subsequent battles in Eastern Virginia. His father, a descendant of George Mason of the Revolution, has been driven from his home & is thus deprived of the means of support for his family. J. Stevens Mason is a private in the 17 Rgt. Virg. Vols. I recommend him for promotion to a Lieut. ce in the C. A. should there be a vacancy or need of additional Lieutenants.

I have the honor to be
Your Obt. Servt.
R. E. Lee
Gen'l.

My Dear Stevens,

I enclose a letter to the Secty. of War as you request. There is great difficulty in getting appointments in the Army. The Pres. will make them in the C. A. Inasmuch as Congress refused to confirm those he had made which was considered as an indication of their wishes on the subject. Appts. on the Staff are usually made upon application of the officers requiring them.

I have not forgotten your Appt. and the services of others of my young kinsmen whom I would like to see rising.

The surest way is to rise in the rgts., get elected Lt. & so advance. Your merit then will soon bring you forward.

I am very truly yours
R. E. Lee

19 July 62

J. Stevens Mason.

In Memoriam: The Faithful Servants

(Continuing the recollections of Fielding Lewis Marshall)

(While countless instances of desertion and abduction could be recited, these pages should not pass without some words of tribute to the loyalty and devotion of countless others who remained, throughout the Southland, trustworthy and faithful, sharing in the tribulation at home and giving care and consolation, in full measure, in hours of greatest need.

(A particular bond grew with those who nursed the children and who were lovingly called "Mammy" as they became an integral part of the household, giving tender care with one hand and unhesitating chastisement with the other when needed. Many a man of renown has stood by the open grave of his childhood's "Mammy" with cherished memories and deep sorrow.

(Specifically, in the family churchyard plot at Emmanuel, "Mammy" lies buried, her name on the same stone with those she loved. In his Recollections, Fielding L. Marshall speaks of her devotion.)

My body-servant, Charles Jenkins, whom I inherited, with many other slaves from my father, was true as steel to me as long as I was in the field. I always felt that he was ready at any time to give his life for me. He was with me in the camp, and washed and cooked for me. He was foster-brother to Tom, who on account of mama's inability from illness to nurse him, drew his milk from the same black breast that Charles Jenkins did. (His mother was afterwards one of my house servants.) Charles, as head-man, managed Ivanhoe for three years of the war, and sent money, as he could, from farm to me, several hundred miles away in the army.

In passing, I must here say that none of my slaves deserted me, or left Ivanhoe during the whole war. Two men-servants, John 'Harrison and Cyrus, a youth, went with my children to take care of them in their exile from home, in '62, '63, '64 and '65.

They had with them also Mammy Sukey and Peggy, a young maid. John died before the war closed, having stayed with my motherless children and Mammy Sukey in the land of the stranger, in Amelia County. His body was buried there by my children, my daughter Mary reading the funeral service. Peggy they left behind, as she had married a man belonging to the estate of Hon. Senator William S. Archer. Cyrus made his way to Williamsburg, where his mother had lived, and where he himself was born. Sukey returned with us to Ivanhoe from Amelia in the spring of '65.

Mammy Sukey (Mammy to Rebecca and all her children), came to me with "Miss Becky", as she called Rebecca, when we were married, and was always with her mistress from her birth to her death. When she was driven from home by the ruthless hand of war to her death at Annandale as well as in her days of affluence, Sukey, the dear negro slave, was at her mistress' side. And night and day watched and guarded "Miss Becky's chil'n" during their three years of exile from home, ready at any moment to die for them.

Let the fanatic write such an epitaph as this, if he can, of any friend who did stick as closely to him and his! When the war closed, I gathered my children and Sukey to go home with what little they had. Sukey scorned so-called freedom. "I'se gwine to die with dese chil'n," were her words. She was very infirm and very fat, and needed the support, frequently, of those whom she had nursed so often and so long; and got it. I never spent more anxious moments in battle, or elsewhere, than I did when I had to support and conduct half-blind and weak old Sukey, leaning on my arm, across the Matoax River on a ruinous bridge of two loose planks, no wider flooring the whole way across. Her lament was touching, as she mourned the death of Miss Becky and saw the pinched life her children had to lead in what she called, in scornful terms, "dis Mealy" (Amelia). After crossing James River in the night, on a pontoon bridge with this helpless set, we worked our dreary journey home. There Sukey lived until you were born, my child; as loving to you, her "wide-eye chile", as she called you, who were so hard to put to sleep, as to any of Rebecca's children.

Sukey died in 1869, when, on her last day, she was shrouded, and her eyelids closed by "Miss Peggy and dem"; faithful into death to her earthly master so to her Heavenly; though she was never baptized or confirmed into any church. But no matter: we committed her to our God and hers too, my daughter Mary reading the funeral services of the church at her grave in our church yard. And when the Trumpet shall sound, Sukey will rise in the white robe of the Lamb.

I make this long tribute to Sukey that my children born since the war may contrast slavery with free-negrodom, and may see it was no sin against God or man to hold the negro in slavery; when he has chosen Abraham, a slave-holder, to be the father of the faithful; and St. Paul sent back Onesimus the runaway slave to his master.

I often think what might have been the condition of the master and slave had there not been a War between the States. Take, for example, the neighborhood in which I was: There was a proper pride of character that obtained amongst our old slaves, and respect for position and rank.

First about "the great house" was the dining room servant. Behind his master's chair at meals, he imbibed information on all the topics of the day discussed between his master and other gentlemen—whether about agriculture, religion or politics. I must here give you an illustration that recurs forcibly to my memory.

Joseph Brent, my father's and afterwards my brother John's dining room servant, was a coal black negro. He was six feet tall, very straight, and graceful in movement, pleasant in expression of face, though not handsome, and noiseless in his close attention to all he waited on. It was amusing to see him in conversation with the boy under him, and with the other servants, when off duty; as intuitively, and without the least effort, he seemed to catch the manner, the tones of voice and modes of expression his master had. He assumed, and without hesitation was accorded by the other servants, a rank superior to their own. When my father or brother was canvassing the county for the Legislature, no white friend was more zealous than Joseph that "we" (including himself as part and parcel in the matter) should succeed; and he would ride many miles, carrying from or bringing to him information more or less important. I remember how outraged he was, when in my father's last election (just before his death, which prevented him from taking his seat), the Democrat who opposed him contested his election. Joseph's words of indignation were unmeasured that such a man should dare to contest "Master's seat". When afterwards he became my Brother John's servant he retained the same post of honor. My brother often entrusted him with large sums of money when he had to send it to a distance, and always with perfect confidence in his integrity. And he was never mistaken. When after Brother John's death the house (Oak Hill) was sold, and Joseph fell to my charge to hire out, I exacted no security from him, but trusted to his honor to bring me his hire; and I never had cause to regret it. I gave him leave to live anywhere he pleased in Virginia.

I will state another incident in his life: My brother being away from home, and no one else in the house, everything was left in charge of the faithful Joseph. He had all the keys. It so chanced that a friend of my brother arrived about dark, and finding no one at home was about to proceed further, when Joseph, with profound respect and politeness, invited him to stay, saying "Marse John" would be much disappointed if he did not. The gentleman consented to remain. He was treated in every respect as he would have been had the master been at home and after breakfast proceeded on his journey to Winchester. Being asked the news and what and whom he had seen on his journey from Fredericksburg, he replied that he had seen but one gentleman on the road, and that was Mr. John Marshall's dining room servant at Oak Hill, and he was a perfect one. How long would it take to make such a one out of any Virginia freed negro of the present day?

Next in rank came the old black mammy of the children. She was always the most indulgent member of the family and loved most devotedly all the children, who heartily returned her warm affection. Many a time have I gone to my mammy's house after breakfast in "the house" and taken another with her. I can taste now the sop and corn-bread!

The cook, after the house servants above named, was the next in rank, whether male or female. The best I remember was Aunt Harvie's man-cook (and grandfather's cook) Henry. I remember the great kitchen fireplace, the huge andirons with rows of supports on them for the spits to revolve upon, as they were turned by the little black scullion, the happiest brat about the house, because when dinner was all done and sent in, he got the sops that were left, and some of the odd bits a cook knows so well how to save. Can you roast or broil with a Yankee stove? You have no fireplace now.

"Old Miss's" maid stood high, too, as well as the "Young Miss's" maids, given them to be theirs both then and when they left home, married women. I remember so well Sally Burwell, Sister Mary's maid. She was as black as the ace of spades. On one occasion, Sally, who had a most beautiful natural voice, seized the opportunity when, as she thought, all the white folks were absent, to steal into the parlor and open the piano. Sitting on the stool, she assumed the gestures and posture and poise of the head of Cousin Lucy Fisher who was a splendid performer, and staying at Oak Hill at the time. Striking the notes with both hands, she sang at the top of her really beautiful voice, "Call Me Miss Lucy Fisher! Piano! Piano!" —words and music her own.

The door was opened upon her, and Sally's improvising came to an end. She had great flexibility of voice, and on many occasions, by assuming the voice of her young mistress, would make Kitty—Sister Agnes' maid—very angry, upon the discovery that Sally and not Miss Agnes was calling her. She would call out Kit-tee! in Sister's voice, with a sharp rising inflection; and Kitty would answer Marm? Then changing her voice to that of a gruff over-servant, she would call out "Kit!" and Kitty would answer like a cat.

A boy of the age of his "Young Master" was likewise given to each of us boys. I remember Melford was given to Brother John, James Cooper to me and John (Mammy Harriet's son) to Tom. James was one of my carriage drivers. He died some years before the war.

The head man was chief among the farm hands. He had frequently to be restrained by the master in his too great rigor of discipline. He "blew the horn" at the crack of day, the year round, to summon all hands to work; and he came to his master the overnight for instructions. My head man Charles Jenkins, although by envious negroes and some of my neighbors accounted a crafty fellow, was always true to me as far as I ever knew. He was my body servant in the war. There was no fellow soldier I could count on as I could count on Charles. At any time he was ready to get between me and danger, aye, death itself.

Among my own slaves I recognized several true and humble followers of the master. I can name Sally Patterson, for one, wife and widow of my old carriage-driver Stirling, who had served my father and mother in that capacity. The last act of his life was done when, one evening, very late, he stuck his spade right by the asparagus bed that he was putting in proper condition, and went home to the couch from which he never rose. The spade was there though, awaiting the hand that never grasped it again. May I be as true to my master, and cherish and nurture the flowers and fruits put under my care, as true old Stirling did.

Others I might name, belonging to me and my brothers and sisters; but these suffice to show to the fanatic what manner of creatures we slave-scourging masters were.

For thirty years of my long life I was a slave holder. My slaves were inherited by me. I never bought one except at his or her request, to be with a husband or wife or near relative. I never sold one but for crime or violent disobedience or insubordination. The master or mistress treated the slaves as children, and loved them, and when they were old or disabled by sickness took care of them, tending them in person, and employing a doctor when necessary. They considered themselves, and were treated by their masters as part of the family, and when they died, they were buried in the graveyards on the farms. I have known many cases of the most devoted affection on their part for the white family.

Tolerably Well Situated In A Yankee Prison

(Excerpts from the correspondence of Lt. T. H. Foster, a prisoner of war with his mother and father, James W. Foster, at The Plains, February 13, 1863, to June 28, 1864.)

Johnson's Island
February 13th 1863.

My dear Ma:

I have written a great many letters to you, all of which have failed to reach their destination. Hope that this one will be received. Nearly all of Father's have come to hand. They afford me great pleasure.

To know that you are all well and have yet more to live upon is a pleasure and satisfaction which can only be realized by those who are in captivity and far from those who are near and dear to them. And while I lament the hard fate that has thrown me in this position, I have great cause to be thankful for my continued good health in this clime where death is reaping a rich harvest.

I wrote Father a short time since stating that I was well supplied with clothes, and that I had not received the "remittances" spoken of by him: that I had learned *that no money had been deposited in Baltimore to my cr;* and that his old and valued friend of that city had sent me nothing, *and has not been able to do so.*

I have received several **very kind** letters from him expressing his regret at his inability to do so. I can do very well without money and hope Father will put himself to no more trouble about my wants in that particular. The next time I write you I expect it will be from another prison. I would like to write you, my dear Ma, a long letter but can not do so. You will excuse this short unsatisfactory letter I know, as it occurs from no fault of mine. With much love to you all. Don't forget to give my love to Aunt Mary—I am,

Your Aff Son
T. H. Foster.

Johnson's Island
March 5th 63.

My dear Father:

I have received none of the remittances which you have mentioned and do not need them. We are tolerably well situated, and have some few sources of amusement. With Chess, Cards, Ball and the few books that have found their way to our enclosure, we endeavor to kill the time that hangs heavily on our hands. Ashby and Chichester have been sent to "Point Lookout". Payne and Randolph are well and desire to be remembered to you. Am in receipt of several letters from your old friend in Baltm. His circumstances are rather bad. That deposit was not made in Baltm. With much love to you all. Give my love to all the relations at The Plains. Tell old Uncle Tom he is not forgotten.

I am, Your Aff. Son

T. Hunton Foster.

(Addressed)
Wm. H. Gaines Esqr.
Care Provost Marshal
2nd Cavalry Division
Warrenton
Virginia.

Johnson's Island
March 31st 63

My dear Father:

Your letter of the 7th came to hand on the 28th of this month. I most earnestly wish you could have succeeded in your endeavors for several reasons. In the first place, I have but little faith in the continuation of the present slow mode of exchange, and fear it will "play out" before any are reached in this prison. In the second place, when reorganizations are taking place, and resignations being made, ones interest is apt to suffer, if not present to look after it in person. I am on this acct., to say nothing of confinement, hardships, separation from friends etc. extremely anxious to be released. But I can bide my time, though it tardily come. As I have never received any of the remittances mentioned in your letters, I was obliged to write to Mr. Brent of Alex. for twenty five dollars, which he very promptly sent me. Tell Ma and Mollie that I am looking for answers to my letters to them. We experienced severe weather this winter. No weather in our country to compare to it. And now bright spring is upon us, with all its joyousness, making captivity more insupportable and harder to bear. Give my love to all relations at The Plains, and to Ma, Mollie, Aunt Mary and the rest, and believe me as ever, Your Affet. Son

T. Hunton Foster.

The Plains Fauq. Cty. Va.
Nov. 20, 1863

To Lt. T. H. Foster

My dear Son

I wrote you recently through our connection Chs. Green Esq. advising that there was deposited with the House of Fisher & Son (formerly Jas. J. Fisher) of Balto. 100$ in par funds subject to your order.

This with the aid others have delivered ere this will make you comfortable.

We must not tax our friends too heavily these hard times but I feel particularly anxious you should be *well clothed,* and hope that you will not neglect yourself in this respect; and will not omit to purchase a *Bible* and *study* it. Your Company is now commanded by Dr. Weaver who has been elected to the third Lieutenancy. Col. Green is restored to his command. Lomax commands the Brigade. We are all well. Tell Willie all are well at his home. We are very anxious to hear from you direct. You can write under cover to Brown & Son near Berlin, Loudoun Cty. Va. Federal Officers assure me that a letter simply giving us information of your health, wants, condition etc. will not be intercepted or objected to. Praying that He who directs and controls all events, will protect you against all *besetting* sins, I remain,

Yr. aff. Father
Jas. W. Foster

Johnson's Island
Decb 6th 1863

My dear Father:

Your letter of Novb 20th informing me of the deposit of 100$ with the house of Fisher & Son of Balt. has just been received. I was surprised as well as pained to learn that you had received none of my letters—for I have written many and through different channels. I am well supplied with good warm comfortable clothes, which have been sent by different parties; which with the money to my credit in Balt. will make me as comfortable as is possible. So far as bodily comforts are concerned I am amply provided, and I hope you will give yourself no more concern about that—I am truly glad to learn that you are all well. Hope that you will write frequently as it is the only pleasure and consolation I have.

I am very well and my health is as good as usual. Willie is also well. Col. Payne writes home today through the same channel that I do and asked that you will forward.

Is there not some mistake about the election of Dr. Weaver to the 3rd Lieutenancy of the company to which I belong?

When I know that you receive my letters regularly I shall write frequently as it is a gratification to communicate with you all even in that way.

With much love to Ma, Aunt Mary & the children & yourself I am,

Yours Affly.

T. H. Foster.

(Addressed J. W. Foster, Care Thos. Brown & Son)

Johnson's Island
Near Sandusky, Ohio
Decb. 12th 1863

My dear Father:

Fearing from your last, which informed me of the deposit of some Money to my cr in Balt, that none of my letters have reached you, I again write you, with the hope that this one will be received. My wants in the way of clothes have all been supplied some time since by different parties. Hence with the money (though now not so useful since the removal of the sutler) I am as comfortable as friends and the kindest of parents can make me. I knew nothing of the report of my death until my attention was called to an advertisement asking for information of my whereabouts by a lady of New York. Previous to that I had written one or two letters home: I then did everything in my power to let you hear from me. It is passing strange to me how such a report found its way in the papers, & I cannot acc. for it. A young man who was captured at the same time and near the same place that I was, was wounded but I do not think he died of his wounds. It could not therefore have originated from that. We are as comfortably situated as could well be expected and if health holds out, hope many of us will return wiser if not better men. Not a day passes that I do not think of you all at home. Willie and Luther Ashby are well. Hoping that you are all well & with much love to Ma, Aunt Mary and all the rest of the family, I am

Yours Affly

T. H. Foster

Glenville Dec. 16, 1863

To Lt. T. H. Foster

My dear Son,

Yours of the 6th Inst is just to hand and is the *first line* from you since your capture. The letter to Mrs. Col. Payne will be forwarded the very first opportunity.

I would dispatch a special messenger with it but Gregg's Division of Cavalry now occupy Warrenton and their Piquets, I understand, will allow no one to pass. I was in Warrenton short time since—Saw Col. W. W. Payne. He seemed in good spirits and said all were very well.

I am very glad to hear you are well and provided with good winter clothing. From what we have learned indirectly from several others it may turn out that you will receive duplicate suits. In which case you had better return the surplus if practicable or sell it to provide the means of payment, as everything you receive *must be paid for* some day and these are hard times.

You ask if there is not some mistake about Weaver's election to the 3rd Lieutenancy. I think not. Have been so informed, and it is the *only vacancy that could be filled by election.* I hear that Major Randolph is to be promoted to the Lieut. Colonelcy in the 4th, which will make your friend Wm. H. full Colnl.

We are all well: so are friends generally. Your uncle Thos. is at home for a week or two. The Black Horse are over here under command of Capt. Payne.

Did you receive the remittance of 75$ and a box of clothes from my old comrade Beverly of Balto.? Have you acknowledged it? Write me fully and frequently. It is a great pleasure to hear from you. When Mrs. Payne writes to Husband I will give it dispatch. Remember me to Willie and Col. Payne & others. All send much love to you.

Yr. Aff Father,
J. W. Foster

Johnson's Island
Jany 5th 1864

My dear Father:

Your last came to hand in due course of mail. I was very glad to learn that at last one of my letters had reached home. I have not received from your old friend Beverly of Baltm. a box of clothes, nor have I recd. from him any money. I am indebted to his kindness for Pants & coat, but not his purse. He is not in a condition to aid his *relations* pecuniarily which I found out and have foreborne to call on him. I have received several letters from him in which he expresses his regret at not having sufficient money to become the banker (which he says he would like to do) of the son of his "oldest and best friend". I learn from him that no money has been deposited with the house of Fisher & Son to my credit. I have just rec'd his letter with this information and hasten to inform you. All money sent to prisoners should be sent *by express.* Hope you will be able to hunt up the money which you informed me had been deposited in Balt; not so much on my account as I can make out without it, but because it is a *heavy* loss these hard times.

The letter which you wrote through Chas. Green Esq. never came to hand. A portion of the contents of your last was gratifying to Col. Payne. He writes again. The thermometer here on New Year's day and the day after was 12 degrees *below* zero. Yet none of us quite froze. It will never be forgotten by us.

Has Capt. W. been restored to his command? He was under arrest when I was captured.

Trusting that the end of this year, unlike its commencement, may find peace spreading its blessings over our now unhappy and distracted land and tell Ma I hope she spent at least a peaceful Xmas, give my love to all,

Your Afft Son
T. H. Foster.

Glenville Jany. 23 64

Dear Hunton,

Yours of 12th and Willie's of 24th Dec. came to hand this evening. We cannot imagine how the advertisement you refer to came to be published in a N. York paper. There was a publication of your death in a Washington paper giving your Regt. & Co. with painful precision. We trust you may continue to be blessed with good health and will use every means to preserve it. Coarse or indeed short rations are not beneficial to the health of the young and robust, with the observance of temperance and *regularity*. Hardships, privations & trials promote the growth of the hardier & more manly virtues as distress and sorrow fit and prepare the heart for the seeds of God's grace. Reversing your quotation, I pray you may return a better (scripturally) as well as a wiser man. Let me know if you rec'd the remittances made or enough to serve you and bring you comfortably Home.

I fear there was a miscarriage of the 100$ to be deposited with Fisher & Son, but expect you have rec'd it from N. York. I should like for you to have enough to come back amply provided with clothes, from head to foot as yours here have all been lost.

I hope you did not omit to write a handsome letter of acknowledgement to my old friend B. C. The families of our friends named above as far as I know are well. We are all well, as is your Uncle Tom's family. All unite in love to you and Willie. Your Mama says write her. Molly says your excuse for not writing her used to be want of time, a plea you cannot make now.

Yr. aff. Father
J. W. Foster.

Glenville, March 25-64

Lt. T. H. Foster

My dear son,

Your letter dated 12th Feb, I found here on my return from Richmond. It is the last rec'd. If you should be removed from Johnson Island and not brought on for exchange, try and communicate with us as soon as possible.

I write this in the hope that it may meet you in Richmond.

I write Edgar to whom I enclose it, to forward if the prospect for a general exchange is not as bright as when I left; and that if he does not expect you soon, to send on another Box of Tobacco and this time to give *your* address. You can share the first with Willie, and he in the second with you. It is the cheapest way we can procure exchange. Tobacco is now the currency and the reserve. The prisoners lately arriving in Richmond had quite an ovation. They were rec'd with the most flattering demonstrations—escorted to Capitol Square where a collation was served, and address made by the President. This is well calculated to produce wild excitement, but every soldier thus honored ought to reflect that the occasion requires more than ordinary *circumspection,* and put a strong curb on his natural impulses. Those who have withstood the temptation, have gone through the fiery ordeal and return to their Country unscathed, with uncorrupted, brave and loyal hearts deserve much honor. You can no doubt get the privilege on coming Home to fix up and get a horse. You might get a brokendown Confed: Cheap of Major Richards at Gordonsville (quondam "Burton of Alex") or of Major Rogers, Orange C. H., and ride him through and turn him out to grass and get a better. It is an investment that pays very well sometimes. All well and enough to live on. All write in messages of love and affection and sympathy for you in your long imprisonment.

Yr. Aff: Father,
Js. W. Foster.

Remember us all to Willie and tell him his immediate family and friends are well.

Glenville March 26-64

Lt. T. H. Foster
My dear Son,

Most of your fellow prisoners that were sent from Johnsons Island have been exchanged. I have seen and talked with several of them. They said the prisoners were being removed alphabetically, and as F stands pretty low down we are in high hopes of seeing you soon. In the mean time write us frequently. Write when you leave. Where you stop if you do not come straight through. From Point Lookout you can write to care of Majr. B. P. Noland, Richmond. From any other point you had better write through Warrenton; and as experience shows under cover to a resident, and to the *care of a Federal Officer of that Post.*

Yr aff. Father
Js. W. Foster.

Point Lookout, Md.
May 5th 1864

My dear Father:

I wrote you when I left Johnson's Island with one hundred and forty sick and disabled soldiers, myself one of them, that I expected to go through direct to Richmond: but have been sadly disappointed. Two exchanges have taken place since we arrived here and unfortunately I am not one of them. Small lots of officers are sent each time.

I suppose my time will come when the fortunes of battle give us the excess of prisoners. That is my only hope now.

I am better than I was when I left Johnson's Island. I have chronic Diarrhea—a very prevalent disease among our prisoners. I have been benifited by the change and hope with prudence and care to continue to improve. I was sorry to learn of your sickness: but hope that this good weather has restored you to your usual health. You can write me by Warrenton, through London or "Flag of Truce" as usual. I am anxious to hear from you, and hope it will not be long before I receive a letter stating your recovery. With the hope that you are all enjoying good health and with much love to you all, I am your Affectionate Son,

T. H. Foster.

(Written on the back)

My friend Col. Wm. Payne, one of the fortunate exchanged, takes this through for me. Address me, Prisoner of War, Ward 2 Point Lookout, Md. T. H. F.

Later. Since writing the within Capt. Duchane informs me that he is going direct to our neighborhood so I send by him as it will reach you sooner. T. H. F.

Glenville June 28-64

Lt. T. H. Foster

My dear Son

We have received but one letter from you (that by Capt. Duchane) since you reached P Lookout. and in that you gave us hope that you w'd get off in the next Boat. Have heard that you had reached Richmond and were too sick to come Home, but we conclude this is but one of the many false rumors that now load the air. Our communication with Richmond is infrequent and uncertain.

I should think you might, on the pleas of long confinement, the state of your health, the fact that you *were selected* at Johnsons Island and shipped as a *proper subject for exchange,* persuade the authorities to let you come away with the first exchange. It can make no difference with them, and common humanity would *dictate a preference in favor of invalids.*

Did you get the Tobacco? There is another box in Richmond, care of Edger if you need it: or, if he is absent with Dept Battn. and you are out of funds write W. N. McVeith, Major Noland, Major Ambler or Wm. H. Fowle.

Your letters care of Brown & Son have generally reached us. A more certain and speedy way w'd be to write a letter to your sister directing it to her on the back care of Mrs. DeBell and addressing the envelope to Miss Hattie Lee, Turberville near Alexandria care of Mrs. Triplett. If however a flag of Truce boat is running it would be as well to send by way of Richmond care Majr Noland. You might try all three media. It would tripple the chances. We are very anxious to hear from you. In Chronic Dyarrhea nothing is so important as temperance in all things, simple wholesome regulated diet and a quiet mind.

Your friends have suffered considerably during the late battles. Col. Randolph and Capt. Weaver amongst the slain, Richd Lewis and the Brents and Granville Smith among the wounded. Commending you to Him in whose hands are the destinies of individuals and of nations,

I am Yr. aff Father

Js. W. Foster.

P. S. All well as usual and send much love.

Hospital "Officers Camp"
July 2nd 1864
Point Lookout

Dear Willie:

Feeling a little stronger and better this morning, I seat myself in an arm chair to try and write you a short letter. Many of our friends and acquaintances have fallen in the late battles around Richmond and in other portions of our state. The letter which you mentioned as having sent me from Father with 3.55 enclosed has not come to hand. I have not heard a word from home since I got here. All the officers save the sick, about fifty in number, have been sent from this point to "Fort Delaware". I think and hope I am improving a little, but it is mighty little if any. I don't think I weigh more than 120 pounds. The weather is excessively hot here; and the water of the most indifferent kind. Hoping you may keep your health good (which is the greatest blessing Heaven bestows on man) while in prison, I am Your Cousin,

T. Hunton Foster.

Died August, 1864
A PRISONER OF WAR
at Point Lookout, Maryland
THOMAS HUNTON FOSTER
Age, 29 Years, 3 Months

Human Screen Against Mosby

(Excerpts from a letter of J. W. Foster of The Plains)

Provost Marshal Office
Alexandria Octo 20th 1864

My dear Nephew

With others I have been taken to travel up and down on the Manassas Gap R. R. for the protection of the same against Mosby's Raiders and this gives me an opportunity which I gladly sieze to give you assurance that all is well at your home and most anxious to hear from you.

The M. G. R. R. is now held by the Union forces, and the country along the line as far as Piedmont in their occupancy. A letter addressed to your Mother at The Plains, care Col. Albright the Commander at that post, would I think reach her. Your sisters are both at home and looking very well. The health of your Mama is not so good. Write soon to some of us.

Yrs. affy.
J. W. Foster.

From Markham to Appomattox With The Fauquier Artillery

By COLONEL ROBERT M. STRIBLING

(Colonel Stribling, a native of Fauquier County and resident of Farrowsville, near Markham, was the father of the late W. C. Stribling and grandfather of W. C. Stribling Jr.)

The Company was mustered into the service of the State of Virginia as an infantry company and named "The Markham Guards" on the first day of July 1861, when composed of barely the minimum number of men required by law, by Major George W. Brent, sent to Markham for the purpose by Gen'l. P. G. T. Beauregard.

It was ordered into barracks in the Old Stone Church (Goose Creek Baptist Church) near that place for the purpose of recruiting, uniforming and drilling, and was recruited to the maximum by July 13th, 1861, as appears from the muster roll of that date, on which there were four commissioned officers and 100 enlisted men.

The County donated the cloth and the ladies of the Markham neighborhood made soldiers uniforms of it.

The caps of the men had painted on the front the number, as each stood in ranks, determined by height, and No. 30 was six feet high.

Frank Kerrick, six feet six inches, was No. 1.

General Jones, when the Company joined his brigade at Centreville, said, "It amused him to watch those great big obstreperous boys at play."

The commissioned officers were: Robert M. Stribling, Captain; James H. Kidwell, First Lieutenant; Wm. N. Green, 2nd Lt.; and Wm. C. Marshall, 2nd Lt.

The company, uniformed and armed with Mississippi rifles, and quite proficient in company drill, was ordered about the first of August to report to Col. William Smith at Manassas, commanding the 49th Regiment of Virginia Infantry, then in process of being organized, to be incorporated in that regiment, and was, according to the date of the Captain's commission, designated "Co. G." Whilst in the regiment it was diligently drilled in the school of the battalion by Lt. Col. William Murray.

General Beauregard, desiring to increase the artillery force of his army, selected this company as one of those to be transferred to that branch of the service, and it was equipped with an armament of two iron 24-pounder howitzers and two iron 12-pounder guns—the only guns that could be obtained that fall.

Lieutenants Kidwell and Marshall were sent to Markham to purchase horses and Lewis Benedict, the Markham saddler and harness maker, made the harness, which was of such excellent quality that the greater part of it was in use at the time of the surrender. As soon as the horses and harness were obtained, the battery, under the name of "The Fauquier Artillery," was ordered to Centreville, and assigned as the brigade battery, to the South Carolina brigade, commanded by General D. R. Jones. This brigade had as its next commander General R. H. Anderson and next to him General Micah Jenkins during the time the battery was with it.

The Fauquier Artillery, in the spring of 1862, went to the Peninsula with its brigade, then commanded by General Anderson, and the next day after its arrival at Lebanon Church was put in position on the line at Winn's Mill, several miles from Yorktown, and remained there until the evacuation of Yorktown, sometimes firing briskly at the enemy and receiving their fire in return.

Our position on the line at Winn's Mill was about the strongest taken during the whole war and we all felt confident of our ability to hold it against any force McClellan might send against it.

Innocent Lamb and Cannon's Roar

Whilst the battery was at Winn's Mill, there was a flock of sheep grazing between the lines of the two armies and when they approached either line, an effort was made to kill or capture them. At dawn, one day, they came close to our line and the men made a dash around them and drove them up to it and quite a number were captured.

A lamb fell to the lot of Sergeant D. M. Mason and was soon gentled and kept as a mascot. During the night of the evacuation, when the thunder of exploding guns and magazines was almost continuous, General Roger A. Prior was with us, prepared to cover the rear of the army with his brigade of infantry and this battery. When, amidst the terrifying sounds and fearful apprehensions, the lamb commenced to bleat, General Prior made us a grand oration, contrasting the horrors that enveloped us with the innocence of the lamb. We will never forget it. The battery remained with General Prior until Williamsburg was reached.

It was then ordered back to its brigade, and on May 5th, about 1 p.m., it was ordered to the front by Col. Jenkins, then commanding the brigade, and in going forward, met litter-bearers carrying from the field General William H. Payne supposed at that time to be mortally wounded. In this stream the excitement of battle dominated all pain from wounds and all doubts and fears and we were urged by it to hasten to the front that we might be participants in the glory of victory.

The battery was ordered into action on the left of Fort Magruder and about half a mile distant from it, from which point a few shots were fired at moving columns of the enemy. The battery was soon ordered to the right and front of Fort Magruder to support a charge of our troops, by enveloping in fire the flank of the enemy's line that was charged. The charge was successful, but the enemy, soon heavily re-enforced, in turn charged and drove back our troops. The battery, then, cooperated with other forces in repulsing their charge, and remained in that position, keeping up an almost continuous fire until dark when it was drawn off, having done excellent work—its first work in an open field engagement.

We lost a great many horses, and several men wounded (J. T. Megeath, Ben Kerrick, John Carter and others), who were left at the house of the Rev. T. M. Ambler in Williamsburg and became prisoners—not one killed. The enemy overshot the guns and the caisson horses received their fire. Many of the bullets fired by them were explosive, but the bullets exploded before they penetrated the chests and did no harm to the ammunition. One of these bullets struck Ben Kerrick, exploded in his clothes and the fragments made 10 or 12 wounds. General Longstreet, in his report of that battle, made very complimentary mention of the battery among others conspicuously engaged.

In this action Lieut. William N. Green directed his section with marked effect. During the night after the battle, the retreat was continued, but our battery, through miscarriage of orders, with its heavy guns and disabled horse force was still in the College grounds when day dawned, and we reached the road just ahead of the rear guard as it was falling back before the advance of the enemy.

The conveying of the guns as far as Burnt Ordinary will ever be remembered by the Company as one of the most arduous tasks of the War, for so many horses had been lost, and those left were so worn out that the guns had to be dragged through the bottomless mud, in great part, by hand. When the batterymen were exhausted and the rear guard of the army were insisting that it must close up or it would be compelled to pass by and leave the guns to fate, the Captain made an appeal to the rear regiment of infantry for help, and it responded in whole and by prolonged effort. The guns were dragged to Burnt Ordinary.

We Lose Men and Horses

When the high ground near the Chickahominy River was reached a much needed rest was given to men and horses. While the Army was at rest, it was mustered into the service of the Confederate States for three years of the War, and the enlisted men of each company were permitted to select its Commissioned Officers. Lt. Wm. N. Green preferred to unite with others in raising a cavalry company and declined to run for re-election. The commissioned officers elected were Robert M. Stribling, re-elected Captain; Wm. C. Marshall, First Lieutenant; Gray Carroll, First Lieutenant; T. M. Archer, Second Lieut.

H. C. Stribling was appointed Sergeant Major, D. M. Mason, First Gun Sergeant, J. A. Marshall, Second Gun Sergeant, P. P. Thomas, Third Sergeant and Garnet Freeman, Fourth Gun Sergeant.

At the Battle of Seven Pines, May 31st, the Battery was again engaged, going into action with Kemper's Brigade. All remember the rain storm of the night before and the terrific condition of the roads that day. As the battery approached the battleground and after going under fire two of the guns stuck in the mud and could not be brought into action. The other two went "in battery" on the right of the Williamsburg road, and about 200 yards beyond the captured woods of Casey's Division. From this position a fire was kept up on the enemy's lines of infantry that advanced in the attempt to retake the works and several times got so near that the flash of their guns was almost in our faces. When driven back their artillery would open upon the guns. We lost men and horses there, but held the position until darkness put an end to the battle of that day.

Carter's and Dearing's Batteries had been, previous to the arrival of this battery, engaged on the same ground but had been so crippled and nearly exhausted that only one or two of Carter's guns were firing and they at long intervals. George Prichard, driving the wheel-horses of one of the guns that stuck in the mud, was belaboring his off-horse that was balky when a musket ball struck it in its throat and the blood spurted.

The horse immediately began to pull with all its might and was moving the gun until it fell dead, much to Prichard's delight; then Prichard received an exactly similar wound in his throat and Martin P. Marshall was sent with him to the field hospital, where he was lost among the dying, and he never could be traced afterwards. General Longstreet made no report of this battle at the time, and in The Records, Kemper's Brigade and this battery are reported to have come upon the field the next day (Sunday) though they had taken a prominent part in the battle of Saturday.

When a line was established on the Williamsburg road and intrenched, the battery was put in position near to and on both sides of the road, and remained there until the Seven Days Battle was in progress and McClellan evacuated that front. At the initiation of the battle when General Lee was moving around McClellan's right flank, the enemy, in front of the battery made a dash and drove off our skirmishers and captured the picket line. Forces were at once disposed to recover it and, from the part of the line on which Lt Carroll's section was in position a regiment of North Carolina infantry, that had just joined the army and had never been under fire, advanced to the charge.

It was badly managed and was broken and driven from the field with heavy losses. Lt. Carroll, then, held back the enemy by the fire of his section, when not supported by any infantry, until the troops, that had recovered the line to the left, swept around and came up in rear of the enemy, and that force of the enemy was pretty nearly annihilated.

Artillery Repels Cavalry

When McClellan moved off, the battery was ordered back to Anderson's brigade, then on the march to Frazer's Farm, and went with it to that battlefield. During this battle, though exposed to a heavy fire, it did not go into action. After the battle, the guns of the battery were exchanged for four that had been captured—two brass light 12-pounders and two 3-inch rifles

About the 1st of August, the battery was ordered to General Tombs, commanding the outpost of the army at New Market on the River Road. During the afternoon of August 4th, it was ordered, together with a regiment of Georgia infantry, on picket at Malvern Hill. The picket-post was attacked at sunrise the next morning, the enemy approaching from the direction of Frazer's Farm, in which direction the roads were observed only by a small force of cavalry that was cut off, and only a few of its stragglers dropped in about light and reported their approach.

Time enough was barely given to get the guns in position and arrange the infantry when there was a cavalry charge, which we met with artillery fire, and it was quickly repulsed by it. At sunrise, two batteries were run out by the enemy about 600 yards distant and an artillery duel ensued, in the open field with no protection on either side, in which The Fauquier Artillery gained so decided an advantage that the guns of the enemy would soon have been completely silenced and the men driven from them, had not their infantry been pressed to the front. This infantry line was composed of three regiments, and heavy bodies of infantry were seen moving in their rear. As soon as the infantry appeared, the fire of the battery was directed upon it, and with such effect that the line was repeatedly thrown into disorder, and when within between one and two hundred yards the men were compelled to lie down in the cover of a ravine and did not emerge from it until we had evacuated the hill and carried off the guns, which was done at 10 a m.

When the infantry appeared, Major Pickett, commanding the Georgia regiment and Captain Stribling of the battery had received instructions from General Tombs to hold the hill, as he proposed to move his whole command down and make that the battleground. At 10 a. m. when it was expected every moment that the enemy would emerge from the ravine, there were not more than a round or two of ammunition left and it was determined to evacuate, which was done so successfully that all the guns were brought off and besides the wounded, no prisoners were lost. When we reached the woods some 800 yards distant, we were met by the 8th Georgia Regiment and a battery on their way to Malvern Hill to relieve the picket, having received no special orders in reference to the attack. These two regiments and two batteries, then, fell back slowly to New Market, checking the progress of the enemy as much as possible. Joe Kendall, John Ball and William

Suddith were left dead on the field and some wounded fell into the hands of the enemy.

During the engagement at Malvern Hill, a gunboat anchored just opposite in James River, and, very near, and in full view, opened upon us from our rear, but the greater part of their shells went over our heads and fell among their own men, in fact, helped us.

General Pendleton, in his report upon the reorganization of the artillery wrote: "This battery in the second affair at Malvern Hill excelled all others in successful daring." General McClellan thought the action of sufficient importance to publicly compliment General Hooker on the field, as appears in the "Official Records."

During this engagement there was an exhibition of heroism by Private Joe Kendall that is worthy of record. His leg was shot off by a cannon ball close to his body. When two of his comrades, by direction of Lieut. Carroll, were removing him over the crest of the hill, he requested them to lay him down near the horses of the limber, and then, asked the driver to take his place at the gun, and told him he would hold the horses. Repeatedly he would call out, "Don't give up, men. Never let them take the guns. Fight to the last." Of his captain, passing by, he asked, "Can we drive them back? How are the men of Lieut. Marshall's section fighting?" When asked if he wanted anything, he answered, "I want a drink of water but don't stop any of the men to bring it, for I will soon be a dead man." Before the action closed he had breathed his last and we left him where he died.

When General Lee moved the troops from in front of Richmond to join Jackson in an attack upon Pope, the battery rejoined its brigade and accompanied it to Culpeper County where it was engaged, at the railroad bridges over the Rappahannock River, in conjunction with Squires' battery of The Washington Artillery and Chapman's battery, thrown together temporarily into a battalion under the command of Major J. Garnett.

This affair was an artillery duel across the river, and the losses in disabled guns and men and horses were very great on both sides. It was brought on by General Lee, apparently, to call off attention from Jackson's march to Manassas, then in progress.

Duel Across The Rappahannock

As Longstreet's Corps was moving up the Rappahannock River on the Culpeper side, the battery was ordered in position on the hill overlooking the Waterloo Bridge. Soon after, the enemy ran out two batteries on the Fauquier side of the river, and the day was spent in another artillery duel; whilst Longstreet's Corps was marching behind the hill, on the Rappahannock Turnpike, to Hinson's Mill, where it crossed. All of the corps having passed by when darkness covered the withdrawal, the battery limbered up and followed after. At Edgeworth, by taking a farm road, so much distance was saved that it emerged from it at the head of all the artillery and trains and rejoined the brigade near Marshall (then Salem).

It was ordered from there to the front and was used in forcing the passage through Thoroughfare Gap and passed through the Gap that evening with the most advanced infantry, and was the only battery that passed through the Gap that night. The next morning, Jenkins' brigade marched through the Gap at the head of Longstreet's Corps, and the battery rejoined it as it passed through.

When the First Army Corps reached Gainesville, the battery was immediately ordered to General J. E. B. Stuart who was watching the movements of Fitz John Porter's corps on the Manassas Railroad, and was used under his directions, in making demonstrations, by rapidly changing positions and opening fire from all prominent points in its front. General Longstreet, in his report of this battle, makes special mention of the fact that this battery by its fire broke and drove back a large body of infantry that was moving against him as he was bringing up his infantry. This was exhausting work to both men and horses, and several men were badly wounded and many horses disabled.

Into Action With Deliberation

About noon the next day, the general advance of Longstreet's Corps was ordered. General Jenkins, whose brigade was on the extreme right of the Corps, ordered the battery to support the brigade in the charge upon Chinn's Hill. The battery advanced with the brigade, in line directly behind it, until Jenkins, finding the brigade extended beyond the flank of the enemy's infantry, made a left wheel with it and came upon the flank of the forces holding Chinn's Hill. As the brigade was making this wheel, General Jenkins cut off two companies of the right regiment and ordered them to report to Captain Stribling to be used by him to keep from the battery the enemy's sharpshooters. The battery, as soon as it could enfilade the enemy's line on Chinn's Hill, went in battery at close range and contributed materially to throwing the lines of the enemy into disorder. General J. E. B. Stuart joined us there and remained with us during the action. At first, he fretted at the deliberation with which the battery went into action, but afterwards was extravagant in his praise of the accuracy and efficiency of the fire.

When the enemy was driven from the hill and their guns captured, Col. Rosser brought up Eshleman's and Rogers' batteries and taking our battery with them advanced on the left flank of the enemy's infantry and between it and their cavalry to support a charge of our cavalry upon the latter. The charge being successful and their cavalry driven away, the batteries were turned upon the Henry House Hill. Being well upon the flank of the troops on this hill, whilst the batteries were engaged in shelling them from a position surrounded by a thick growth of young pines, a force of the enemy, as prisoners stated, "taking them for their guns," marched upon their flank with the purpose of taking position behind them. This force had approached within 100 yards before discovered. When seen, the guns were turned upon them and canister and musket balls by the two companies of infantry were poured into their ranks. It was quickly dispersed. From the "Official Records", it appears this was Don Peat's command, that met with heavy losses and was much disorganized. Generals Stuart and Rosser, in their reports, give much space to the important services of these three batteries on that occasion in which they give the highest praise to Rogers' Battery. General Jenkins was wounded and made no report.

The battery remained with the brigade until the army reached Leesburg on its way into Maryland, where, having lost a great many horses and the company being much reduced by the casualties of the campaign, it was ordered back to Winchester to recruit and from there to Staunton to be equipped with guns and horses, and did not rejoin the army until December 1st at Fredericksburg.

Whilst at Winchester, after the Battle of Sharpsburg, the artillery of the army was reorganized and Lieut. M. M. Rogers and forty-two men of The Loudoun Artillery (Rogers' Battery) were assigned to The Fauquier Artillery and the company was still further increased in numbers by 40 or 50 new recruits and had present for duty when it reached Fredericksburg about 200 men. Its armament was two brass 24-pounder howitzers and four Napoleon guns, all of which had been captured at Harpers Ferry.

According to the plan of re-organization, batteries that were reduced below a certain standard of efficiency were disbanded, and the men distributed among those that came up to the standard brigade batteries, that had served with the infantry at the front, had been greatly reduced by casualties in battle, by forced marches and irregular issues of rations and forage, while reserve batteries, that had seen but little service, had made regular marches and had issued to them rations and forage with comparative regularity, as a rule. Consequently the injustice to brigade batteries produced more dissatisfaction than was produced by any other act of the authorities.

The Fauquier Artillery fortunately escaped the fate that befell many others. The Loudoun artillery, that was at the First Battle of Manassas and served with marked distinction on the Henry House Hill in the line with Stonewall Jackson's brigade, and from that time had been the brigade battery of one of the brigades of Longstreet (afterwards Pickett's) Division, fell a victim to the rule, and the Fauquier Artillery was fortunately the recipient of more than 40 seasoned artillerymen, that, under the command of the gallant officer and accomplished gentleman, Lieut. M. M. Rogers, made up a section of the battery, than which there was none better or more efficient in the Army of Northern Virginia.

At the Battle of Fredericksburg the battery was with Pickett's Division near the redoubt in which General Lee made his headquarters and nearly in the center of the Army, from which position an unusually good view of Jackson's engagement to the right was had. The battery was but little used there. Whilst at Fredericksburg, all the batteries were organized into battalions, and this battery became Company A of the 38th Battalion of Virginia Artillery to the command of which Major (afterwards General) James Dearing was assigned.

Gunboats Shall Not Pass

In February, 1863, the battalion was sent to Petersburg and from there went with General Longstreet's Corps to Nansemond County where it was expected that the capture of Suffolk would be attempted. Not many days after arriving in front of Suffolk, the battery was ordered to General French, who commanded the left wing of the army which fronted the Nansemond River below the town.

His chief of artillery placed it in position in an old earth work that jutted out into the river, from which the channel of the river was well commanded. The orders given were that no gunboats were to be permitted to pass either up or down the river, and that was to be the sole duty of those in the work. Its protection from an attack on land devolved upon the infantry held behind the hill in its rear. The day following the night in which the guns were placed in position, two gun boats attempted to run by. Owing to the unfinished condition of the embrazures, the first one passed unmolested, but the second was plowed through from stem to stern by shot; the pilot house and pilot in it were shot away, and the boat drifted out of range and sank. From that time, an incessant fire was kept up on the battery by the gunboats above and below, and by land batteries and sharpshooters on the opposite side of the river, but no gunboat again attempted to run the gauntlet.

The injury done to the works during the day was repaired during the night and any weak points that had developed were strengthened, and it became evident that unless the battery was captured the river could not be used.

Lieutenant Lawson, of the Union Navy, who commanded one of the gunboats arranged to capture it by throwing suddenly a force of 700 or 800 picked men across the river above, together with a battery of howitzers, quickly and very quietly deploying it across the narrow strip of land and charging upon the work which was semi-lunar and open in that direction.

The attack was made late in the afternoon of the 5th of April. Through the mistake of someone—General French charging General Hood with it, and General Hood charging it upon General French—the pickets had been withdrawn from the river above and no intimation of the landing of this force was given to those in the work until it was seen deploying at a double-quick in their rear, and the force, placed in the rear over the hill to meet an attack on land, did not make even a demonstration to assist the small body charged upon.

Captured by The Enemy

There were heavy traverses between the guns, and the gun platforms were so narrow that the guns were turned with great difficulty.

There were in the work, besides the artillery company, only two small companies of the 44th Alabama regiment, with about 75 men in them. The unexpected attack made it almost impossible to bring at once into use the full strength of this small force. Notwithstanding this, it succeeded in holding back and would have eventually repulsed the main body had not a detachment passed around to the river front and mounted over the parapet that was then the rear. The guns and infantry companies at the time were engaged in firing to the land front. Five guns and every man in the work were captured.

With the battery, four officers (Capts. Marshall, Rogers and Archer) and 62 men were captured, and Lieut. Carroll in command at the time of the supernumeraries and drivers in camp reported that there were with him present for duty 100 men. These men were at once armed with rifles and as mounted infantry, commanded by Lieut. Carroll, were ordered to the left of the line to protect the flank of the army and the foraging parties from the enemy landing from gunboats.

There are very voluminous reports, both Union and Confederate, of this capture in the Official Records and also in The Union Records of the Navy. Captain Stribling now has his sword that was surrendered. It has been recently returned to him by Captain Lawson of the Navy who had kept it through all the years as his special trophy of that victory, and in his letter returning it stated he was induced to do so because of his high appreciation of the gallant fight we made when our situation was desperate. The equal of this cannonade has rarely, if ever, been recorded in the annals of war.

Within half an hour after all the guns on our line opened fire, the enemy's caissons were exploding in the air and their return fire was slowing and mild and we knew the men were flat on the ground, hugging Mother Earth, with that tired feeling of "Rock Me to Sleep, Mother, Rock Me to Sleep" creeping over them and we thought we were to be the ministering angels to bear them to the haven prepared for them at Libby. But, alas! General Longstreet did not seize the opportunity, and waited after our ammunition had been exhausted before he ordered the infantry to advance to the charge and consequently their charge was met by fresh guns and fresh infantry, that had been hurried to the front as soon as our ammunition was exhausted, and Pickett's Division, that was the pride of our hearts, was almost annihilated.

To Gettysburg and Back

The enlisted men of the artillery were exchanged at once, and the four officers within a month by a special agreement, and then the company was reorganized in Richmond and equipped with six Richmond made Napoleon guns and went with Pickett's Division to Gettysburg. There, it was on Pickett's line and participated in the great cannonade that preceded the charge of the Division.

The following day, the battery was with the skirmish line and several times assisted in driving back the advance of the enemy's skirmishers, then assisted in repulsing a cavalry charge that sought to capture them near Falling Waters. After the army crossed the River, the battery was sent forward with Corse's Brigade to Chesters Gap and was in position there to resist the occupation of the gap by the enemy.

It then went with Pickett's Division to Petersburg and wintered there. In the latter part of the winter the battery went with the expedition commanded by General Pickett to New Bern and was engaged in forcing the outposts of the place. The next day Col. Chew with his regiment of infantry (about 200 strong) and Capt. Stribling, with Rogers' Section of his battery and a section of the "Fayette Artillery" commanded by Lieut. (later Judge) Clopton, were sent to capture a redoubt some miles to the left. When the guns were placed for opening the attack upon it, a white flag was sent out from the redoubt and, after some parleying, it was surrendered to Capt. Stribling during the absence of Col. Chew, who, with his regiment, was moving through the woods to turn the front of the works. With it were taken more than 400 prisoners, two 3-inch rifles completely equipped, some wagons and a large store of army supplies.

Upon the return of General Pickett to Kinston, Capt. Stribling received notice of his promotion and orders to report to Ewell's Corps, then on the Rapidan River, and Lieut. William C. Marshall, of his promotion to be captain of the battery. H. C. Stribling, who had been sergeant-major of the company, was now elected lieutenant.

General Hoke was soon after ordered to the command of the forces at Kinston, and quickly arranged for the capture of Plymouth. The Fauquier Artillery, now Marshall's Battery, took part in the capture of Plymouth, which, with its garrison of 2834 officers and men, surrendered on the 20th day of April 1864. During the engagement of the 19th which caused the surrender, the battery dashed up to the redoubt below the town that had, up to that time, successfully resisted all efforts for its capture, and going "in battery" just outside the moat, threw canister into it until it surrendered. The men of the battery then turned and served the enemy's guns in it upon other parts of the line of defenses until they too surrendered.

Some acts of heroism deserve special attention. Private Wm. H. Riley of Sergeant Mason's gun, who lost an arm and leg, when brought into our lines about 10 p. m. said, "I knew the men could not come after me until the fight was over, but, after the firing ceased, I had been looking out for them." He was soon among the dead. Private A. M. Weaver, in the charge, after being twice wounded, still continued on, until he received the third wound that proved to be mortal, within 100 yards of the redoubt, and when one of his friends stopped to assist him, he told him, "Don't stop with me but go on with your gun." Sergeant F. W. Powell was killed in the charge, when within 60 yards of the redoubt, by shrapnel penetrating the limber-chest and bursting in his face as he was carrying the last round of ammunition from the chest to his piece. His gallantry had been conspicuous throughout the engagement. Lieut Archer received a wound in this engagement that disabled him for the rest of the war.

The battery marched from Plymouth with Hoke's command back to New Bern, Gen'l. Hoke feeling confident that he would capture that place also. But on the eve of the attempt, the critical conditions about Richmond caused his recall, and he hastened with all speed to Petersburg.

The battery was next engaged in the afternoon of May 18th on the Bermuda lines, assisting in the repulse of the enemy when an attempt was made by them to recapture the works that had been taken from them. In this engagement Capt. Marshall was wounded and Corporal Joe Pearson was wounded. Capt. Marshall as the result of the wound did not rejoin the battery until the spring of '65 for about six weeks.

The battery, commanded by Lieut. Carroll, during the absence of Capt. Marshall, marched with Hoke's Division to Cold Harbor and was engaged on the line with the division in the Battle of Cold Harbor on June 3rd, 1864. Hoke held the part of the line against which the strongest and most persistent assaults were made and the battery was in the thickest of the fight, the enemy repeatedly charging up to the chevaux-de-frise before being repulsed, and, in its front, the dead of the enemy laid thickest. During their charges and when the fire was at its height, the second gun was spiked by the priming wire. Corporal Sillman jumped upon the trunnion and by the exercise of great courage and wonderful strength, drew out the priming wire and thereby brought the gun into immediate action. Towards the close of the engagement General Hoke reported to General Lee that in his front the ground was thickly strewn with the enemy's dead and that up to that time he had not lost a single man. Richard E. Pearson was wounded there and Wortman shot in the shoulder.

When Grant moved his army across the James, Hoke's Division, carrying the battery with it, was hastened to Petersburg, and during the night of June 15th was placed in position on Hare's Hill upon which part of the line the assaults of the next day were specially directed. The battery remained in this position until the retreat to Appomattox where the two lines were closest together and where it was under constant fire, day and night, from the enemy's sharpshooters, guns and mortars. During this time the battery lost many gallant soldiers, among them Sergeants John W. Birkby and John H. Fouch and Privates Wm. H. Harding and George Saunders killed, all excellent soldiers. Sergeant J. A. Marshall was temporarily disabled by a shot through the shoulder and lungs and Hugh L. Kerrick was among the wounded. General Pendleton in his report of the campaign of 1864 gives a detailed statement of the casualties during the campaign in each battalion of Artillery in the Army of Northern Virginia, and our battalion (the 38th) suffered the heaviest losses of them all in killed and wounded.

Lt. Col. Stribling who was assigned to the command of the battalion in November, 1864, selected two detachments from this battery led by Lt. M. M. Rogers and two from each of the other batteries of the battalion and with them charged with the sharpshooters of General Gordon's command when Fort Steadman was captured.

The captured guns were turned upon the enemy and served against them until General Gordon ordered the withdrawal of the troops. In this engagement Sergeants Hath Brent and Frank Cable, two splendid soldiers, whilst in the captured works directing the fire of their guns, were killed and Frank Hoffman was shot in the throat and carried to the hospital in Petersburg.

Cough Up a Musket Ball

When the army retreated, he was left in an unconscious condition and the surgeon in charge reported that he could not possibly recover. More than six months after the war closed and he had been mourned for as dead, his father received a letter from him at Ft. Monroe, stating that he had been discharged from the prison hospital and was too weak to walk or work for money to pay for his passage home. His father went for him and brought him home, apparently a complete wreck, but several years after reaching home in a violent fit of coughing he coughed up a musket ball and immediately a rapid recovery set in and now he is a hale, hearty man.

General Lee sent one of his last official dispatches to the War Department to bring notice to the services of the battalion on this occasion, as follows:

"Headquarters of Second Army Corps, Mar. 27-65. I desire to bring to the attention of the commanding General the admirable conduct of Col. H. P. Jones, commanding artillery on my line, and the officers and men of his command during the action at Hare's Hill, on the morning of the 25th instant. Col. Jones remained at the front, personally superintending the management of the artillery, and a select body of officers and men, under the command of Lieutenant Colonel Stribling, charged the enemy's breastworks with the sharpshooters of this Corps and at once turned upon the enemy the captured guns.

"I am, Colonel, very respectfully, Your Obt. Serv't. J. B. Gordon Maj. Gen'l. Commanding. Col. W. H. Taylor A. A. Gen'l, Army of N. Va."

GENERAL LEE'S DISPATCH

"Headquarters March 28th 65

"General Gordon informs me that in his report of the action at Hare's Hill, on the 25th instant, he omitted to mention that Col. H. P. Jones, commanding the Artillery on that portion of the line, was at the front superintending, in person, the operations of the artillery, and that a select body of officers and men, under the command of Lieutenant Colonel Stribling, carried the enemy's breast-works with the sharpshooters of the Corps, & immediately turned upon the enemy the captured guns.

"R. E. Lee

Hon. John C. Breckinridge
Secretary of War"

April 2nd 1865, when Gen'l. Lee's line was turned and broken and he was forced to retreat, the guns on the line in front of Petersburg were brought out without any loss. Capt. Wm. C. Marshall with some of the guns of the battery had been sent a short time before to General Anderson on the right side of the line, and was with that part of the army on the retreat to Amelia C. H. where the two wings united, and, though in the engagement and in the retreat, General Anderson lost almost all of his command, Capt. Marshall brought off two of his guns and rejoined the rest of the battery at that place. At Amelia C. H., this battery with the battalion was ordered to Genl. Gordon, who brought up the rear of the army, to Sailors Creek. At Sailors Creek, Gordon's line, on which the battery was used, held firmly until the lines to its right and left were captured. Gordon then joined the remnant of the army at High Bridge near Farmville, but this was accomplished with heavy losses.

Off For Home and Parole

At Farmville the battalion, with the battery, was ordered to the head of the column of the army on its march to Appomattox, and, about mid-day of the 8th of April, passed through the village and halted about one and a half miles beyond it, on the road to Lynchburg.

During the afternoon, the enemy charged up the road from the railroad depot to the village and got in between the battalion (together with a number of battalions of artillery that had passed beyond the junction of the roads) and the infantry of the army.

This artillery—the artillery of Anderson's Corps, commanded by Col. H. P. Jones and the artillery of A. P. Hill's Corps, commanded by Gen'l. Lindsay Walker—about one half of the artillery of the army was then moved around the flank of the force interposed, in an effort to rejoin the army. After marching the greater part of the night in that attempt and finding it impossible to rejoin the army, the artillery of Anderson's Corps, to which the battery belonged, passed for Lynchburg and reached there about noon of the 9th day of April, that fatal day to the Confederate States, and reported to General L. L. Lomax, commanding at that place, who had heard of the surrender of General Lee's army, and the artillery was ordered by him to disband.

The officers and men of the Fauquier Artillery made their way to their homes in Fauquier and Loudoun and after Johnston's surrender received their paroles from General Hancock at Winchester.

SUPPLEMENT

In this War, all reward a Confederate Soldier expected was that his manhood should be recognized, for love of home and of Country was his inspiration. Though he marched and fought with bare feet and tattered clothes, and with nothing but a small ration of corn meal and coarse pork for his diet, and with worthless money for his scant pay, he wrote, in the record of his acts, with what bravery and fortitude it is possible for manhood to assert itself.

R. M. STRIBLING

Aftermath

WITH LEE'S FAREWELL WORDS at Appomattox, "My men, we have fought through the war together. I have done my best for you," the war was over, and the men of Fauquier, who had also done their best, began the road back home to the heartrending task of beginning life anew.

With their wounds of defeat stark and fresh, and their countryside ravaged, the return home called for courage almost equal to that demanded on the field of battle.

(Channing M. Smith lightened the dreary memory with this story of courage. A group of old soldiers were sitting around swapping tales of real and ofttimes imagined deeds of heroism when it was noticed by a little girl that one of the group sat in silence. Such an unusual attitude prompted the inquiry, "What did you do? You were there." Unhesitatingly, to the wonder of all, he replied, "I was the bravest man in Lee's army." When astonishment had somewhat abated, he added, "I was scared to death the whole time, but I never ran.")

Indicative of the emotional tensions abroad in the aftermath of the war was the useless tragedy of New Baltimore during the first postwar election held in that village.

Two brothers, Thomas and Ernest Hunton of Kenmore near New Baltimore, were among Mosby's men when the attempt was made to capture their leader at Lake's Farm near Upperville in 1864. This raid was said to have been led by one Wash Fletcher of Prince William who acted as a Yankee spy.

Thomas Hunton was captured and held prisoner until the end of the war. Ernest hid under the steps and escaped, saying he could never forget the black eyes of the supposed spy.

At the first election held in New Baltimore after the close of the war, Ernest attended against the wishes of his father who sensed there might be trouble. Amid the crowd, Hunton again saw those coal black eyes and promptly accosted Fletcher.

"Aren't you the grand rascal who led the Yankees into Lake's Farm?" he asked.

Whereupon Fletcher, without a word, drew his pistol and shot young Hunton dead on the spot.

His defense was that Hunton had reached for his pistol and he feared for his life if exposed, with feelings running high, in a hostile group.

It turned out, however that young Hunton was completely unarmed—not even a pocket knife.

Fletcher was detained in the Warrenton Jail for two months, when as a result of a petition for his clemency he was released. Hunton's father William Hunton signed the petition with the explanation that too much blood had already been shed and no expiation could bring back his son.

A lonely grave in the lonely Hunton graveyard at Evergreen near New Baltimore bears this inscription,

Ernest G. Hunton
born April 5, 1847
Wantonly assassinated
Oct. 22, 1867

Fletcher is said to have been a haunted and unhappy man until his death near Haymarket many years after the War.

There seems a scarcity of letters extant relating to this period of "the return home", but one story of hardship bespeaks the kinship of all.

The story is excerpted from the report of Dr. William H. Gardner, rector of Emmanuel, Grace and Trinity Churches, Piedmont Parish, to the convention in Richmond in September 1865:

"This Parish has suffered heavily during the war. Farms have been laid waste, barns burned, dwellings pillaged, and more, many valuable lives have been lost. Among the departed it is proper to mention Col. John A. Washington and Col. Thomas Marshall, both vestrymen of this parish, both gallant men and sincere Christians, slain in battle.

"The members of the parish are much reduced in means, and the church buildings were much injured by the Union troops. All three churches were sadly defaced and two of them now stand mere naked walls, roofed over . . ."

The names of soldiers from different regiments, scratched into the plastered walls of the woodroom, confirms the story handed down that Emmanuel was used as a hospital. It has been told that sometimes it served as a stable.

These are the names discernible—

(illegible) 8th Illinois Cavalry
P. B. Johnson—Rockport
Charles Gillem, 51 New York Volunteers, Rockport
Sgt. C. W. Johnson, 63 Reg. Ind. Cav.
C. B. Adams, 86 Reg Mass. Vol.
Benj Hill
George Adams, N. Y.
48th Reg. Pa. Vol.

It can be assumed that they are the names of soldiers of McClellan's command and were inscribed there when McClellan was on his way to Rectortown where he was relieved of his command . .

"The visitor strikes and the vanquished go down. But the years cover them both."

Now, in these anniversary years 1961-65, the long passage of time has healed many wounds. Scars remain. But the alleviated sharpness is fast being obliterated in the onward demand of life which belongs to the future.

The Blue and The Gray

(A TALE OF COMPASSION)

By CATHERINE P. WISER

Many years ago in Ohio, when I was a child of seven, my cousin Alice, who was two years younger, and I were being cared for by her "other grandpa" during a long cold winter afternoon while the rest of the family attended a funeral.

He was a tall, fine-looking old man, with a shock of snowy-white hair. The hours passed quickly as he regaled us with stories of his Civil War experiences. One incident stands out vividly in my memory because after all those years, he became quite excited as he recounted it, and his excitement was contagious.

He enlisted in the Union Army (possibly from New Burlington, Ohio), when he was just past eighteen, a farm boy with firey-red hair and freckles. His first assignment was with the Army Supply Train in the Valley of Virginia. When not on duty the men were supposed to make their beds on top of the boxes in the wagons and travel along. On one of the first mornings he was rudely awakened by someone shaking him by the shoulder, and he looked up into the face of a Confederate soldier.

Visions of a firing squad flashed through his mind. The young "rebel" marched him off to his commanding officer. After asking him a few questions and not feeling disposed to putting a sleepy and very much frightened boy to death for his innocent involvement he ordered him to be released. The terrified young Yankee was blindfolded and led back through the Confederate lines and turned loose, with instructions as to get back to his own group.

Fourteen years later I was teaching at The Plains, Virginia, in Fauquier County, and boarding in the home of Dr. and Mrs Robert Shakelford. Mrs. Shakelford's mother and father, Mr. and Mrs. Bartlett Bolling, were living there also during part of the winter. One night at the dinner table Mr. Bolling told us one of his earliest experiences in the war.

His boyhood home was Bollingbrook, a beautiful estate at the foot of the Blue Ridge on the east side. His father and older brothers were in the Confederate Army, but because of the fact that he was only sixteen he was delegated to stay home with his mother and help with the duties of the large plantation. They raised fine horses, and of course the necessary crops to supply them.

However, the Union soldiers descended upon them and stripped the place of everything in the way of food, took all the horses, cattle, hogs, poultry and grain. Fortunately, they did not burn the beautiful mansion. The faithful and devoted old colored man, who had been his "bodyservant" as he grew up, had foresight and had hidden two of the horses deep in the thicket where he was sure the Union men would not find them. He prevailed on Bartlett to stay hidden also, lest he cause his mother and himself more trouble by his impulsiveness. Soon after the raid young Bartlett left with his man-servant and joined Mosby's men.

Colonel Mosby, with his complete knowledge of the countryside, was able by his raids on the Yankee Supply Trains to keep the women and children of that section from starving. This was literally true. Aside from sweet potatoes, which were not recognized as food by many northern men, the gardens and orchards were laid bare.

Mr. Bolling said that he was a young recruit when he found a young, lanky, red-headed Yankee asleep in one of the Union wagons that had been captured and hidden in a well concealed spot. He didn't know what to do with the other "boy" so he took him to Colonel Mosby. The Colonel ordered him to be blindfolded and taken through the Southern lines to where he could make his way back to his friends.

I do not know why I should have been fortunate enough to hear the story from both sides of the Mason-Dixon Line. But having known and loved both of those wonderful old men, and knowing the well-deserved place of respect they held in their respective communities, I can only say "I hate war."

And I am so thankful for the gentle compassion shown by the brilliant soldier, Colonel Mosby. May each of us in these days of propaganda, of hate and fear, and insecurity, hold our hearts and minds open so that we may exercise a comparable understanding of human values.

The Rosters

We call The Roll again
With none to answer, "Here!"

During The War, eleven companies were formed in Fauquier County with a total strength of about 1100 men. Although no large battles were fought in her territory, Fauquier was the scene of numerous engagements and her railroads were constantly employed in the movement of troops and supplies.

On July 18, 1861, General Joseph E. Johnston with 9,000 men marched through Ashby's Gap and bivouacked at Paris. The next day, the infantry took train at Piedmont Station, now Delaplane, while the cavalry, artillery and supply wagons moved over the road. This army was engaged in the first battle of Manassas, fought July 21.

On June 26, 1862, three divisions of General Pope's army encamped at Warrenton.

On August 22, 1862, J. E. B. Stuart swept with irresistible force to Catlett's Station where he destroyed General Pope's supply train.

On August 24, 1862, Jackson with 20,000 men marched through Salem, now Marshall, on through Thoroughfare Gap to Manassas where General Pope was defeated in the second battle of Manassas, fought August 29 and 30.

In October, McClellan's army was encamped near Warrenton and General Meade's headquarters were established there on July 26, 1863.

Fauquier was also the scene of many of the operations of Mosby's men who rendered distinguished service during the last two years of the war.

Few other military engagements were carried out in Fauquier, but the county, with Loudoun and Fairfax, comprised what was known as Mosby's Confederacy, the arena of his Ranger activities.

The constant presence of soldiers in this pathway for the continuous passage of regular troops, north and south, east and west, brought the full import of war to the home front.

MR. and MRS. AUGUSTUS diZEREGA JR., MISS SUSIE A. SMITH

COMPANY B, EIGHTH REGIMENT, HUNTON'S BRIGADE

This company was organized at Rectortown on 17 April 1861 by Richard H. Carter who served as Captain until he was transferred to the Quartermaster Department in September, 1862. The company was known as the "Piedmont Rifles."

Carter, Richard H. Captain

Ashby, John T. Captain
Enl. as Private, 2nd Lt., Capt, 22 Aug. 1864. Wdd 3 times

Skinner, Charles E. 1st Lieut.

Herrington, E. M. 2nd. Lieut.

Washington, John H. 3rd Lieut.
1862, assigned to duty with Genl. J. E. Johnston

Turner, Thomas B. 1st Sgt.

Carr, William 2nd Sgt.
Pro. to 3rd Lt., Killed at Seven Pines

Hutchison, T. B. 3rd Sgt.

Pierce, Abner C. 4th Sgt.

Reid, Wm. T. 5th Sgt.
Cpt'd 1863

Clancey, William 1st Cpl.
Moss, Hubert 2nd Cpl.
Kincheloe, Wickcliff 3rd Cpl.
Harding, M. Smith 4th Cpl.
Blackwell, S. Haley
Enl. at Orlean, by Capt. Wingfield, 1861*
Acrie, Chas. H. Private
Sur. at App'tx

Allen, George T. Private
Pro. to 3d Lt., June '62, Killed at Seven Pines
Ashby, James S. Private
Killed at Gettysburg
Bowie, John N.
Ballard, Albert Private
Wdd. Gettysburg
Brummet, Jonathan M. Private
Balthrope, Jas. Frank Private
Pro. 2nd Cpl. '64
Bonnell, Wm. A. Private
Pro. 3d Cpl. '64
Ballard, Abner Private
Bowles, Jos. H. Private
Pro. Sgt.
Brook, Robert Private
Killed at Williamsburg, 1862.
Brown, Calvert Private
Barker, Coleman C. P. Private
Carter, Fauntleroy Private
Carter, Alexander Private
Carter, Albert Private
Carter, Benton Private
Carter, Henry Private
Carter, Bushrod Private
Enl. at Orlean by Capt. Wingfield
Calvert, Joseph

Carter, Ezekiel Private
Creel, Elijah Private
Campbell, ——— Private
Cornwell, Beverly Private
Cpt'd. at Winchester, 1865

Downs, Cicero Private
Dixon, Collins Private
Deserted to the enemy
Fletcher, Wesley Private
Buried at Mt. Jackson

*"Orlean Rifles—This company is composed of Young men living near Orleans, Fauquier County, Virginia, passed through this city yesterday evening, en route to Leesburg. They were commanded by Capt. Wingfield." (Alexandria Gazette, 23 May 1861). No further information on this company with the exception of the names of former members being a part of Co. B at later dates.

Fletcher, E. W. Private
Glascock, Nimrod Private
Pro. 4th Sgt. 1864
Green, Daniel H. Private
Surr'd at App'tx.
Gray, J. D. Private
Gill, William H. Private
Gill, John A. Private
Enl. 1 Nov. 1863, Petersburg
Harrington, Daniel C. Private
Haley, Richard D. Private
Haley, Blackwell Private
Haley, Poke Private
Haines, George Private
Hibbs, B. Private
Ingle, Wm. H. Private
Iden, John R. Private
Iden, Samuel Private
Iden, Joseph J. Private
Jewell, Henry L. Private
Deserter
James, Samuel Private
Jerrell, William J. Private
Kennedy, A. J. Private
Kincheloe, William Private
Capt'd & wdd. at Williamsburg. POW at Ft. Monroe where he died, 2 Sept. 1862
Kerfoot, Wm. F. Private
Wdd. Gettysburg
Kincheloe, Elisha D. Private
Kincheloe, Conrad B. Private
Knight, William Private
Enl. at Orlean. Died 4 July 1864
Kerr, William Private
Kidwell, Newton J. Private
Lanham, Manley Private
Lanham, Thomas L. Private
Laws, Thomas L. Private
Lake, Luther B. Private
AWOL, 2/25/64 — 5/2/64, performed hard labor 3 hrs. per day for 30 days, court martialled
Lewis, Frank W. Private
Matthews, Albert E. Private
McArthur, John Private
Killed at Gettysburg
McAten, John R. Private
Milton, Charles A. Private
Milton, A. H. Private
Discharged
Meador, Thos. P. Private
Newton, George Private
Killed at Gettysburg
Newland, Kent Private
Killed at Gettysburg
Newland, James Private
Owens, Kent Private
Killed at Williamsburg, 1862
Pope, Henry E. Private
Pierce, J. William Private
James W. Pierce, 2nd Lt. at the organization of the company was killed by a train at Enfield, N. C.
Preble, Caswell J. Private
Prillaman, John Private
Pettigrew, Wm. B. Private
Surrendered at Appomattox
Pennington, Levi Private
Killed at Gettysburg
Pennington, John Private
Killed at Gettysburg
Phillips, Charles E. Private
Trans. to 7th Va. Cav.
Phillips, Hunter Private
Died in hospital
Payne, Fielding F. Private
Pro. to 3d Lt., Killed at Gettysburg
Pike, Ira H. Private
Died 25 June 1864
Reese, H. C. Private
Royston, Z. V. Private
Wdd. at Gettysburg
Rawlings, J. Wesley Private
Royston, Lewis W. Private
Died in hospital
Robinson, Milton Private
Died in prison
Reed, John Private
Richards, Thomas Private
Put in substitute & joined Mosby

Sampsell, F. Columbus — Private
Sullivan, J. F. — Private
Strother, Lewis — Private
Put in substitute & joined 12th Va. Cavalry
Shacklett, Sewel — Private
Killed at Williamsburg, 1862
Spencer, E. H. — Private
Spencer, Wm. D. — Private
Trinell, Frank — Private
Triplett, Reuben — Private
Tibbetts, Alfred G. — Private
Trans. to 7th Va. Cav.
Triplett, Sydnor — Private
Triplett, Albert — Private
Triplett, Madison — Private
Triplett, Addison — Private
Put in substitute & Joined Mosby

Turner, Thomas B. — Private
Trans. to cavalry
Taylor, Thomas — Private
Utterback, Ferdinand — Private
Whitmore, J. Wesley — Private
White, H. W. — Private
Wright, J. S. — Private
Whitmer, John — Private
Died & buried at Pt. Lookout, Md.
White, Chas. W. — Private
White, Hugh — Private
Weaver, Virgil — Private
Made Lt. in 6th Va. Cavalry
Wade, Wm. C. — Private
Weeks, Hezekiah — Private
Yates, Joseph B. — Private
Discharged

COMPANY H, FOURTH VIRGINIA CAVALRY,

FITZHUGH LEE'S BRIGADE

"THE BLACK HORSE TROOP"

This company was organized in 1858, with John Scott as Captain and Robert Randolph, Charles H. Gordon and A. D. Payne, as First, Second and Third Lieutenants, respectively. The company was at Harper's Ferry or Charles Town at the time John Brown was hanged, December 1859. In January or February, 1861, Captain John Scott resigned and went to Alabama and entered the Confederate Army. First Lt. Robert Randolph went with the Company to Harpers Ferry, April 16, 1861, as commander. After staying about a week at Harpers Ferry the Company returned to Warrenton, at which time W. H. Payne was elected Captain. He commanded the Company until September 1861, at which time he was promoted and Robert Randolph made Captain and served in that capacity until December 1863, at which time he was promoted to Major of the 4th Va. Cavalry and soon thereafter to Lt. Colonel. He was killed May 12, 1864 at Meadow Bridge near Richmond while in command of the Regiment.

The Company constituted a part of the force of Virginia Volunteers and were called into the service of the State by the Governor under an ordinance of the State Convention, adopted April 17, 1861, and were to serve for the term of one year from the 25th day of April 1861, unless sooner discharged. The Company was enrolled for active service by Lieutenant Randolph the 7th day of May 1861, at Warrenton and was mustered into service by Colonel Eppa Hunton.

THE YEARS OF ANGUISH

As Company "H", 4th Virginia Cavalry, the Black Horse Troop took part in many bloody engagements, including the following: First Manassas, July 21, 1861; Seven Days Battles around Richmond, June 1862; Second Manassas, August 1862; Antietam, September 1862: Fredericksburg, December 1862; Chancellorsville, May 1863; Wilderness, May 1864; Second Cold Harbor, June 1864; and Five Forks, April 1, 1865.

From October, 1863 until the surrender at Appomattox on 9 April, 1865 Captain Alexander Dixon Payne, well known Warrenton lawyer, served as commanding officer.

Payne, William H.	Captain
Pro. Brig, General	
Randolph, Robert	1st Lt.
Pro. Lt. Col.	
Gordon, Charles H.	2nd Lt.
Payne, Alexander D.	3rd Lt.
Pro. Captain	
Smith, William R.	O. Sgt.
Childs, James H.	2nd Sgt
Cap'td., Morris Island, S. C. prison, became blind while POW	
Mitchell, Robert	3rd Sgt.
Lewis, Richard	4th Sgt.
Million, Wellington	1st Cpl.
Tyler, Madison C.	2nd Cpl.
Shumate, George H.	3rd Cpl.
Clopton, Nathaniel A.	4th Cpl.
Ashton, Lawrence	Private
Able, George	Private
Capt'd.	
Armstrong, J. E.	Private
Alston, Harold	Private
Abel, C. T.	Private
D. in Elmira, N. Y., & buried in Woodlawn Nat'l Cemetery	
Bowen, William A.	Private
Wdd.	
Bailey, Joseph	Private
Beale, Severe F. G.	Private
Baggarly, Baldwin B.	Private
Boswell, Peter K.	Private
Boteler, Joseph	Private
Pro. 4th Cpl.	
Beale, L. D.	Private
Beale, John G.	Private
Brown, R. A.	Private
Brown, Martin B.	Private
Balch, W. C.	Private
Butler, M.	Private
Butler, E. L.	Private
Enl. at Bealeton	
Baggott, James	Private
Enl. but did not serve	
Balinger, J. W.	Private
Barbour, J. E.	Private
Scout for Gen'l Fitz. Lee	
Ballinger, B. G.	Private
Beale, James A.	Private
Bowen, P. B.	Private
Brown, Henry	Private
Boteler, James S.	Private
Chichester, Thomas T.	Private
Wdd.	
Colbert, Austin	Private
Crittenden, James L.	Private
Cooke, James F.	Private
Lost leg at Raccoon Ford	
Campbell, F. M.	Private
Carter, George H.	Private
Carter, Shirley	Private
Carter, Cassius	Private
Caynor, W. O.	Private
Childs, F. A.	Private
Clarke, Geo. W.	Private
Deserted, 1863	
Colbert, J. W.	Private
Colbert, B. P.	Private
Collins, T. E. B.	Private
Cologne, E. M.	Private
Courtney, M. F.	Private

Crain, P. K. Private
K., Stevensburg
Crosson, R. E. Private
Killed, 1864
Curtis, Charles P. Private
Scout, General Stuart
Cockrell, F. H. Private
Enl. but did not serve
Collins, J. B. Private
Downman, Rawley W. Private
Downman Robert H. Private
Downman, John Joseph Private
Digges, T. Henry Private
Digges, C. G. Private
Digges, C. W. Private
Duke, Frank R. Private
Wdd. at Cold Harbour
Downs, J. A. Private
D. & buried at Pt. Lookout, Md.
Eastham, J. R. Private
Edmonds, G. D. Private
Lost arm at Raccoon Ford
Edmonds, J. R. Private
Edmonds, R. H. Private
Wdd.
Embrey, Hugh T. Private
Embrey, J. J. Private
Epling, D. H. Private
Fant, John S. Private
Wdd. at Winchester, 1864
Fant, Thomas A. Private
Ficklen, William L. Private
Pro. 2nd Lt.
Fitzhugh, George Warren Private
Fletcher, Benton V. Private
Served 2 yrs., discharged
Fisher, E. L. Private
Ficklin, J. M. Private
Fones, Henry Private
Scout for Gen'l Wickham
Florence, C. G. Private
Florence, R. C. Private
Folin, J. M. Private
Fitzhugh, Thomas Private
Green, Nimrod M. Private
Glascock, Armistead Private
Gordon, William C. Private

Gordon, Samuel H. Private
K. 1861
Gaskins, Thomas T. Private
Detailed to purchase cattle
Gaskins, William E. Private
Company quartermaster
Gaskins, J. A. Private
Captured
George, J. G. Private
George, O. C. Private
George, M. Private
Gordon, Dallas P. Private
Wdd. Sailors Creek
Glascock, O. F. Private
Green, John A. Private
Green, T. R. Private
Green, M. M. Private
Gresham, E. C. Private
Captured
Gray, Robert A. Private
Trans. from 9th Va. Cav.
Green, B. P. Private
Pro. 2nd Cpl.
Greiner, C. C. Private
Gordon, I. J. Private
D. in service
Hart, Robert A. Private
Helm, Erasmus Private
K. 1862
Hamilton, Ferguson Private
Pro. 4th Sgt.
Holland, George L. Private
Hunton, William S. Private
Hunton, J. G. Private
Hunton, Henry Private
Hunton, W. S. Private
Hunton, Thomas Private
Captured
Hamilton, Hugh Private
Wdd. twice
Hansborough, J. F. Private
Horner, S. L. Private
Wdd.
Helm, Wm. P. Private
Helm, Harvey Private
K. 1864
Hunter, Alexander Private

Hite, C. R. Private
Capt'd., POW Elmira Prison
Holmes, M. C. Private
Helm, Woody Private
Hunton, Alexander Private
Holtzclaw, Charles E. Private
Holmes, C. F. Private
James, Marshall K. Private
Pro. 2nd Lt.
Jones, Strother S. Private
Bugler
Johnson, William Private
Johnson, Horace Private
Johnson, John Private
Captured
James, T. F. Private
Jones, Lawrence B. Private
Jones, W. B. Private
Johnson, George W. Private
Honorably dischg'd. 1864
Keith, Isham Private
Keith, James Private
King, George R. Private
Lewis, William H. Private
Leach, Charles H. Private
Captured
Lunceford, Thomas R. Private
Lear, Robert Private
Lee, William F. Private
K. 1863
Lewis, Richard Private
Lewis, W. H. Private
Lewis, J. H. Private
Lee, H. H. Private
Love, J. M. Private
Wdd. Fairfax
Lucas, R. W. Private
K. Trevillians Station
Latham, Charles Private
Latham, Robert Private
Loving, R. J. Private
McCormick, Robert Private
Lost leg at Stevensburg
Martin, Robert E. Private
Pro. 1st Sgt., wdd.
Martin, J. Richard Private
Scout for Gen. Fitzhugh Lee

Moffett, James H. Private
Meredith, Richard M. Private
Marshall, J. Markham Private
Markell, George H. Private
Marsteller, A. A. Private
Martin, Edward Private
Martin, J. M. Private
Martin, George W. Private
Mason, B. R. Private
McDonald, Elias H. Private
Mitchell, Robert Private
Captured
McVeigh, James H. Private
Millon, W. R. Private
Newhouse, John P. Private
Payne, John Scott Private
Payne, John D. Private
Priest, James G. Private
Porter, John M. Private
Payne, J. F. Private
Peters, J. M. Private
Detailed courier for Mosby
Pilcher, T. C. Private
Pegram, W. M. Private
Payne, John W. Private
Payne, E. S. Private
Riley, John W. Private
Rector, James W. Private
Read, Joseph S. Private
Pro. 3rd Sgt., scout for Gen'l. Stuart
Riley, J. T. Private
Rector, L. T. Private
Ransdall, G. C. Private
Robinson, J. P. Private
Ricketts, H. A. Private
Wdd. Raccoon Ford
Robinson, William Private
Killed, 1862
Smith, John P. Private
Smith, William A. Private
Smith, Channing M. Private
Scout for Gen'l. Stuart
Skinker, William K. Private
Schwab, Antonio Private
Smith, Sands Private

Smith, Wm. B. Private
K., 1864, Spotsylvania C. H.
Smith, Thos. J. Private
Smith, Isaac Private
Smith, Boyd M. Private
Smoot, W. A. Private
Stewart, C. W. (W. C.) Private
Butcher for the Reg't.
Shepherd, A. J. Private
Sowers, J. Kerfoot Private
K. Spotsylvania C. H., 1864
Stribling, A. J. Private
Stribling, W. E. Private
Sedgwick, Charles Private
Spilman, W. M. Private
Scott, W. W. Private
Sisson, E. B. Private
Stone, Peter Private
Drowned in Rappahannock River
Stone, John W. Private
D. in prison
Smith, A. D. Private
Wdd.
Sarver, J. M. Private
Simms, Walter Private
Smith, W. E. Private
Tyler, Lyttleton Private
Triplett, W. H. Private
Lost arm, Bridgewater
Tongue, Johnzie Private
POW, Pt. Lookout Prison
Taliaferro, John K. Private
Wdd.
Taylor, Geo. W. Private
Thorn, W. N. Private

Towson, J. W. Private
Turner, John R. Private
Turner, B. B. Private
Tyler, Madison Private
Killed, 1861
Taliaferro, Robert Private
Killed, 1861
Taliaferro, Charles Private
Tate, J. F. Private
Vass, James Private
Wdd. in Maryland
Vass, Geo. F. Private
Killed, 1862, Meadow Bridge
Vass, Townsend D. Private
Killed, 1864, Charles City Co.
Wayman, J. J.
Wise, W. A.
Captured
Wheatley, George
Weeks, Wm. H.
Willis, C. B.
Captured
Ward, Boliver
Withers, Melville
Wheatley, James G.
Washington, George A.
Washington, Courtney
killed, 1863, Williamsport
Ward, Ellis
Ward, Henry S.
Washington, Malcom
Yancy, James E.
deserted from the Federals and then went back to them

COMPANY I, ELEVENTH REGIMENT, KEMPER'S BRIGADE

Known as "Rough and Ready Rifles," this company was organized 25 May 1861 at Morrisville, Fauquier County, Va. The members were natives of Fauquier and Culpeper Counties.

Jamison, James Henry Captain
Jones, Andrew J. 1st Lt.
Pro. Captain
Taylor, James E. 2nd Lt.
Barker, John E. 2nd Lt.
Dropped, 21 Jan. '64

Stringfellow, Bruce W. 3rd Lt.
Wd. Seven Pines, POW
Allen, Joseph W. 1st Sgt.
Reduced to ranks, AWOL
Eskridge, Henry W. 2nd Sgt.

Tyack, Joseph L. 2nd Sgt.
Trans.

Embrey, Judson J. 3rd Sgt.
Pro. 1st Lt.

Jones, John W. 4th Sgt.

Berryman, Wm. N. 1st Cpl.
Reduced to ranks, AWOL

Bowen, James 2nd Cpl.

Edwards, James H. 2nd Cpl.
1 year's service

Edwards, Joseph H. 4th Cpl.

Anderson, James M. Private
D. in hospital, 9 Sept. 61

Allen, Jos. H. Private

Allen, David W. Private

Bennett, Oscar H. Private
D. of wds, Drury's Bluff, 10 May, 1864

Burton, James W. Private

Bowen, Peter B. Private
enl. at 18 yrs. of age

Brown, Jesse Private
Wdd. Gettysburg

Berry, Charles Private

Beard, R. N. Private

Brown, James W. Private
Wdd. Williamsburg

Blankenship, J. A. Private

Beale, James A. Private
Pro. 4th Sgt, wdd. 2nd Manassas

Brown, Thomas Private
Pro. 4th Cpl.

Cooksey, James W. Private
Capt'd.

Coppage, Lewis J. Private

Claxton, Henry H. Private
Capt'd., Gettysburg

Crews, I. G. Private

Callahan, J. A. Private

Courtney, Basil Private
D. & buried at Pt. Lookout, Md.

Cain, Peter Private

Childs, Zachariahs Private
Wdd. at Gettysburg

Covington, Robt. F. Private
Deserted

Claxton, Robert P. Private

Courtney, Crawford Private

Courtney, James E. Private

Courtney, Calvin Private

Drummond, M. H. Private

Embrey, Charles E. Private

Embrey, Norman Private
Pro. Sgt. & 2nd Lt., capt'd.

Embrey, Addison S. Private
Wdd., Seven Pines

Embrey, Robert E. Private
Wdd. Manassas

Embrey, Thomas R. Private

Embrey, Wm. M. Private
Wdd. Boonesboro, Md.

Embrey, James T. Private
D & buried at Point Lookout, Md.

Embrey, A. G. Private

Embrey, Charles O. Private

Edwards, Inman R. Private
Wdd. Gettysburg

Edwards, Henry F. Private
Wdd. Gettysburg

Edwards, John T. Private

Edwards, Jessie C. Private

Elliott, Wm. Private

Evans, John R. Private

Freeman, Sam'l S. Private

Freeman, Allen Private

French, Matthew M. Private

Gilliam, Walter F. Private
Wdd.

Glassell, James S. Private
Wdd. Gettysburg

Guthridge, Wm. E. Private

Hansbrough, Elizah T. Private

Huffman, Ludwell S. Private

Heflin, Robert Private

Huffman, Thomas Private
MIA, Gettysburg

Huffman, Whitson Private

Humphrey, Robert F. Private
Pro. Cpl. 27 Aug., 1861

Humphrey, David Private

Jones, George H. Private
D. at his home in Fauquier, 7/31/61
Jones, John W. Private
Jones, Henry F. Private
Jones, A. J. Private
Wdd. Gettysburg
Jones, Lewis Private
D. in hospital
Jones, Thomas E. Private
D. in prison
James, John B. Private
D. in Elmira Prison & buried in Woodlawn Cem.
James, Charles H. Private
James, Benjamin D. Private
Wdd. Gettysburg
Jacobs, Welford C. Private
Jacobs, Henry P. Private
Wdd. Melford Station
Jacobs, Spicer W. Private
Kemper, James G. Private
Kennedy, J. A. Private
Pro. Lt., d 2/29/1903
Lee, Thomas A. Private
Wdd. Gettysburg
Lindsay, J. Private
Prisoner at Newport News, d & buried at West Farm
McConchie, John Private
McConchie, Wm. A. Private
McConchie, James A. Private
McConchie, William Private
MIA, Gettysburg
Mayhew, Hampton Private
Moore, George J. Private
Martin, Wm. T. Private
K. at Munsons Hill, 8/27/1861
Oliver, Bernard Private
Obenshain, Walton Private
Palmer, J. H. Private
Wdd. Wilderness
Porter, Wm. S. Private
Pro. 1st Cpl., 5th Sgt.
Payne, Daniel J. Private
Rector, Alfred W. Private
Rector, Thomas M. Private
Stringfellow, M. R. Private
Smith, Robert Private
Wdd. at Seven Pines
Stribling, Robert H. Private
D. & buried at Point Lookout, Md.
Stigler, Joseph P. Private
Pro. 2nd Cpl., 7/27/1861
Stephens, Wm. A. Private
Stribling, James G. Private
Tate, Wm. H. Private
Torrent, Lewis C. Private
Capt'd. at Williamsburg
Taylor, J. E. Private
Tulloss, Wm. H. Private
Timmons, Franklin Private
Deserted from Capt. Green's Co., 6/17/1861
Urquhart, John J. Private
Woodward, B. Private
Wdd., near Richmond
Walker, John S. Private
Dischgd., 31 Aug., 1861, rendered no service
Willingham, Alexander Private

COMPANY K, EIGHTH VIRGINIA REGIMENT
HUNTON'S BRIGADE
"BEAUREGARD RIFLES"

This company was organized at Warrenton on 1 April 1861 by Robert Taylor Scott who was elected Captain. The company was in the Battle of First Manassas and in August 1861 assigned to the Eighth Virginia Regiment, commanded by Colonel Eppa Hunton.

Robert Taylor Scott Captain
Pro. Major, QM, Pickett's Div.
Smith, T. Towson 1st Lt.
Pro. Captain

Fant, Edward L., Jr. 2nd Lt.
K. Gaines Mill, 27 June 1862
Carter, Edward 3rd Lt.
C Gettysburg, pro. Captain
Lake, John L. 1st Sgt.
Pro. 1st Lt. 1862
Garrison, John N. 3rd Sgt.
Wd. Gaines Mill & Gettysburg
Miller, G. A. 2nd Sgt.
C
Brooke, George W. 4th Sgt.
Gaskins William H. 1st Cpl.
Pro. 1st Sgt. K. Gettysburg
Rothrock, Champ 2nd Cpl.
Harrington, Elias M. 3rd Cpl.
Wd. Gettysburg
Lawrence, L. Mason 4th Sgt.
Pro. 1st Sgt. K Cold Harbor
Athey, Samuel Milton Private
Pro. 2nd Sgt.
Able, Robert Private
K 2nd Cold Harbor
Anderson, French Private
Alley, Adolpheus Private
Alums, Wilson Private
Bayne, George W. Private
Pro. Cpl., Wdd. Gettysburg
Baggett, Richard Private
Ball, Edward J. Private
Buchanan, C. H. Private
Pro. Cpl.
Botts, Edward Private
Botts, Samuel Private
Burchett, J. W. Private
Burchett, W. H. Private
Cochran, Michael Private
Cook, John T. Private
Carter, Benton Private
Caynor, ———— Private
Candler, John W. Private
Dennis, Frank Private
K. Gettysburg
Didlake, Andrew J. Private
Drake, Jas. Private
Furr, Joseph Private
K. Balls Bluff

Furr, Chapman Private
Deserted
Fields, Charles W. Private
Wdd. Gettysburg
Fewell, Charles H. Private
Pro. Cpl.
Fewell, Ben Private
Fletcher, Charles Private
Buried in Brooklyn Nat'l Cemetery
Fletcher, Erasmus Private
Wdd. Balls Bluff
Furr, Charles W. Private
Lost arm at Gaines Mill
Follin, Patrick Private
Wdd. Gettysburg
Gillispie, Ralph Private
Dischg'd. 1862
Glascock, Minor Private
D. 1863
Garrison, R. A. Private
Heflin, A. M. Private
Hanback, S. B. Private
Harris, J. Edward Private
K. near Richmond
Heflin, James M. Private
Pro. Cpl.
Heflin, Morgan A. Private
Wdd. Gettysburg
Hinson, George Private
K. Gettysburg
Hollins, John B. Private
Jones, John Private
James, Waverly Private
Dischg'd.
Jewell, John Private
Julian, Ralph Private
Kirkpatrick, Joseph Private
Wdd. Gettysburg
Kearns, Jackson Private
Leach, Peter T. Private
K. near Richmond
Lunceford, Evan O. Private
Legg, William Private
Lowry, ———— Private
Milton, Wm. L. Private
Moffitt, Robt. F. Private
Pro. Lt.

Miller, G. Allen — Private
Moore, John A. — Private
Magonola, Patrick — Private
McClanahan, Armistead O. — Private
McClanahan, James T. — Private
Died & buried at Pt. Lookout Maryland
McClanahan, Presley — Private
McClanahan, Willis A. — Private
Moore, J. — Private
Enl. 1862
Monroe, George — Private
K. Gettysburg
Mabe, Leander — Private
Mason, Smith — Private
O'Brien, Michael — Private
O'Roark, ———— — Private
Pence, Frank K. — Private
Pillers, J. — Private
Quana, Dennis — Private
Deserted to enemy
Rector, William E. — Private
Wdd. Ball's Bluff

Redman, Elisha — Private
Wdd. Seven Pines
Roark, A. W. — Private
Spinks, C. W. — Private
Swayne, William E. — Private
Wdd.
Swain, John H. — Private
Wdd. Seven Pines
Siddall, ———— — Private
K. Gettysburg
Smith, A. — Private
D. Ft. Delaware
Self, F. — Private
Taylor, William F. — Private
Pro. Cpl., 1862
Timmons, Alex. T. — Private
Utterback, John N. — Private
Cook
White, J. H. — Private
D. in Camp Morton, buried in Green Lawn Cemetery
Yates, Wm. W. — Private
Pro. Cpl., Sgt., 2nd Lt.

COMPANY A, 6th REGIMENT CAVALRY BRIGADE

This company was organized at Unison, Loudoun County, in June, 1861 and is included in the rosters of Fauquier County organized companies because many of the men were residents of the latter county. This company was known as the "Loudoun Dragoons."

Note: Luther W. Hopkins, a member of this company, wrote a memoir entitled: "From Bull Run to Appomattox; A Boy's View" (Baltimore, 1908). Concerning his military connections he says, "I was in Company A, first commanded by Col. Richard H. Dulany, who served a few months and was promoted. He was succeeded by Bruce Gibson of Fauquier County, Virginia, who served during the entire war, and was once knocked from his horse by the concussion of a shell, but sustained no other injuries. Was a prisoner from June, 1864, to the end of the war."

Dulany, Richard H. — Captain
Afterwards Lt. Col. 7th Va. Cav.
Dulany, H. G. — 1st Lt.
Resigned, 1862
Plaster, George E. — 2nd Lt.
Served as Capt., Capt'd.

Carter, Robert — 3rd Lt.
Pro. Captain

—Reorganization 1862—

Gibson, Bruce — Captain
Captured, Yellow Tavern
Armistead, Bowles E. — 1st Lt.
Wd Cold Harbor

Gibson, Joseph A. 2nd Lt.
Wd Yellow Tavern
Laws, J. Newton 1st Sgt.
Wd Stoney Creek
Edmonds, B. S. 2nd Sgt.
Wd Five Forks
Reed, Oscar 3rd Sgt.
Wd Fairfield & capt'd.
Rector. Asa 4th Sgt.
Wd Spottsylvania
Armistead, Walker
Ord. Sgt. of Regt.
Palmer, Frank Cpl.
Wd Cold Harbor
Rector, Harvey Cpl.
Wd Cold Harbor
Peake, B. F. Cpl.
Marshall, R. A. M. Cpl.
D in Elmira, N. Y. & buried in Woodlawn Nat'l Cemetery.
Atwell, Johnson Private
Wdd. Snickersville
Alder, Frank Private
Wdd. Spottsylvania, capt'd Brandy Station
Alder, Nathan Private
Wdd. Cedarville
Alder, Flavius Private
K. Brandy Station
Ashby, Edward Private
Armistead, Walker Keith Private
Son of General Armistead
Anderson, __________ Private
Dischg'd.
Alder, Geo. F. Private
Bray, __________ Private
Boggs, John Private
Balthis, Charles Private
Bailey, William Private
Capt'd.
Brent, Mont. Private
K. Brandy Station
Ball, John Private
K. Upperville
Beavers, Benjamin Private
Barber, Thomas Private
Brathan, Charles Private
Beavers, R. E. Private
Carter, Thomas Private
Wdd. & capt'd. Brandy Station
Carter, James F. Private
Capt'd. Brandy Station
Carter, Thomas Goody Private
Carter, Robert Private
Carter, Delwin Private
K. at Trevillians Station
Carr, Thomas Private
Capt'd. Yellow Tavern
Carrol, Thomas Private
Carrol, R. Private
Carrol, Lewis Private
Dischg'd. over age
Chappelear, George W. Private
Wdd. Five Forks. Pro. Cpl. for gallantry
Chappelear, J. Armistead Private
Chappelear, Pendleton Private
Trans. to Mosby K. Dranesville
Dennis, Joseph Private
Capt'd. Cold Harbor, d. in prison
Deacon, William Private
Capt'd. Shepherdstown
Dickens, Frank Private
Dowdell, Flavius Private
Lt. White's Btn, Capt. Co. C
Dowdell, Thomas Private
Driscoll, Richard Private
Capt'd. Yellow Tavern, d. in prison at Pt. Lookout, Md.
Deakins, Robert Private
Trans. to Maryland Line, 1864
Evans, Robert F. Private
Edmonds, E. G. Private
Wdd. near Yellow Tavern
Eliason, Rutledge H. Private
Wdd. Spottsylvania, trans. to inactive duty
Edwards, John Private
Edwards, Benjamin Private
Furr, John W. Private
Wdd. near Five Forks
Furr, James Private
Wdd. Brandy Station

Ferguson, Sewell Private
Ferguson, William Private
Fleming, Joseph Private
Feltner, Joseph Private
Frazier, Herod Private
Dischg'd. over age
Fitzhugh, Champ Private
Fowler, Everard Private
Gibson, John N. Private
Gibson, Douglas Private
Gibson, Gilbert B. Private
Wdd. Culpeper C.H.
Gibson, John E. Private
Griffith, William Private
Deserted
Gossum, Edward
(or Edwin) Private
D. in hospital, 1861
Gordon, George A. Private
Galleheur, George Private
Capt'd. at Upperville
Gregg, William H. Private
Green, Wirt W. Private
Wdd. Fairfield
Hough, Jackson Private
Disch'd, over age
Henry, Edward Private
Disch'd., over age
Hope, Theodore Private
Hopkins, Luther Private
Capt'd. Upperville
Hannoran, John Private
Wdd. Fairfield and Trevillians
Hummer, Mason Private
Deserted
Hummer, John Private
Hoskiss, William Private
Regt. blacksmith
Hall, Snowden Private
Wdd. Trevillians
Hunton, Henry Private
Trans. to Engraving Dept.
Howdershell, Humphrey Private
Hoge, George D. Private
Hill, Laban L. Private
Capt'd. near Petersburg

Hesser, Mason Private
Hesser, C. C. (or Bud) Private
Hunt, ———— Private
D. in prison
Hixson, William Private
Killed near Aldie
Hedgeman, Grayson Private
Trans. to Infantry
Homer, Alex Private
Hixson, William A. Private
D. and buried at Pt. Lookout
James, Robert M. Private
Courier to General Lomax
James, Fleet Private
Jenkins, Edward Private
Keane, John Private
Kline, John A. Private
Knight, Bud Private
Trans. to White's Batt'n
Knight, D. M. Private
Keys, John Private
K. Cedarville
Kirkpatrick, M. Private
Wdd. Brandy Station
Leslie, Thomas Private
Accidentally killed near Strasburg
Laws, Norval Private
Capt'd. near Paris
Lipscomb, Robert Private
Lock, Jack Private
Deserted
Lock, William Private
Deserted
Luckett, Cook D. Private
Leith, Theodore Private
Wdd. at Fairmont
Leith, Lawrence Private
Wdd. near Culpeper
Leith, Dallas Private
K. Spottsylvania
Lawrence, John Private
Deserted
Lovett, Mort Private
Dropped from the roll
Love, Landon Private
Dropped from the roll

Leake, Benjamin F. Private
Lawrence, Jno. W. Private
D. in Elmira, N.Y., & buried in Woodlawn Nat'l. Cemetery
Miley, H. T. Private
Color Sgt.
Martz, Samuel Private
Teamster
Martz, Albert Private
Deserted
Miley, Thomas Private
Capt'd. at Yellow Tavern
Moorehead, William Private
K. Yellow Tavern
Moulden, Jeremiah Private
Dischg'd. for inability after 3 years of faithful service.
Marlow, George W. Private
Marlow, James Private
Deserted
Marlow, Jeremiah Private
McArtor, Frank Private
McArtor, Henry Private
Capt'd. at Upperville
McArtor, Thomas Private
Mercer, Jesse Private
Mercer, Nathan Private
Deserted
Marshall, Robert Private
D. in prison
McLeary, John Private
Deserted
Myers, Henry Private
K. near Strasburg
Murphy, J. F. Private
Moreland, Wm. Private
McClaughrey, Jno. Private
Maby, Alpheus Private
Neal, Fauntleroy Private
Nightingale, ———— Private
Nevett, Edward Private
D. in prison at Pt. Lookout
Osborne, Herbert Private
Capt'd.
Osborne, James M. Private
Owens, Mason Private
K. Harpers Ferry
Powell, William Private
Trans. to 11th Va. Cav.
Peake, John Tip Private
Headquarters orderly
Peake, Frank Private
Patton, John Private
Dischg'd.
Pine, George Private
Redmond, Wilford Private
Deserted
Reed, John Private
Wdd. Stoney Creek
Rector, Caleb C. Private
Cpl., capt'd. at Yellow Tavern. D. at Pt. Lookout Prison
Rose, Custis Private
Capt'd. near Culpeper. D. in prison
Ripley, ———— Private
Roszel, deButts Private
Capt'd., Cold Harbor
Robinson, John G. Private
Robinson, Robert Private
Capt'd. near Culpeper
Robinson, Melbourne Private
Capt'd. Yellow Tavern, d. in prison at Pt. Lookout
Rollins, J. H. Private
Reid, S. D. Private
Wdd. at Yellow Tavern
Sowers, William Private
Wdd. at Upperville
Sowers, James Private
Wdd. at Spottsylvania
Sowers, Robert L. Private
Settle, J. M. Private
Wdd. at Culpeper
Shores, Alfred Private
Stewart, William Private
Deserted from picket post
Smith, L. W. Private
Strother, John W. Private
Trenary, E. S. Private

Trenary, Thomas — Private
Discg'd.

Thorne, ———— — Private
K. at Strasburg

Thompson, George — Private
K. in Loudoun

Taylor, John — Private
K., Cold Harbor

Taylor, Andrew — Private
Dischg'd, over age

Taylor, A. J. — Private

Tutwiler, W. P. — Private

Teppett, Hy — Private

Vandeventer, Isaac — Private

Wilmouth, Jack — Private
Wd. Cold Harbor, Capt'd. Luray

Whiting, Clarence — Private
Pro. Adjt. 7th Va. Cav.

Wilson, Crosby — Private
Capt'd. Yellow Tavern

Wiley, H. T. — Private

Wiley, Cornelius — Private

Willingham, Jno. — Private

Young, Samuel — Private
Capt'd. Brandy Station

COMPANY K, 17th VIRGINIA INFANTRY REGIMENT

THE WARRENTON RIFLES

The Warrenton Rifles were mustered into service on 27 April 1861 at Dumfries, by Major Kerr. The Company was organized in 1859. On 17 April 1861, the day Virginia seceded, this company marched to the front under command of Captain John Q. Marr. After performing various duties, by order, it reported to General Beauregard at Manassas, who made it his infantry vanguard. The company was ordered forward to Fairfax Court House, at which place it reached 31 May and went into camp. At two o'clock in the a. m. of 1 June, while it was pitch dark, the command was routed out by an attack by a company of U. S. Dragoons, under Capt. Tompkins. The enemy was driven off with loss in munitions, horses and Capt. Tompkins wounded. But the brave Capt. Marr was mortally wounded and Col. R. S. Ewell shot through the shoulder. Captain J. Q. Marr was the first to be slain—the first blood to stain the soil of the South in the War Between the States.

Marr, John Quincy — Captain
Killed in skirmish at Fairfax C.H., 1 June, 1861. Had been sent pro. to Colonel

Shackleford, B. Howard — 1st Lt.
Pro. to Capt. 3 June, 1861. Wdd. Blackburn's Ford, disch'd

McGee, J. W. — 1st Lt.
Elected Captain 1 March, 1862. Served with distinction until April, 1862

Withers, H. C. — 2nd Lt.
Honorably disch'd, fall, 1861

Graham, D. E. — 1st Sgt.
Reduced to ranks

Brodie, A. M. — 2nd Sgt.
Wdd. 25 Aug., 1864, pro. to 1st Lt.

Tompkins, J. H. F. — 3rd Sgt.
Made Lt. Fairfax C. H., later honorably disch'd, 10 Oct., 62

Turner, John R. — 4th Sgt.
Pro. 2nd Lt., 1 March, 1862

Kemper, Hugh T. — 1st Cpl.

Lear, William — 2nd Cpl.
Trans. to another service

Beckham, John — 3rd Cpl.
Pro. 1st Sgt. 31 Aug., 62. Trans. to Stuart, 7 Apl., 64. Wdd. Sharpsburg

Hamme, L. E. — 4th Cpl.

Bragg, William M. — Ensign
Trans. to Mosby. D. in prison

Allison, R. H. — Private

Allison, Richard S. — Private

Allen, Henry — Private

Bragg, Charles P. — Private
Trans. to Med. Dept.

Bennett, Henry T. — Private
Pro. Cpl.

Bowling, Egbert T. — Private

Bowling, William — Private

Brooks, Thomas D. — Private

Briggs, Henry C. — Private
Wdd. Drury's Bluff

Cromwell, Oliver — Private

Cole, Francis M. — Private
Wdd. Frazier's Farm, dischg'd

Cole, Joseph N. — Private
Dischg'd

Carter, Charles S. — Private
Trans. to cavalry, 4/18/63

Cologne, John A. C. — Private
Pro. 2nd Sgt., POW 8/30/64

Day, Henry — Private

Day, Alexander — Private
Died

Davis, Lancaster Cook — Private

Digges, Charles W. — Private
Dischg'd, ill health

Digges, George W. — Private
Wdd. Sharpsburg, 9/17/62. Trs. to Black Horse Cav., 1863. Made Lieut.

Davisson, Hugh N. — Private
Dischg'd, 19 Aug., 1861

Embrey, Albert G. — Private
K.I.A., Second Cold Harbor

Edmonds, Elias, Jr. — Private
Wdd. & discharged

Francis, Aaron B. — Private
Made Color Cpl. Wdd. at Dinwiddie Court House

Fisher, John E. — Private
Wdd. Seven Pines, dischg'd

Fisher, Edward L. — Private

Fisher, James A. — Private
Pro. 1st Sgt., Co. G, 17th Va. Regiment

Fletcher, Robert H. — Private

Fletcher, Harrison — Private

Florance, Benj. F. — Private
Pro. 3rd. Sgt. 12/14/61

Fletcher, Edwin — Private
Wdd. Second Manassas

Fletcher, Albert — Private

Fant, John E. P. — Private

Field, William H. — Private
D. 19 August, 1862

Frankland, Walter — Private
Trans. to Mosby, pro. Capt.

Foster, William G. — Private
Pro. to 2nd Cpl., Sgt.

Golway, William — Private
Dischg'd

Groves, Robert H. — Private
Pro. Cpl., d. from disease

Hughlett, Richard K. — Private
Dischg'd

Hughes, George N. — Private
Pro. Sgt.

Harris, Albert — Private
Wdd. at Howlett's House

Hope, James W. — Private
D. 15 Sept., 1861

Hoffman, Otterbine — Private
Wdd. at Suffolk, dischg'd

Hansbrough, Peter C. — Private

Hansbrough, John G. — Private

Hart, Thomas G. — Private

Jeffries, Frederick — Private

Jeffries, Joseph A. — Private
Detached service, Med. Dept.

Jenkins, George F. Private
Wdd.

Jones, Elcon (Elkton) Private
Trans. to Signal Corps, pro. Capt.

Kemper, George N. Private

Kirby, James D. Private
Elected 3rd Lt., 17 Sept., 1861, 1st Lt., 1 March, 1862; Capt., 26 Apl., 1862; dist for gallantry; wdd. Dinwiddie C. H.; present at surrender

Kloeber, Chas. C. Private

Kane, Thomas F. Private
K.I.A., Seven Pines

Lindsay, Stephen C. Private
Elected 2nd Lt. 4 June, 1861, resigned 1 Sept., 1861

Leitz, George Private

Lear, Alpheus Private
Trans.

Love, Robert Private
K.I.A., Seven Pines

McConchie, Benj. F. Private
Dischg'd

McLearen, Thos. C. Private
AWOL, July 1862

McClanahan, George W. Private
Wdd. & died, 5 May, 1862

McIlhany, Hugh M. Private
Trans. to Mosby, pro. Lt.

McIntosh, Charles R. Private
Wdd.

Mays, Jefferson Private

Moore, Joseph E. Private
On detached service

Mooney, Nicholas R. Private

Mooney, Gallemus T. Private
Wdd. at Drury's Bluff

Marable, Champion Private
Wdd. 25 Aug., 1864

Murray, Daniel Private
Trans. to Capt. Murray's Fauq. Guards, 15 July, 1861

Murray, Thomas J. Private
Pro. Sgt., made Lt. of Irish Bn.

Marshall, Robert T. Private
Trans. to Washington Arty. 2 Oct., 1861. K.I.A.

Minter, William H. Private
Wdd.

Nelson, Joseph H. Private
Trans. to Mosby, pro. Lt.

Norris, Wm. C., Jr. Private
Detached service, Ord. Dept.

Parkinson, John W. Private
Dischg'd

Pattie, James S. Private

Pemberton, James O. Private
Wdd. 5 May, 1862, dist. for gallantry

Payne, Richards, Jr. Private
2nd Lt. in Irish Bn., 26 Sept., 1864

Payne, Richard Private
D. from wounds, 8 May 1862 (battle of Williamsburg)

Payne, Henry Private
Wdd. Seven Pines

Risdon, William J. Private

Reynolds, Lewis H. Private
Dischg'd

Saunders, Thomas B. Private
Wdd. Suffolk, dischg'd

Sedwick, John F. Private
Deserted, 18 Nov.,1864

Smith, Edwin Private
Made Capt. & Ass't. Commissary 49th Va. Regt, Sept. 1861

Smith, Norman E. Private
Trans. to Black Horse Cav., later trans. to Mosby, pro Lt. K.I.A.

Singleton, James A. Private
Wdd. Williamsburg, POW Made Sgt. K.I.A., Drury's Bluff

Stanfield, Henry A. R. Private

Suddoth, Patrick H. Private
Wdd. Seven Pines

Suddoth, Robert A. Private
Wdd. 5 May, 1862

Sinclair, Albert G. Private
Wdd. Blackburn's Ford, dischg'd

Stout, James H.	Private
Spilman, William M.	Private
Wdd. Williamsburg	
Slaughter, Lewis	Private
Pro. 3rd Lt., April 1862; wdd. Sharpsburg	
Smith, Albert G.	Private
Made Adj., 38th Va. Regt.	
Smith, John J.	Private
Tapp, Henry J.	Private
AWOL, July 1862	
Thomas, John P.	Private
Made Cpl., Co. K	
White, Frank	Private
Weaver, Richard A.	Private
D. typhoid fever, Richmond, 15 May, 1862	
Walden, Richard E.	Private
Wdd.	
Weaver, Mason A.	Private
Pro. 4th Cpl., 17 Sept., 1861	
Wall, William	Private
Dischg'd	
Withers, Andrew F.	Private
Whitescarver, George H.	Private
Trans. to Mosby, pro. Lt., K.I.A.	
Washington, Mason	Private
Wheeler, John V.	Private

BATTERY A, 12th BATTALION. "Brooke's Battery"

Organized at Warrenton, March, 1862 by James Vass Brooke. The battery was attached to Poague's Battalion of Artillery, Jackson's Corps. (Bulletin, Fauquier Historical Society, July, 1924, pp. 464-465).

Brooke, James V.	Captain
disabled, 1862, resigned July 1863.	
Utterback, Addison W.	Captain
Pugh, John W.	Lieut.
Brown, Wm. Judson	Lieut.
Wdd., Gettysburg	
McCarty, Wm. T.	Lieut.
Fry. Hugh N.	Lieut.
Barnett, Jas. N.	Sergt.
Killed, 1863, near Furnace	
Booth, Jas. S.	Sergt.
Campbell, Alex. S.	Sergt.
Carson, Andrew J.	Sergt.
Chilton, James V.	Sergt.
Groves, Wm. B.	Sergt.
Henson, Wm. H.	Sergt.
Louthan, Carter M.	Sergt.
Dischgd, July 1862, illness	
Bayne, William	Sergt.
Barnett, J. Edward	Sergt
Ashton, Henry	Sgt. Major
Tulloss, Jos. D.	Sergt.
Downing, Charles W.	Corpl.
Jones, John W.	Corpl.
Kemper, Leigh R.	Corpl.
Suddith, John R.	Corpl.
Wdd. 2 May, 1863, Furnace	
Tyler, Richard B.	Corpl.
Weems, John C.	Corpl.
Wells, Joseph E.	Corpl.
Wdd. 14 Oct., 1863, Bristow Sta.	
White, John W.	Corpl.
Rawson,	Corpl.
Ames, John C.	Private
Wdd. Chancellorsville, 1863	
Amiss, Carroll	Private
Kd. Petersburg, Va., 1864	
Anderson, Herod	Private
Aylor, Henry L .	Private
Back, Bumbrey W.	Private
Bailey, James H.	Private
Bailey, William	Private
Bailey, Richard	Private
Wdd. Dec. 1864, Dutch Gap	
Bartlett, James	Private
Died 1862, at Camp Lee	
Bridwell, Wm. T.	Private
Britton, Wm. C.	Private
Brown, David H.	Private
Bryant, George	Private

Burgess, James M. Private
Butler, James Private
Baker, Jacob H. Private
Buckner, J. A. Private
Wdd. at Petersburg
Barnes, J. H. Private
Bell, Jos. F. Private
Barnett, George N. Private
Baggarly, Nimrod W. Private
Browning, Mark A. H. Private
Carroll, John C. Private
Caynor, William O. Private
Claggett, Isaac N. Private
Clarke, Robert Private
Carey, James Private
Colvin, James F. Private
Crawford, ———— Private
Curtis, Jesse Private
Campbell, Alexander Private
Corbin, Edmund Private
Dixon, Thomas Private
Edwards, John Private
Embrey, John A. Private
Embrey, Pollard F. Private
Wdd., May 1864, Wilderness
Eveleth, John Private
Embrey, Edgar A. Private
Faulconer, William Private
Finchum, James Private
Fletcher, John T. Private
Deserted, took U.S.A. oath of allegiance.
Fletcher, James H. Private
Fletcher, Townsend Private
Gaines, Benj. F. Private
Gallehugh, Andrew J. Private
Gray, W. Fitzhugh Private
Green, George M. Private
Gallehugh, G. W. Private
Glascock, Roger C. Private
Hackley, Benj. F. Private
Hackley, Francis M. Private
Harris, William P. Private
Helm, R. Henry Private
Wdd. June 1864, at Trevillians Sta.

Hobson, James E. Private
Wdd Chancellorsville, May 2, 1863
Died at Richmond, May 1863.
Holtzclaw, C. Taylor Private
Huffman, John W. Private
Henson, W. H. Private
Harwood, E. L. Private
Heflin, Amos Private
Howison, Thomas Private
Jenkins, Appleton Private
Johnson, C. McLean Private
Jenkins, Church Private
Jeffries, Enoch Private
Jeffries, Lemuel G. Private
Kemper, Peter Private
Kemper, William D. Private
Wdd. 14 Oct., 1863, Bristow Station
Kemper, Leigh R. Private
Louthan, Carter M. Private
Dischgd, July 1862. POW
Lloyd, Columbus Private
Lillard, Sinclair M. Private
Lillard, John W. Private
Served 3 mos. 1863
Lloyd, J. H. Grattan Private
D. June 1862, Richmond
Leathen, E. Private
Leathen, John W. Private
Leathen, W. H. Private
May, John E. Private
May, Robert Private
Martin, Alfred C. Private
Mauzy, John P. Private
McCormick, Jos. B. Private
McCormick, William Private
Minter, John B. Private
Mitchell, Lovelace Private
Mooney, Luton A. Private
Morris, Wm. A. Private
May, Lewis Private
Munn, Jas. W. Private
May, William R. Private
Newman, John T. Private
Norris, Jas. French Private
Discharged. 1862, illness

Nicholson, William	Private
Olinger, Grayson E.	Private
Phillips, Richard H.	Private
Plunkett, John T.	Private
Reamer, Marion F.	Private
Rector, Henry	Private
Rector, Thomas B.	Private
Cpl., 1862	
Ross, Price H.	Private
Wdd. 2 May, 1863, Furnace	
Rasson, Henry H.	Private
Rasson, Jno. D. E.	Private
Rasson, Wm. A.	Private
Cpl. 1862.	
Routt, Peter A.	Private
Rush, James J.	Private
Rush, John	Private
Rosser, G. H.	Private
Rosser, Sam	Private
Shirley, J. Richard	Private
Shotwell, Albert	Private
Shotwell, George C.	Private
Shotwell, Reuben H.	Private
Sluyter, Benj. F.	Private
Soaper, William R.	Private
Sutphin, James	Private
Sinclair, James A.	Private
Teasley, William W.	Private
Tharpe, George W.	Private
Wdd. at Petersburg, Apr. 2, 1865	
Thayer, James M.	Private
Thomas, Joseph D.	Private
Tyler, Winfield S.	Private
Utterback, Addison W.	Private
Promoted to Captain	
Utz, Augustus S.	Private
Enl. Madison County	
Utz, Joseph P.	Private
Enl. Madison County	
Utz, Toliver S.	Private
Enl. Madison County	
Wayland, Fielding H.	Private
Enl. Madison County	
Weakley, Carnott	Private
Wdd. at Gettysburg	
Webb, James R.	Private
Wdd. at Gettysburg	
Weems, A. Wellington	Private
Weems, O. Taney	Private
Welch, Richard	Private
Wells, Patrick T.	Private
Willis, William L.	Private
Wine, James	Private
Enl. Madison Co.	
Weakley, B. F.	Private
White, Jno. W.	Private
Yowell, James D.	Private
Enl. Madison County	
Yowell, C. Storey	Private
Enl. Madison County	
Yowell, J. Frank	Private
Enl. Madison County	

COMPANY A, SEVENTH REGIMENT, VIRGINIA CAVALRY

Some years prior to the War Between the States, General Turner Ashby had organized a company of cavalry to protect the neighborhood of his home (Markham) from the sprees of the Irish who were employed to construct the Manassas Gap Railroad. This organization was known as "The Mountain Rangers". When John Brown made his attack on the arsenal at Harper's Ferry this company was mustered into the Virginia Militia. Captain Turner Ashby's payroll dated 30 January 1860 is in the Flowers Collection, Duke University, Durham, N. C. After witnessing the execution for treason of John Brown the company returned to Fauquier and remained active, holding musters and serving "as a patrol for the County of Fauquier. . . . The limits of (which were) the districts of Farrowsville, Rectortown, The Plains and that portion of Salem district above Carters Run to the River." (Minute Book, 24 Dec. 1860).

On 17 June 1861, The Mountain Rangers became Company A of the newly organized Seventh Regiment, Virginia Cavalry, known as The Laurel Brigade. Before leaving Fauquier the Company was presented with a handsomely embroidered flag, by the "Ladies of Salem" . . . the flag, which always remained by Ashby's side on the march and outside his tent on bivouac, is preserved in the Confederate Museum, Richmond.

PAY ROLL CAPTAIN ASHBY'S COMPANY (MOUNTAIN RANGERS) Pay of officers and soldiers rations, use of horses, emoluments, etc. Jany. 30th 1860. (Flowers Collection, Duke University).

Turner Ashby, Capt. $196.00, pay per month
William F. Turner, 1st Lieut.
Dan'l Hatcher, 2nd Lieut.
T. L. Settle, Surgeon
Bush Grigsby 1st Sgt.
Jos. C. Gibson, 2nd Sgt.
J. Chap Little, 3rd Sgt.
Rich, Ashby 4th Sgt.
Rich. C. Horner 1st Cpl.
Luther R. Ashby, 2nd Cpl.
H. C. Hathaway, 3rd Cpl.
Jno. Fletcher, 4th Cpl.
Thomas H. Payne

PRIVATES

Jas. L. Adams, H. C. Adams, J. W. Brent, Rich. P. Buckner, Charles Berkeley, Milt. Byone, W. B. Collins, Edw. Carter, Collins Dixon, Thos. H. Foster, Oswell Foley, Bush Garrison, Ths. W. Glascock, Nat. Grigsby, Alf. Glascock, D. B. Harrison, Harry Hatcher, F. B. Hutchison, K. G. Hicks, Wm. H. Ingle, H. B. Jones, Jno. W. Kincheloe, E. D. Kincheloe, E. H. Kidwell, C. B. Kincheloe, R. C. Lawler, John H. Lewis, Wm. Marshall, Chs. Manning, Jas. Marshall, Jas. T. Mageath, F. W. Maddux, Wm. C. Marshall, T. W. Maddux, Ths. E. Martin, T. T. Milton, H. B. Phillips, Jno. M. Phillips, R. H. Rixey, J. H. Rector, Jos. H. Reid, Wm. A. Rector, A. H. Rector, Jno. M. Stewart, R. M. Stribling, Jr., D. O. Smith, Wm. Shumate, Jas. A. Sutton, Jas. E. Templeman, F. R. Welch, Wm. T. Weaver, Rich. Ashby.

Ashby, Turner Captain
pro. Lt. Col., Col., Brig. Gen'l. k. near Harrisonburg, 6 June 1862

Ashby, Richard Captain
succeeded his brother, wdd. at Kelly's Island, 1861. died of wounds.

Fletcher, John W. Captain
Killed, Buckton Station, 23 May 1862

Turner, William F. Captain
Retired 1862

Hatcher, Daniel C. Captain
Enl. as Private, pro.: Lt., Captain, 1862; Major, 1865.

Smith, Granville T. 1st Lt.
K. 1864

Smith, Sullivan 2nd Lt.
Served 4 years

Glascock, Alfred 3rd Lt.
Pro. to Capt. in Mosby's Bn.

Potterfield, Thomas L. Ord. Sgt.
Served 4 years

Payne, Thos. Henry — Ord. Sgt.
POW, Pt. Lookout Prison, d. in prison & buried there, 1864

Fletcher, Joshua C. — 2nd Sgt.
Wdd. Nov. 1864

Welch, F. Rush — 3rd. Sgt.
Wdd. Buckton Sta., 1862

Fravel, David H. — 1st. Cpl.
Enl. July 1861, Rockingham Co.

Ashby, Vernon — Private
Cptd. Sept 25, 1863

Ashby, Luther R. — Private
Pro. 2nd Lt., cptd. July 5, 1863, Boonesboro, Md., POW

Athey, Waynefield S. — Private

Anderson, E. W. — Private

Anderson, Edward — Private
Captd. in Maryland, 1862

Ashby, J. William — Private
Trans. to Co. I, 12th Va. Cav.

Barnes, S. Jacob — Private

Blackmore, Robert — Private

Byrne, H. Milton — Private

Brent, J. Warren — Private
K. Upperville, 7 June, 1863

Brent, William A. — Private
Wdd. Buckton Sta., 1862

Brent, Hugh — Private
Wdd. Buckton Sta.

Bruce, Charles — Private
K. 28 June, 1864, Sappony church

Buckner, Richard C. — Private
Discharged, 1861.

Brent, James A. — Private
Trans. to Wicker's Bn. 1862

Cochran, Thomas B. — Private

Crane, Major — Private

Cornwell, Silas — Private
D. fever, 1862

Carter, George S. — Private

Carter, J. Pitman — Private
K. Wilderness, 1864

Clem, A. W. — Private
Blacksmith

Chancellor, George W. — Private

Coffman, A. — Private
Wdd.

Carter, Cassius — Private
Discharged, 1861

Crane, Smith — Private
Discharged 1862, over-age, joined Co. I, 12th Va. Cav.

Diffendaffer, George — Private
Discharged 1861

Donnelly, John B. — Private
Wdd. at Slaughter Mt., Aug. 9, 1862

Dean, Thomas W. — Private

Darnell, J. B. — Private

Dawson, Nicholas — Private
Wdd. Brandy Station

Dufenderfer, J. M. — Private
In Lawton, Okla., 1913

Engle, Bub — Private
Discharged 1861

Eastham, Henry F. — Private

Eskridge, H. R. — Private
Discharged 1861

Evans, Caswaller — Private
Joined Co. at 13 years & served 4 years, one horse killed under him. He was the youngest member in the Company.

Flynn, Henry — Private

Flynn, John — Private
Dischgd, 1862, joined Mosby

Fletcher, Clinton — Private
K. Greenland Gap Raid, 1863

Fletcher, Robert — Private
Wdd. First Manassas

Foster, William — Private
Capt. in Mosby's Bn.

Francis, George W. — Private
Served 4 years

Foley, Oswald — Private
K. Kelleys Island, 1861

Foster, Hunton — Private
Trans. Co. H, 6th Va. Cav.

Geiman, Jesse C. — Private

Gibson, Gurley — Private
Captd., Slaughter Mt. 1862

Glascock, Robert T. Private
Discharged, 1861
Glascock, J. Samuel Private
Discharged, 1861
Grigsby, Bushrod Private
Discharged, 1863, overage
Glascock, Thomas W. Private
Grigsby, Nathaniel Private
Wdd. Upperville
Garrison, Bushrod T. Private
Garrison, Tip Private
Wdd. Kelley's Island
Garrison, Albert Private
Gilmore, Howard Private
Gilmore, Harry Private
Pro. Maj. & Lt. Col. 2 Bn. Maryland Cav.
Gilmore, Richard Private
Graybill, J. C. Private
Gaines, Lucian (colored) Wagon driver
Haws, ———— Private
Holmes, Charles A. Private
Wdd. Greenland Gap
Hitt, Jas. W. Private
Blacksmith for company
Harman, John D. Private
Harrison, Daniel B. Private
Wdd. several times
Hathaway, C. H. Private
Horner, Richard H. Private
Discharged, 1861
Hoffman, W. A. Private
Wdd. 1 June, 1864
Hughes, Charles Private
Discharged, 1861
Hatcher, Harry Private
Pro. Sgt. Maj., wdd.
Hatcher, William P. Private
wdd. Buckton Sta.
Herndon, John G. Private
Hackley, James Private
Henderson, Jno. D. Private
Heflin, John Private
Hicks, Kimball Private
D. near Upperville, 1863

Hunton, James Private
Discharged, 1861
Jacobs, Diven T. Private
Jones, Scott Private
K., Bolivia Heights, 1861
Jones, Henry Private
Discharged, 1861
Jones, Philip Private
Discharged, 1861
Jeffries, James A. Private
Jordan, J. H. A. Private
Keys, James Private
Wdd. Buckton Station, 1862
Kincheloe, John W. Private
Kincheloe, Elisha Private
Trans. to 8th Va. Inf. 1861
Kidwell, Evan H. Private
Captd. Markham
Kirkpatrick, W. S. Private
Discharged 1863
Ladd, John A. Private
Wdd. Kelley's Island, 1861
Leslie, Thomas Private
Long, E. Pendleton Private
Lawler, Robert Private
Discharged, 1861
Lake, F. Marion Private
Lake, Luther B. Private
Trans. to 8th Va. Inf. 1861
Lake, Bladen Dulaney Private
D., fever, 1862
Larkin, Richard D. Private
Discharged 1862, ill health
Lacy, W. J. Private
Lee, William Private
Lewis, John F. Private
Discharged, 1861
Marlow, Richard Private
Trans. to White's 35th Va. Bn.
Marlow, John Private
Trans. to White's 35th Va. Bn.
McClennahan, Samuel B. Private
Marshall, Richard C. Private
Wdd. Trevillians Station
McArthur, T. H. Private
Wdd. Kelley's Island, 1861

Marshall, Thomas Private
Joined 12th Regt. Va. Cav. 1862
Marshall, Polk Private
Joined 12th Regt. Va. Cav. 1862
Marshall, James Private
Trans. to Co. E, 12th Va. Cav.
Martin, Gibson Private
Middleton, John W. Private
Middleton, Campbell Private
Last recruit in March, 1865
Mitler, Proff Private
Discharged, 1862, over age
Mitchell, James W. Private
K. Wilderness, May 1864
Mitchell, John Hugh Private
Maddux, F. Webster Private
Detached service, all war
Maddux, Weadon Private
K. Salem (now Marshall)
Martin, Thomas Private
D. 1862
Morrison, D. B. Private
Middleton, Humphrey Private
Meyers, Frank Private
Discharged 1861
Melton, H. Private
POW, d. in prison, Ft. Delaware
Noell, J. M. Private
Owens, Morgan Private
Owens, Cuthbert Private
Wdd. Wilderness
Payne, Hugh G. Private
Payne, Robert W. Private
Wdd.
Price, John H. Private
Price, James Polk Private
Potterfield, W. H. Tyler Private
K. Brandy Station

Known as Payne's Legion

Payne, Richard C. Private
Wdd.
Payne, Robert J. Private
K. Fredericksburg, 1863
Payne, Robert B. Private
Payne, Wallace J. Private
Payne, Edward A. Private
K. Wilderness, 1863
Payne, Wilson V. Private
K. Haws Shop, 1864
Payne, Lafayette Private
Payne, John T. Private
K. Beverley, W. Va., Jan. 1865
Payne, Upton Private
Payne, Mason Private
Payne, Rice W. Private
Wdd.

Peyton, Robert E. Private
Pendleton, David E. Private
Captd. Ream's Station, 1864
Phillips, Evan D. Private
Phillips, Charles E. Private
Phillips, John E. Private
Discharged in 1861
Packard, William Private
D. Pt. Lookout, 1864
Pickett, Albert Private
Discharged 1862
Reid, Joseph H. Private
Rector, William F. Private
Rector, Howard N. Private
Rector, Abner Private
Rector, Columbus Private
Left to bury the dead at Greenland Gap
Rector, Asa Private
Trans. to Co. A, 6th Va. Cav.
Rector, W. A. Private
Rust, H. Clay Private
Trans. to 12th Va. Cav. 1862, killed
Rust, John R. Private
Trans. to Co. I, 12th Regt. Va. Cav.
Robinson, W. S. Private
Wdd. Brandy Station
Rogers, William S. Private
Wagoner
Royston, John Private
Smith, R. S. Private
Scanlon, Dade Private
Trans.

Skinner, Wm. Jeff — Private
Served 4 years
Skinner, Charles G. — Private
Wdd. Buckton Station
Stewart, John W. — Private
Sutton, James — Private
Silcott, Landon — Private
Smith, H. Golder — Private
Smith, Seldon — Private
Smith, Horace — Private
Smith, D. O'Connell — Private
D. during the war
Settle, T. L. — Private
Promoted to Surgeon, 1861
Smith, Thomas B. — Private
Discharged 1862, claimed to be a Marylander
Strother, Lewis — Private
Trans. to 8th Va. Inf., 1861
Strother, John W. — Private
Trans. to 8th Va. Inf., 1861
Shippey, W. D. — Private
Sutton, James — Private
Discharged in 1862, over age
Seely, George W. — Private
K. Slaughter Mts., 9 Aug., 1862
Taylor, Rufus — Private
Q.M. Sgt. last 2 yrs.
Templeman, James — Private
Trans. to Co. I, 12th Va. Cav.
Triplett, Leonidas — Private
Templeman, Robert — Private
Courier for Gen'l. Stuart
Templeman, James — Private
M.D., acted Surgeon, all war
Turner, Thomas — Private
D. during war
Turner, Hezekiah — Private
Tebbetts, Albert — Private
K. near Edinburg, 1864
Utz, J. J. — Private
Wdd., Orange C. H.
Violett, Elijah — Private
K. near Ream's Station, 1864
Wigfield, Wm. H. — Private
Wigfield, James — Private
Captured at Orlean, 12 Feb., 1864
Wigginton, Isaac — Private
Wigginton, Geo. W. — Private
Welch, Sylvester M. — Private
Wdd. in Maryland, 5 Sept., 1864
Wilson, James — Private
Wilson, William — Private

At the close of the war there were the following officers:

Capt. Daniel C. Hatcher
First Lt. Sullivan Smith
Second Lt. Luther Ashby
Orderly Sgt. T. L. Potterfield
2nd Sgt. J. C. Fletcher
Cpl. Wallace Payne
2nd Cpl. J. W. Middleton

ROSTER OF THE FAUQUIER ARTILLERY

Compiled from the roster of Lt. Col. Robert M. Stribling and the records in the National Archives. *(*-Loudoun Battery).*

Letter from M. M. Rogers, Commanding, Loudoun Battery, to J. A. Marshall, Esq., dated: Dover, Loudoun County, 4 Sept. 1884:

"My Dear Sir: Yours of the 29th ulto. duly rec'd. The enclosed list of Loudoun men (included in the above roster, marked *) turned over to the "Fauquier Battery" was made by Sergeant Joseph L. Norris, and although from memory, as he writes, I am confident that it is correct. He also writes me that many have died and others have followed "Greeley's" advice and gone West, so that but few are now living in this county. This may account, partly, for the absence of the Loudoun members from the reunion which I regret.

"Regarding suggestion that there may be a 'wish to preserve a separate record of the Loudoun Battery', I doubt if it has ever entered into the mind of a single member. Certainly, it has never occurred to me. They were so thoroughly identified with the 'Fauquier Battery', by reason of long service, etc., that, I feel sure, every man will esteem it a privilege to have his name preserved on the roll of that organization.

"If publication is made of your proceedings be kind enough to send me copy."

Stribling, Robert M. — Captain
pro. Major/ Lt. Col.
Marshall, William C. — Lt.
pro. Captain
Green, William N. — 2nd Lt.
Rogers, M. M. — Lt.
Trans. from Loudoun Arty.
Kidwell James H. — Lt.
Carroll, Gray — Lt.
Archer, J. M. — 2nd Lt.
assigned to duty with provost marshal
Stribling, Henry C. — 2nd Lt.

*Ankers, William S. — Private
Ash, J. A. Delbert — Private
wdd. Seven Pines
Ash, B. Harrison — Private
Ash, Henry — Private
wdd.
Ash, James — Private
Ash, Littleton — Private
died
Aylor, Frank — Cpl.
*Adrain, John A. — Pvt.
Adrain, John M. — Pvt.
Tr. to Mosby
Atkins ———— — Pvt.
*Ayres, Samuel — Pvt.
Barron, James — Pvt.
Barbee, Wm. H. — Pvt.
Brown, John W. — Pvt.
Bowie. Bushrod — Pvt.
Bowden, Daniel — Pvt.
Bowden, David F. — Pvt.
tr. to Pr. Geo. Cavalry
Bussey, James — Pvt.

Bales, Joseph — Pvt.
Berryman, Douglass — Private
Berryman, Silas — Private
*Birkby, John M. — Cpl.
K.I.A.
*Benjamin, Wm. H. — Private
Blair, James A. — Private
*Benedum, Jas. H. — Private
K.I.A.
*Benedum, E. Hammett — Private
K.I.A.
Brierwood, Robert — Private
*Brent, J. Heth — Sgt.
Beach, Charles — Private
Ball, William — Private
d. at Yorktown
Ball, Frank — Private
Ball, George — Private
died
Ball, John T. — Private
K.I.A.
Ball, B. F. — Private
Blackwell, Joe — Private
Coleman, John — Private
Carter, James W. — Private
wwd. at Gettysburg
Carter, Arthur — Private
wwd. at Gettysburg. Res: Rappahannock County
Carter, John E. — Private
Carter, George H. — Private
Res. Fairfax
Carter, Richard — Private
Cornwell, Jonas — Private
Cornwell, Joseph S. — Private
Res. Clarke County
Cornwell, Thornton — Private

Campbell, James	Private
*Carruthers, John E.	Private
*Carruthers, Wesley	Private
*Carruthers, Thomas N.	Private
Res. Cumberland County	
Conrad, J. W.	Private
Canard, William	Private
Corder, Allie	Private
Cabell, J. W.	Private
*Crim, A. M.	Private
Cable, Frank	Cpl.
K.I.A.	
Conner, George W.	Private
Conner, Joseph	Private
Creel, Peyton	Private
*Cridler, J. W.	Private
sometimes spelled 'Crigler'	
Cockrell, Richard	Private
*Cockrell, Thomas	Private
*Caylor, S. Thomas	Private
Chamberlain, Wm. C.	Private
died at Soldiers Home, 1912	
Dike, Nathan	Private
*Dove, Thomas	Private
*Drish, Wm. H.	Private
Dennis, Lorenzo	Private
Dennis, D. J.	Private
wwd. at Gettysburg	
Evans, George	Private
died	
Easley, D. J.	Private
Res. Bedford County	
Easley, J. N.	Private
Res. Bedford County	
Ford, James	Private
Fouche, John H.	Sgt.
K.I.A., Gettysburg	
Freeman, J. Garnet	Private
Freeman, Wm. T.	Private
Franklin, ______	Private
Fairfax, ______	Private
*Gentle, David L.	Private
*Grimes, Jack H.	Private
Groves, James	Sgt.
Groves, Albert	Private
Gladson, Daniel	Private
Glascock, John	Private
K.I.A.	
Glascock, Leroy B.	Private
Gordon, Jim Tom	Private
Gordon, Arlic	Private
Harrington, Mike	Private
died	
*Harding, Wm. H.	Private
wwd. & died	
*Howser, Wm. C.	Sgt.
Heflin, Thomas	Private
Hankins, W. E.	Private
Hoffman, Frank W.	Private
wwd. 26 March 1865, P.O.W.	
Hall, Jack R.	Private
*Heffner, Stephen	Private
*Hutchinson, Cuthbert	Private
*Hunt, ______	Private
Iden, Abner	Cpl.
Iden, John N.	Private
*Jenkins, Charles W.	Private
*Jenkins, J. W.	Private
Jett, Peter	Cpl.
Johnson, Thomas	Private
Johnson, Smith	Private
Kerrick, Benj. F.	Private
Kerrick, Frank M.	Private
Kerrick, J. T.	Private
wwd. at Seven Pines	
Kerrick, W. T.	Private
Kerrick, H. L.	Private
Kerns, John	Private
died	
Kemper, John J.	Sgt.
wwd. Gettysburg	
Kemper, Dudley	Private
Kemper, Joshua	Private
Kane, Ambrose	Private
Kane, William A.	Private
Kendall, Joe	Private
wwd. & died	
Kendall, George W.	Private
Kines, Daniel	Private
Kinnie, H.	Private
*Lane, Wm. H.	Cpl.
*Lefevre, Samuel	Private
Martin, Elias B.	Private
Mason, D. M.	Sgt.

Mageath, J. T. Private
Marshall, Martin P. Cpl.
Marshall, E. C. Private
Marshall, William Private
Marshall, J. A. Private
Moore, Thomas F. Private
*McClanahan, John Private
Melton, W. T. Private
Moore, R. S. Private
Moore, Jack Private
Moore, James W. Private
*Morass, H. W. Private
*Moran, Frank Private
*Moran, Josh. Private
Maupin, Jack Private
Maupin, Jessie C. Private
Mahoney, James Private
wwd. Malvern Hill
McBee, Lock Private
McMahey, Thomas Private
(McNealey?)
*Majors, George C. Private
Mathews, Jeff Private
McMahey, Alexander Private
d. & buried at Pt. Lookout, Md.
Newton, Robert M. Private
*Norris, Joseph L. Sgt.
O'Donnell, Thomas Private
Phillips, A. W. Private
Phillips, J. T. Private
Payne, Arthur Private
Payne, Bernard Private
Wdd. Sharpsburg & Appomattox
Payne, J. F. Private
Payne, Wm. E. Private
Payne, Wm. H. Private
Payne, Thomas Private
D. & buried at Pt. Lookout, Md.
*Powell, Frank W. Sgt.
Pearson, James S. Private
Pearson, Joseph Private
K.I.A.
Pearson, Richard E. Private
Pierce, John Private
Pritchard, George Private
K.I.A., Seven Pines
Pritchard, Henry Private
Pritchard, Thomas Private
Rector, Alban Private
Rector, Charles H. Private
Rector, Marion Private
Robinson, John Private
Robinson, George C. Private
Redman, Tilghman Private
Served 1 yr., discharged
Riley, William H. Private
K.I.A.
Riley, William Private
Russell, Thomas Private
Rawls, Thomas Private
Ross, ------ Private
Swayne, John Private
Swayne, Thomas Private
Silliman, Charles L. Private
Symington, John Private
*Smith, Dr. Wm. F. Cpl.
Wdd. First Manassas
Strother, A. B. Private
Sealock, Thomas Private
*Saunders, George Private
K.I.A.
Selden, Wilson Private
Suddith, William Private
K.I.A.
Suddith, Martin Private
Suddith, Joseph T. Private
Thompson, Thomas Private
Thomas, P. P. Sgt.
Thomas, Henry Private
Thayer, John R. Private
Thorpe, Frank Private
Turner, Henry Private
*White, George W. Private
Wright, Henry Private
K.I.A.
Wright, William Private
*Wynkoop, P. Henry Private
*Wynkoop, Simeon Private
Wiser, Joseph Private
*Wortman, James W. Private
Wilford, Wm. N. Private

Weaver, Mason wdd. & died	Private	Weeks, John	Private
Weaver, Wm. S.	Private	Weeks, Joseph	Private
Welch, Elias	Private	Weaver, John d. during War	Private
Wines, A. L.	Private	Wine, Dorsey	Private
*Wilson, William	Private	Wrenn, Virginius	Private
Wines, Sewell	Private	White, Daniel	Private
		Wine, Elias	Private

MOSBY'S REGIMENT, VIRGINIA CAVALRY, PARTISAN RANGERS

(Notes Compiled by Lee A. Wallace Jr., for the Virginia Civil War Commission)

Mosby, John S., Col., 1864-1865. Formerly the 43rd Bn. Va. Cav., Partisan Rangers, organized in 1863, this command was increased to a regiment about December 7, 1864. The battalion companies did not change their lettered designation when the regiment was formed.

Co. A, Capt. James William Foster's Co.; organized June 10, 1863; formerly Co. A, 43rd Bn. Va. Cav., Partisan Rangers. Parole Records indicate two Co. A's, Capt. Foster's and John A. Belvin's; how the latter company was formed, or when organized, has not been ascertained.

Co. B, Capt. William R. Smith's Co.; organized October 1, 1863; formerly Co. B, 43rd Bn. Va. Cav. Partisan Rangers. Captains: William R. Smith (killed), Adolphus E. Richards (to maj.), William H. Kennon.

Co. C, Capt. William H. Chapman's Co.; organized December 7, 1863; formerly Co. C, 43rd Bn. Va. Cav., Partisan Rangers. Parole reports indicate two companies were paroled as Co. C, those of Capt. A. J. Hobson and Capt. William Suttles, neither of whom has been identified as of the 43rd Bn. Captains: William H. Chapman (to lt. col.), C. S. Jones (?). A. J. Hobson (?), William Suttles (?).

Co. D, Capt. R. P. Montjoy's Co.; formerly Co. D, 43rd Bn. Va. Cav. Partisan Rangers. Captains: R. P. Montjoy (killed November 27, 1864), Alfred Glascock.

Co. E, Capt. Samuel F. Chapman's Co.; organized July 28, 1864; formerly Co. E. 43rd Bn. Va. Cav. Partisan Rangers.

Co. F, Capt. Walter E. Frankland's Co.; organized September 19, 1864; formerly Co. F, 43rd Bn. Va. Cav. Partisan Rangers. Parole records indicate that no companies were paroled as Co. F of this command, commanded by Capt. Frankland and Capt. John Harris. How, or when, the latter company was formed has not been ascertained.

Co. G, Capt. T. W. T. Richards' Co.; formerly Co. G, 43rd Bn. Va. Cav. Partisan Rangers.

Co. H, Capt. George Baylor's Co.; formerly Co. H, 43rd Bn. Va. Cav., Partisan Rangers.

Co. I, K and L, No commissioned officers reported for these companies. Enlisted men are reported as having been paroled as of these companies.

Artillery Co. Personal papers of Col. John S. Mosby show that upon his application, the Sec. of War granted him authority, July 4, 1864, to organize a company of light artillery for his battalion. This company is reported to have been commanded by Capt. Peter Frankland.

Capt. James C. Kincheloe's Co. A&IGO Letters (1055-R-1864) and S. O. No. 187, A&IGO., dated August 9, 1864, report that this company was serving in the 43rd Bn. It is found to have been assigned as Co. H, 15th Regt. Va. Cav. No authority has been found that it was recognized as a company of this battalion. It appears to have been serving within the Federal lines and claimed to have belonged to this command in order to continue as Partisan Rangers and escape service as regular cavalry. It was disbanded because the company failed to comply with the order assigning it to the 15th Regt. Va. Cav.

COMPANY H, 6th REGT., CAVALRY BRIGADE, C. S. A.

This company was originally organized at Salem on 1 April 1861 by Dr. John A. Adams who served as Captain until he resigned on 8 January 1863. He was succeeded by Captain Virgil Weaver and the company became known as "Wise's Dragoons."

NAME	RANK	ENLISTED
John A. Adams	Capt.	1 April 1861
(Resigned 8 January 1863)		
Virgil Weaver	Capt.	
Coleman (J. C.) Davis	1st Lt.	
Milton Morehead	2nd Lt.	
(Promoted to 1st Lt.)		
Turner D. Scott	2nd Lt.	
T. H. Foster	2nd Lt.	
(Died and buried at Pt. Lookout, Md.)		
F. Lewis Marshall	1st Sgt.	
W. R. Welch	2nd Sgt.	1861
(Served 4 yrs., Promoted to 1st Lt, 1862, Captain)		
R. Singleton Rust	3rd Sgt.	
(Served 4 yrs.)		
H. C. Barbee	4th Sgt.	
George E. Lewis	1st Sgt.	1861 4 yrs.
John T. Moffet	Sgt.	
(Maryland Line)		
E. T. Adams	1st Cpl.	1861 4 yrs.
(Wounded)		
John W. Mountjoy	2nd Cpl.	1861 4 yrs.
(Captured)		
John C. Pearson	3rd Cpl.	1861 4 yrs.
Jesse Moffett	4th Cpl.	
N. T. Ashby	Private	1 April 1861
(Served 3 yrs.)		
John T. Allison	Private	1 April 1861
(Served 3 yrs.)		
Bertrand Ashby	Private	
Basil Allison	Private	
(Died in Person and buried at Pt. Lookout, Md.)		
Bailey Allison	Private	
Samuel A. Barbee	Private	
Bert Bishop	Private	
Hezekiah Bishop	Private	Sept. 1862
(Served 6 mos., wounded twice)		
H. S. Bishop	Private	1861 4 yrs.
(Wounded)		
C. T. Brown	Private	
Jeremiah Balthrope	Private	
Joseph Ballard	Private	April 1862 3 yrs.
Robert Barbee (or R. S.)	Private	
George Barbee	Private	
(Wounded at Winchester)		
Horace P. Burgess	Private	April 1861 4 yrs.
John (S.) Brown	Private	3 yrs.
Gurley W. Cocke	Private	March 1862 3 yrs.
William Cockrill	Private	1 June 1861
(Served 1 yr., discharged)		
Frank Crouch	Private	
(Killed at Trevillian, 11 June 1864)		
Joseph Cockrill	Private	
Addison Creel	Private	(Wounded)
Benton Chinn	Private	1862 3 yrs.
Frank R. Carter	Private	Nov. 1861 3½ yrs.

Benjamn Cooper	Private	
George E. DeNeale	Private	1862 3 yrs.
Benjamin Dawson	Private	
George W. Davis	Private	1861
(Promoted to 2nd Lt., lost leg, resigned 9 May 1864)		
Landon C. Edmonds	Private	
Phil. Edmonds	Private	
Benj. Ferrel	Private	
T. Hunton Foster	Private	
(Died in prison, Pt. Lookout, Md.))		
William A. Fynn	Private	
Henry J. Francis	Private	
James Glassocke	Private	
(Killed at Winchester, 19 September 1864)		
John (or J. W.) Griffith	Private	
(Wounded at Twin Oaks)		
William E. Griffith	Private	1862 3 yrs.
Hugh R. Green	Private	
(Appointed Hospital steward of the Regt, 3 August 1863)		
Benjamin R. Green	Private	1861 4 yrs.
C. W. Hinson	Private	2 yrs.
John P. Holmes	Private	
M. D. Herrell	Private	
T. L. Herrell	Private	1861, at Orange
(Served 4 yrs., wounded at Brandy Station)		
D. B. Harrison	Private	
(Severely wounded at Millfords, trans. from 7th Cav.)		
Benj. Harrison	Private	
Charles W. Holtzclaw	Private	
George Holtzclaw	Private	
(Deserted)		
W. H. Heyl	Private	
(Deserted)		
W. C. Holmes	Private	1861 4 yrs.
Richard Horner	Private	
George Hackley	Private	
(Killed, Culpeper, September 1863)		
Louis Herrell	Private	
Benj. (S.) Herrell	Private	
(Died in Prison at Ft. Delaware, buried at Ferris (?) Point National Cemetery, New Jersey)		
Tince Herrell	Private	
Middleton Herrell	Private	
John A. Herrell	Private	April 1862 3 yrs.
Lewis T. Herrell	Private	1862 3 yrs.
Wm. S. Herrell	Private	1862 3 yrs.
John Hiet	Private	14 March 1862
(Deserted, 25 May 1862)		
Wilbur Jackson	Private	
Samuel Jones	Private	
Addison Jeffries	Private	
Enoch Jeffries	Private	
George A. Jeffries	Private	
William R. Jeffries	Private	
John T. Jones	Private	
George W. Kirby	Private	April 1861 4 yrs.
(Promoted to Sgt.)		
Marcellus Kilpatrick	Private	
James R. Kirby	Private	1861
(Transferred to Mosby)		
James R. Lawrence	Private	
T. F. Lawrence	Private	
Wesley Lloyd	Private	
Bladen Lake	Private	
John H. Larkin	Private	

NAME	RANK	ENLISTED
James Milstead (1)	Private	
(Killed at Five Forks, April 1865)		
George Milstead	Private	
George Metcalf	Private	
Alexander Maxwell	Private	
Reuben Murray (or R. J.)	Private	
(Deserted)		
James Milstead (2)	Private	
(Captured, died in prison, buried at Arlington)		
J. B. W. Macrae	Private	
James M. Morehead	Private	
Richard Coke Marshall	Private	1861
(Transferred to Co A, 7th Regt, Cav. 1862)		
Thomas (A.) Nelson	Private	1861 4 yrs.
John T. Newman	Private	
Cuthbert Owens	Private	
(Killed, Yellow Tavern, 11 June 1864)		
S. K. Owens	Private	
(Transferred to Piedmont Rifles, 21 August 1861)		
Henry Renoe	Private	
(Killed, Back Road, 30 October 1864)		
James Rust	Private	
Nimrod Rust	Private	
Wlliam Rust	Private	
(Killed, 1 September 1864)		
Battle Rector	Private	1862
Samuel Redmond	Private	May 1861 4 yrs.
A. P. Ramey	Private	April 1862 3 yrs.
Tom Ramey	Private	
William Ramey	Private	
Ed. Ramey	Private	
Sam D. Reid	Private	April 1861 4 yrs.
Alpheus Robinson	Private	
Elzey Strother	Private	
William Strother	Private	
James Sherman	Private	
Laflavius Shaffer	Private	
Jacob Symons	Private	
Alfred (A. O.) Sudduth	Private	
J. W. Shackelford	Private	April 1861 4 yrs.
Thomas Sephenson	Private	
Sol. Stone	Private	
John B. Stone	Private	
(Promoted to 2nd Sgt, Killed, Brandy Station, 1863)		
D. W. Strother	Private	
James H. Simons	Private	
(Died and buried at Pt. Lookout, Md.)		
B. W. Van Horn	Private	
James Wines	Private	
A. D. Walker	Private	
Arthur Walker	Private	
Luther Welch	Private	
Rich'd. Woodward	Private	
Horace Weaver	Private	
Henry Wines	Private	
(Wounded at Lacy's Springs, December 1864)		
W. H. Winn	Private	
Virgil Weaver	Private	
(Promoted to Captain, Killed at Todd's Tavern, 7 May 1864, succeeded by W. R. Welch)		

INDEX